THE INTEGRAL PHILOSOPHY
OF SRI AUROBINDO

SRI AUROBINDO

THE INTEGRAL PHILOSOPHY
OF
SRI AUROBINDO

A Commemorative Symposium

EDITED BY

HARIDAS CHAUDHURI
FREDERIC SPIEGELBERG

Ruskin House
GEORGE ALLEN & UNWIN LTD
MUSEUM STREET LONDON

FIRST PUBLISHED IN 1960

PRINTED IN GREAT BRITAIN
in 11 *on* 12 *point Old Style type*
BY UNWIN BROTHERS LIMITED
WOKING AND LONDON

TO SRI AUROBINDO

Whose word was the voice of the dynamic world spirit
Whose vision was the light of the cosmic truth

ACKNOWLEDGEMENTS

GRATEFUL acknowledgement is made to the following publishers for the inclusion in this volume of excerpts from the publications indicated:

Alfred A. Knopf Inc., New York, and George Allen & Unwin Ltd., London: Oswald Spengler, *The Decline of the West*, 1945.

Sri Aurobindo Ashram Press, Pondicherry: Sri Aurobindo, *Last Poems*, 1952; *Letters of Sri Aurobindo, First Series*, 1950; *The Renaissance in India*, 1946; *Savitri*, 1954. Haridas Chaudhuri, *The Philosophy of Integralism*, 1954.

Sri Aurobindo Ashram, Pondicherry, and E. P. Dutton & Co., New York: Sri Aurobindo, *The Life Divine*, 1953; *Essays on The Gita*, 1950; *The Human Cycle*, 1949; *The Ideal of Human Unity*, 1953.

The Beacon Press, Boston: Pitirim A. Sorokin, *The Ways and Power of Love*, 1954.

The Commonwealth Fund, New York, and Harvard University Press, Mass.: Andras Angyal, *Foundations for a Science of Personality*, 1941.

The Duke University Press, N.C.: Andras Angyal, 'A Theoretical Model for Personality Studies', in *Journal of Personality*, September 1951.

Harper & Brothers, New York: S. Radhakrishnan, *The Bhagavad-gita*, 1949.

The Macmillan Co., London and New York: F. S. C. Northrop, *The Meeting of East and West*, 1950; Howard H. Brinton, *The Mystic Will*, 1930; Milton, *Paradise Lost*, 1934.

Pantheon Books, New York: C. G. Jung, *Psychology and Religion*, 1958.

John Wiley & Sons, New York: Calvin S. Hall and Gardner Lindzey *Theories of Personality*, 1957.

*

PREFACE

THE idea of this Commemorative Symposium on the integral philosophy of Sri Aurobindo was first conceived while celebrating his birthday anniversary at San Francisco Ashram in August 1957. It was felt that the time was ripe for the message of Sri Aurobindo to be increasingly known to the wider public in different parts of the world. It is a message which silently took shape over a long period of time in the medium of a life such as transcended all geographical and national boundaries, and unconditionally offered itself at the altar of human welfare, or rather at the altar of the Divine in human evolution. The message is one of human unity, and of 'the out-flowering of the Divine in collective humanity'. Occasioned by an intermingling of the two broad streams of culture, eastern and western, it envisages a new world-order of peace, progress and international harmony, broadbased upon a radical change of man's collective consciousness. It indicates the lines along which the unification of all human races is to be achieved through increasing participation in the creative adventure of the world-spirit. It utters forth the secret of collective and co-operative living toward the fulfilment of the ultimate destiny of man.

The present symposium consists of various articles contributed by some eminent scholars of Aurobindonian literature. It cannot possibly claim to cover all the aspects of Sri Aurobindo's teaching. Nor is the list of contributors included herein to be taken in any way exhaustive of the vast and ever-growing volume of scholarship in the field. Different contributors had full freedom in expressing their own interpretation and evaluation of the approach and outlook which has now come to be known as integral nondualism (*pūrṇa-advaita*). Editors have proceeded on the assumption that truth in its creative aspect lies, not in reproducing a static thought structure, but in the free self-expression of different individuals in the application and evaluation of a dynamic spiritual message.

The symposium has five parts: Philosophy, Epistemology and Psychology, Yoga and Ethics, Literature, and Miscellaneous. The part called 'Miscellaneous' includes tributes to Sri Aurobindo, an outline of the historical setting in which his message was formulated, his political thoughts on freedom and world unity, and a brief sketch of his life.

Dr Frederic Spiegelberg's article 'Sri Aurobindo and Existentialism' is based upon one of the three talks which he gave at San Francisco Ashram on August 21, 1958, in connection with the celebration of Sri Aurobindo's birthday. Dr Pitirim A. Sorokin's article, 'The Integral Yoga of Sri Aurobindo', is taken from his book, *The Ways and Power of Love* (Boston: The Beacon Press, 1954), pp. 371–6. Editors wish to take this opportunity of expressing their grateful thanks to Dr Sorokin and his publisher for their kind permission in this respect. Professor Richard P. Marsh's paper, 'The Organismic Psychology of Andras Angyal in Relation to Sri Aurobindo's Philosophy of Integral Nondualism', represents the essay which won him the first prize in the Aurobindo Essay Contest which was held in 1958 among the students of Indian philosophy in Northern California. Sri A. B. Purani's brief life-sketch, 'Sri Aurobindo', was first broadcast from the B.B.C., London, in December 1955, and has been incorporated here by courtesy of the B.B.C.

No words would be adequate to express the gratitude of the editors to the eminent contributors who have most graciously co-operated with them by joining this symposium. Editors are also grateful to Cultural Integration Fellowship, San Francisco, for sponsoring the symposium. Finally, sincere thanks are due to Bina Chaudhuri, Esther Weissman, Bernice Littlewood, Myrtle Vepsala, and Blanche Beat, who have assisted in various ways in the preparation of this volume, and to the Mother of the Sri Aurobindo Ashram of Pondicherry for permission to quote extensively from the works of Sri Aurobindo.

HARIDAS CHAUDHURI

San Francisco　　　　　FREDERIC SPIEGELBERG

October 15, 1958

CONTENTS

The Integral Philosophy of Sri Aurobindo

PART ONE

PHILOSOPHY

I

HARIDAS CHAUDHURI

The Integral Philosophy of Sri Aurobindo

THE philosophy of Sri Aurobindo is all-comprehending in its integration of the past, and prophetic in its vision of the future. As a connected view of the totality of existence, it brings to light the ultimate unifying principle of life. On the basis of a balanced appreciation of the multifarious values of life, it shows how to reconcile the various conflicts of our human existence. Out of a broad survey of cosmic evolution it evolves a creative idea which bids fair to impart a new rhythm to the historical order. In reaffirming the eternal truths of ancient wisdom in the context of our present-day problems, it creates new values and opens up new vistas of human progress. In an endeavour to meet the challenge of the present age, it gives a new dynamic form to the spiritual heritage of the human race—a unified and integrated form to the highest cultural values of East and West. With a penetrative insight into the profound meaning of life it lays the foundation for a complete art of harmonious and creative living.

When a great idea is born, it shows limitless capacity for transcending fixed moulds of thought, and for reconciling diverse viewpoints. It goes on growing and expanding, refusing to be confined within the stone walls of any rigidly fixed thought structure. As a living spiritual force it goes on fertilizing the spiritual soil of the world, giving rise to varied forms of practically useful self-expression. Remaining the same in its central truth-vision it may undergo changes and modifications with the passing of time in accordance with the divergent needs of the human psyche and the changing requirements of social growth. Sri Aurobindo has given to the world such a living spiritual force, a dynamic truth-vision.

We are living today at a critical juncture of human history. It is a transitional phase of the development of human culture. The traditional cultural values of the past have been thrown into the melting pot, creating a large spiritual vacuum in the minds of thinking people. But nothing new and positively satisfying to the human soul has clearly emerged to fill the vacuum. There are some who think that philosophy is a kind of sublimated mythology. Some maintain that philosophy, dealing as it does with such trans-empirical concepts as God, soul, immortality, essence, etc., is a mighty fabric of meaningless propositions or contentless emotional ejaculations. Some again hold that philosophy is a kind of escape mechanism for those who shudder to face the responsibilities of independent and mature living. But after everything has been said against philosophy, the fact remains that the most glorious periods of human history have been those which were animated by a lofty world-view (*Weltanschauung*), inspiring men to high creative endeavour and to noble deeds of self-sacrifice at the altar of truth and beauty and justice. Consciously or unconsciously, every man is guided by some kind of philosophic outlook, whether positive or negative, self-coherent or inchoate and incoherent. Only a satisfactory world-view can sustain man through all the storm and stress of life, release the most creative energies of his soul, and channel them toward the fulfilment of the higher ends of evolution. As Dr Albert Schweitzer puts it: '. . . all human progress depends on progress in its theory of the universe, whilst, conversely, decadence is conditioned by a similar decadence in this theory. Our loss of real civilization is due to our lack of a theory of the universe.'[1] Now, a soul-satisfying theory of the universe or world-view has to come to terms with the recent developments in science and psychology, and with recent changes in man's social structure. So, what we most imperatively need today is a comprehensive and dynamic world-view based upon a critical revaluation of the values of life and a thinking reconsideration

[1] Albert Schweitzer, *The Philosophy of Civilization* (London: A. & C. Black Ltd., 1950), p. xii.

of the fundamental concepts of ethics and religion. The philosophy of Sri Aurobindo is a world-view of precisely that nature which takes into account the challenge of the present age, the variety of human experience, the fundamental demands of the human psyche, and the indications of the evolving world-spirit. An outline of that philosophy will be briefly presented here by the writer in his own way.

INTEGRAL NONDUALISM (PŪRṆĀDVAITA)

The philosophy of Sri Aurobindo may aptly be described as integral nondualism (*pūrṇa-advaita*), or integral idealism (*pūrṇa-vijñāna*), or just integralism (*pūrṇavāda*). Nondualism is the dominant keynote of Indian culture, and, on the whole, of Oriental culture. It is prompted by an intuitive approach to life and existence—an approach which seeks to understand reality in its undivided wholeness and fundamental oneness. Differences which we observe are looked upon as developments taking place within the framework of the all-inclusive unity of the Real. Turning to the West we find that dualism has been for long the dominant keynote of Western philosophic thinking. As Dr Schweitzer rightly says: 'That (the world-view) of India is monistic and mystical, ours is dualistic and doctrinaire.'[1] The dualistic outlook of European thought has been prompted by the rationalistic approach to life and existence—the approach which stresses the relational or logical structure of reality, and converts the rationally defined polarities of existence into separate entities. For instance, spirit and nature, god and world, mind and matter, good and evil, the divine and the undivine, and the like, are, to the rationalistic-dualistic way of thinking, separate metaphysical principles and eternally fixed values. Integral nondualism integrates the significant distinctions of ethics, religion, logic and metaphysics in its nondualistic philosophical outlook, without deprecating their value and importance. It reconciles the dualities of thought and existence in the unity of integral experience, integral living, and the integral sweep of cosmic evolution. According to

[1] Albert Schweitzer, *Indian Thought and Its Development* (London: A. & C. Black Ltd., 1951), p. 10.

rationalistic dualism the value-distinctions of reality and appearance, good and evil, god and devil, etc. are eternally fixed and absolute, whereas according to integral nondualism such distinctions are valid but not eternally fixed—they are real, but not indicative of any ultimate division in existence. Fully acknowledging the validity of the ethico-logical approach, integralism sublates it in a higher standpoint of identity-consciousness (*advaita-jñāna*).

THE BASIC CONVICTION OF NONDUALISM

Common to all forms of nondualism is the conviction that reality in its inmost essence is non-dual, non-verbal, and non-conceptual. It is indeterminable and logically indefinable, but accessible to direct experience on the non-verbal level, to the penetrative insight of spiritual intuition born of the integration of human personality. As non-dual, reality is beyond the scope of application of all human categories including that of number. Strictly speaking, monism, unitarianism, trinitarianism, pluralism, etc., are our different human ways of intellectual comprehension of the various aspects of reality. Even monism, which utters a profound truth in proclaiming the fundamental unity of existence, commits the rationalistic fallacy of identifying reality with a conceptually formulated principle or intellectual scheme. Rationalistic monism interprets the essence of reality in terms of the concept of unity, and endows the One with a determinate logical or dialectical structure, or a sum of well-defined powers and qualities. Nondualism is opposed to such identification of reality with a *determinate* principle of unity. The conceptually formulated One, whether the infinite substance of Spinoza, or the absolute idea of Hegel, represents only a particular metaphysical standpoint, a specific rationalistic way—one among many ways—of comprehending the nature of reality. According to nondualism (*advaita*), reality is beyond one and many, beyond substance and quality, beyond cause and effect, and beyond any rigidly conceived thought structure. It is not to be equated with any conceptual formulation or logical construction, or system of words and symbols. It is this conviction which is expressed in the concept of Nirguṇa Brahman in Vedānta, in the concept of Sūnyatā in Buddhism, in the concept of Tattvātīta in Tantra, in the concept of Tāo in Chinese philosophy, and in the concept of Zen in Japan. Sri Aurobindo shares the same conviction and holds that reality is in essence *indeterminable*. Reality is 'indefinable and inconceivable by finite and defining Mind; it is ineffable by a mind-created speech; it is describable neither by our negations, *neti neti*—for we cannot limit it by saying it is not this, it is not that—nor by our affirmations, for we cannot fix it by saying it is this, it is that, *iti iti*'.[1] The concept of the *indeterminable* implies that no metaphysical system or conceptual scheme can be equated with ultimate reality and regarded as the last word of wisdom. It implies that the multiform fullness of reality can hardly be exhausted in any logically differentiated system of terms and relations, however comprehensive. That would make reality limited. Nor can reality be regarded as 'a vacancy of pure existence . . . a mystery of infinite blankness . . . a supreme sum of negations',[2] or a colourless and featureless void incapable of self-determination. That would make reality limited too, identified with a determinate notion of the human mind.

The nondualistic view of reality as the indeterminable and inexhaustible plenum of pure experience has been subjected to varying degrees of misunderstanding and inadequate comprehension. It has been interpreted by some as the sum-total of the sensuous world disclosed in its not-yet-differentiated all-embracing oneness to man's aesthetic intuition. Professor F. S. C. Northrop says: 'Brahman in Hinduism is the same immediately apprehended, undifferentiated aesthetic continuum which was found to be Tāo in Tāoism, *jen* (human-heartedness) in Confucianism, and Nirvāṇa in Buddhism.'[3] Further on he says: 'Chit or Ātman, the undifferentiated aesthetic continuum, is in the immediately apprehended natural object in its empirically given aesthetic character as much as it is in mind.'[4] Now, Professor Northrop is perfectly

---

[1] Sri Aurobindo, *The Life Divine* (Pondicherry, Sri Aurobindo International University Centre, 1955), p. 292.   [2] *Ibid.*, p. 291.
[3] F. S. C. Northrop, *The Meeting of East and West* (New York: The Macmillan Company, 1950), p. 367.   [4] *Ibid.*, p. 368.

right in his contention that Oriental culture is nondualistic in its outlook, emphasizing as it does the fundamental oneness of existence. It is also true that the basic unity of existence is revealed to some kind of immediate experience. But that immediate experience is not sensuous or aesthetic intuition conceived as the prius of logical differentiation. It is not sentient immediacy but some kind of supersensuous and supra-rational immediacy in which sense and intellect are consummated in a higher unity of consciousness. It is that deeper spiritual intuition variously called *bodhi, prajñā, Brahma-jñāna*, etc., in which the immediately apprehended datum and the mediation of rational thinking are both transcended and transformed. Likewise, the basic unity of existence revealed to such spiritual insight is not a continuum of sense-experience but that higher unity in which the sensuous total and the differentiations of the conceptual understanding are brought together in a higher synthesis. Professor Northrop is grievously mistaken in interpreting the central concept of nondualism as 'the immediately apprehended aesthetic continuum'. Vedānta clearly and emphatically maintains: 'Brahman is unseen but seeing, unheard but hearing,'[1] that it cannot be the *object* or *datum* of any sensuous intuition, because it 'cannot be seen or seized'.[2] The immediate datum of sensuous apprehension (*idam*), as distinguished from the knower (*aham*), has been called in Hindu philosophy *Prakṛti* (the matrix of becoming). Puruṣa, Ātman, Brahman, etc. (pure existence) is that deeper unity in which the dualistic experience of knower and known, self and not-self, *aham* and *idam*, is transcended and integrated. Brahman is not to be identified either with the undifferentiated aesthetic continuum or with the theoretical continuum of modern experimental physics. Brahman is pure existence or ultimate reality. Both the aesthetic continuum and the theoretical continuum are different phases in the creative-evolutionary self-expression of Brahman.

In recent times Dr Carl G. Jung has made a signal contribu-

---

[1] Swami Vireswarananda, trans., *Brahma-Sutras* (mayavati: Advaita Ashram, 1948), pp. 86–9. *See also* Haridas Chaudhuri's article, 'The Concept of Brahman in Hindu Philosophy' in *Philosophy East and West* (Honolulu: University of Hawaii Press, April 1954), pp. 57–9.   [2] *Ibid.*, p. 88.

tion to the understanding of the spiritual wisdom of the East. His notion of 'the collective unconscious' throws a flood of light upon some of the basic concepts of Eastern thought. He interprets Brahman as the true centre, essence or energy (libido) of the collective unconscious, and interprets the Vedāntic doctrine of the identity of Self and Reality (Ātman and Brahman) as 'a deeper layer of unity in the unconscious below or beneath the world of personal fantasies and instincts'.[1] Dr Jung talks of 'the remarkable agreement between the insights of yoga and the results of psychological research', and says: 'Modern psychology knows that the personal unconscious is only the top layer, resting on a foundation of a wholly different nature which we call the collective unconscious . . . the images in the deeper unconscious . . . (are) of a purely supra-personal nature and are therefore common to all men.'[2] The aim of Indian yoga is, as Jung sees it, to realize this deeper layer of unity in the collective unconscious, which is reflected in the great Upaniṣadic statement, 'That art thou'. The individual realizes at this stage his essential oneness with the All of existence. The collective unconscious is 'a universal and homogeneous substratum whose homogeneity extends even into a world-wide identity or similarity of myths and fairy tales'.[3]

Now, Jung shows profound psychological insight in interpreting the concept of Brahman as the universal psychical or spiritual substratum of our human existence, the individual being existentially and essentially one with it. But a proper understanding of the concept of Brahman would reveal that the blanket-term 'collective unconscious' is too inadequate for this universal spiritual substratum. We have seen that the undifferentiated aesthetic continuum and the differentiated theoretical continuum are different phases in the creative self-expression of Brahman which is pure existence. Similarly, the collective unconscious, the rational-ethical consciousness of the civilized man, and the cosmic consciousness of the

[1] C. G. Jung, 'Psychology and Religion' in *Collected Works*, Vol. XI, (London: Routledge & Kegan Paul Ltd., 1958), p. 573.   [2] *Ibid*, p. 573.
[3] C. G. Jung, *Psychological Types* (London: Routledge & Kegan Paul Ltd., 1949), p. 624.

religious mystic, are different phases in the creative self-expression of Brahman which is pure consciousness (*cit*).[1] Pure consciousness or intelligence is egoless unobjective consciousness, beyond all categorized and verbalized expression. It is essentially different from mental consciousness, which is characterized by the polarized subject-object structure. It is also essentially different from the unconscious, which, as unrealized potentiality, seeks higher fulfilment on the conscious level. The unconscious appears darker by comparison with the conscious rational mind. But pure consciousness is that unobjective light[2] which on the one hand lights up the darkest corners of the unconscious mind, and on the other hand represents the supreme fulfilment of the gropings and aspirations of the rational mind. Moreover, this pure consciousness which is also pure existence (*sat-cit*), is the ultimate ground of both the psychological and the physical orders of existence. According to Dr Jung, egoless consciousness is a contradiction in terms, because, in his view, relatedness to 'the ego' is an essential condition of consciousness. 'I cannot imagine a conscious mental state that does not relate to a subject, that is, to an ego',[3] says Jung. This is because Jung considers the objective and empirical consciousness of the rational mind as the prototype of all consciousness. Actual realization of what Dr Jung himself has called 'a deeper layer of unity in the unconscious' would make it possible for anyone to grasp the profound meaning of egoless consciousness, which is otherwise incommunicable and inexpressible. Brahman, the principle of pure intelligence, is, in the collective unconscious, in a state of self-alienation or involution in apparent opposites. Conscious personality emerges out of the collective unconscious in the course of evolution. Higher religious, mystical, and yogic experiences are different modes of self-expression in the human medium of the structureless light of Brahman. Since the egoless consciousness of Brahman is radically different from the polarized consciousness of the mind as well as the darkness of the unconscious, Sri Aurobindo has called it 'the luminous

[1] *Brhadāranyaka Upaniṣad*, 4.5.13.
[2] *Brahma-Sūtras*, *op. cit.*, pp. 115–16. See also *Mundaka Upaniṣad*, 2.2.11.
[3] Jung, 'Psychology and Religion', *op. cit.*, p. 289.

uttermost Superconscience' as distinguished from 'the Night of inconscience'.[1] 'The conscious existence is . . . stretched out as it were horizontally between two other extensions; below is the dark sleep of the subconscient, above is the luminous secrecy of the superconscient. These are the upper and the lower oceans,'[2] says Sri Aurobindo. A failure to distinguish properly between these two layers of the universal psychological substratum of human existence is responsible for Jung's inadequate, although otherwise remarkable, comprehension of the ultimate objective of Indian yoga. His inadequacy of understanding is reflected in passages like: 'The European seeks to raise himself above this world, while the Indian likes to turn back into the maternal depths of Nature.'[3] This clearly shows Jung's failure to understand the concept of Brahman as the unity of above and below, as the transcendent unity of maternal Nature (*Māyā*) and the heavenly Spirit (*Iśwara*). The highest ideal of Indian yoga is neither to turn back into the maternal depths of Nature, nor to rise up to the heavenly Spirit, rejecting Nature, but to discover that ultimate ground of existence in which Nature and Spirit are unified. In realizing the ultimate ground of existence (*Brahman*), one has to come to terms on the one hand with the forces of the unconscious mind, and develop to the highest limit, on the other hand, the rational and ethical consciousness of human personality. It is such an integration of the unconscious psyche and the rational-ethical consciousness—and not a falling back into the depths of the unconscious—which has been affirmed by Indian sages as the pathway to that yogic union with ultimate reality which is the source of all wisdom, love and peace.

DIFFERENT TYPES OF NONDUALISM

It has already been stated that the nondualistic outlook which is inspired by the intuitive apprehension of reality in its undivided wholeness and fundamental oneness is not the same as rationalistic monism. Rationalistic monism identifies the

---

[1] Aurobindo, *The Life Divine*, p. 289.
[2] Aurobindo, *On the Veda* (Pondicherry: Sri Aurobindo Ashram Press, 1956), p. 123.   [3] Jung, 'Psychology and Religion', *op. cit.*, p. 570.

essence of reality with a conceptually formulated determinate principle of unity. It has assumed various forms in Western thought, e.g. naturalism, pantheism, voluntarism, vitalism, absolute idealism, etc. Naturalism designates the essence of reality as Nature with her unconscious physical energy and blind mechanical causation, and seeks to explain mind, spirit, value, etc., as accidental by-products of the interaction of physical forces. Pantheism designates the essence of reality as a logically defined spiritual substance wholly immanent in the realm of Nature. Voluntarism designates the ultimate unifying principle of existence as universal Will. Vitalism conceives of the ultimate unifying principle as the cosmic life force (*élan vital*). Absolute idealism envisages the ultimate unifying principle as Absolute Idea or a unified thought structure, or some kind of cosmic mind. But according to the nondualistic philosophical outlook, unconscious nature and conscious spirit, matter and mind, cosmic will and absolute idea, universal life-force and cosmic mind, etc., are different interrelated factors in the creative self-expression of the indeterminable reality. Since reality is essentially indeterminable, it is not to be identified either with any one of them exclusively, or with all of them collectively.

It follows from the above that according to intuitional nondualism, the multiform fullness of reality refuses to be exhaustively formulated in terms of any particular philosophical system or theological scheme. But nondualism also has assumed various forms in the East, e.g. Vedānta, Tantra, Vaiṣṇavism, Tāoism, and Zen (which is an offspring of Mahāyāna Buddhism coupled with Tāoism). Common to them all is the conviction that the ultimate essence of existence, variously designated as Brahman, Tattvātīta, Puruṣottama, Tāo, Śūnyatā, etc., is beyond exhaustive conceptual formulation or verbalized expression, but accessible to intuitive realization. It is also readily perceived that there can naturally be different lines of approach to the intuitive apprehension of that pure existence. That is why a Chinese can at the same time be a Buddhist, a Confucian, and a Tāoist. A Japanese can at the same time be a Buddhist and a Shintoist. An Indian can at the same time be a Vedāntist, a Vaiṣṇava and a Tāntrist.

Differences between various thought systems are readily understood in the East to be differences in emphasis, relative value, local suitability, etc. They are not construed as radical and disjunctive distinctions. They are ultimately unified in the multiform richness of reality. They are also capable of being reconciled in the dynamic spiritual growth of individuals. It is this nondualistic, all-embracing outlook which has produced the conviction that different ethico-religious systems or yoga techniques are various spiritual pathways leading to the same supreme goal. Likewise, in the practical sphere, nondualism is productive of the belief that different socio-political ideologies such as capitalism, socialism, communism, etc., may be accepted as mutually compatible ruling principles of social existence, relatively valid with reference to the varying social, economical and political conditions obtaining in the different countries of the world.

Let us now have a little closer look into the main points of distinction between the traditional nondualistic systems of the East. They are fundamentally agreed upon the ultimate goal of life, which is immediate experience of pure existence in which the individual and the universal, the sensuous and the rational, and the intellectual and the emotional are reconciled and unified. One major difference between them, specially noteworthy from our standpoint here, is that which arises from their respective predilections for different paths or lines of approach leading to the same goal.

Tāoism recommends the method of *wei wu wei*, effortless and spontaneous living, intelligent co-operation with the spirit of Nature. The concept of *wei wu wei*, which is a key concept in Chinese mysticism, implies, 'acting without action ... it means to get along as Nature does: the world gets created, living things grow and pass away without any sign of effort'.[1] As one lives thus in effortless harmony with the spirit of Nature, the latter gradually and unconsciously leads him on to higher levels of experience and achievement. Zen Buddhism in its most revolutionary form of development recommends the method of 'non-clinging' to any form, object, or state of

[1] Lao-Tzu, *The Way of Life*, R. B. Blankey trans. (London: Frederick Muller Ltd., 1956), p. 39.

consciousness, and thereby attaining the 'Samādhi of formless-ness',[1] the spiritual freedom of 'no-mind' (*wu-hsin*).[2] It is 'the self-seeing type of meditation'[3] which consists in 'seeing into nothingness', and not clinging to even purity, tranquillity, illumination, emptiness, etc. It is the art of seeing things and doing deeds, without clinging to any of them, and without allowing the mind to be defiled or stained by any of them. Tantra recommends that one can best advance spiritually by awakening the central psycho-physical power latent in man, by rousing his dynamic spiritual potential called the *Kunda-linī*.[4] When this spiritual potential or fundamental psychic energy is mobilized and channelled along higher constructive lines, living becomes effortless and spontaneous, attuned to the ultimate goal of existence. Vaiṣṇavism recommends the method of love and devotion, i.e. whole-hearted self-surrender (*bhakti*) to God,[5] who is the sovereign reality and the synthetic unity of the higher values of life. Christian mysticism and Sufism have close resemblance to Vaiṣṇavism in this respect. 'Let Thy Will, not mine, be done' is the secret of spiritual growth here. Vedānta lays stress upon the method of critical self-inquiry. It includes discrimination between truth and falsehood, or between the self and the not-self (*viveka*) and also detachment or renunciation of emotional attachments to, and fixations on, the not-self (*vairāgya*). As soon as false identifications with, and emotional attachments to, the not-self are removed, the indwelling light of truth revealing the nature of pure existence which is also pure consciousness and pure bliss is revealed.[6]

THE DISTINCTIVE CHARACTER OF INTEGRALISM

According to integralism the opposition between the so-called lower nature and the higher nature develops within the cosmic self-expression of the same ultimate reality. The lower nature is the source of physical forces in the world, and of instinctual

[1] Suzuki, *Zen Buddhism*, William Barrett ed. (New York: Doubleday & Company, 1956), p. 177.   [2] *Ibid.*, p. 163.   [3] *Ibid.*, p. 178.

[4] Sir John Woodroffe, *The Serpent Power* (London: Mizae & Co. Ltd., 1953), pp. 245-6.

[5] Swami Tyagiśānanda, trans., *Narada Bhakti Sūtras* (Madrās: Sri Ramkrishna Math, 1952), p. 6.

[6] Sri Saṅkarāchārya, *Vivekachuḍāmani*, slokas 149-55.

drives in the unconscious mind. The higher nature comprises man's rational self-consciousness and his ethical and religious aspirations. The lower nature is the realm of brute fact and blind energy, whereas the higher nature is the realm of intelligence, value and ideal. In spite of all apparent opposition between them, the higher nature evolves out of the matrix of the lower nature through the operation of the superconscient creative dynamism (*śakti*) of ultimate reality. This superconscient dynamism is not to be identified with either the drive of the unconscious or the power of the self-conscious; it is vastly superior to both, and immanently operative in both. Unconscious material nature as well as the self-conscious human nature is ultimately derived from it, the supernal nature (*parā prakṛti*) of the Absolute.[1] Having brought forth into manifestation the rational-ethical-religious being that man is out of the depths of material nature, the superconscient dynamism seems now to be steadily working toward the transformation of man into a still higher form of self-expression such as supermanhood,[2] or a new world order of abiding peace, international harmony and unimpeded human progress. It is this superconscient creative force of evolution, called the Divine Mother by Sri Aurobindo, with which man has fully to co-operate in order to attain integral and dynamic realization of ultimate reality. Such co-operation implies a balanced integration of our relations to material nature on the one hand, and to the ethico-religious or spiritual ideal on the other hand. We can afford neither to suppress material nature nor blindly to follow all her promptings. Similarly, we can hardly afford either to ignore the demands of the spirit, or to be carried off by them in utter disregard of the elemental forces of material nature. Tantra and Tāoism, in course of their historical development, tended at times to yield in too much to the urges of the unconscious, encouraging spiritual malpractice and bringing disrepute upon themselves. This happened when the spirit of unconscious nature had been endowed with special significance as revelatory of the nature of ultimate reality. Vedānta and

[1] Anilbaran Roy ed., *The Message of the Gita* (London: George Allen & Unwin Ltd., 1946), pp. 108–13.
[2] Aurobindo, *The Life Divine*, pp. 5–7.

Buddhism, in the course of their historical development, encouraged at times the ascetic life-negating tendency, over-emphasizing the ideal of renunciation, and thus undermining the foundations of social, economical and political development. This happened when the self-transcending spiritual aspiration or longing for the infinite had been endowed with special significance as revelatory of the nature of ultimate reality. Integralism stresses the concept of balanced harmony between the material and the spiritual. An intelligent organization, controlled fulfilment, and constructive channelling of the material unconscious, can bring it more and more in line with the spiritual ideal. On the other side, an intelligent bridling of the spiritual yearning consistently with one's firm stand on mother earth and one's firm hold on the concrete realities of the physical environment would place it in the proper setting of material evolution. As Sri Aurobindo puts it: 'The touch of Earth is always reinvigorating to the son of Earth, even when he seeks a supra-physical Knowledge . . . the supra-physical can only be really mastered in its fullness—to its heights we can always reach—when we keep our feet firmly on the physical.'[1] The urge of the unconscious material nature, and the ideals of man's ethical and religious consciousness, are different modes of manifestation of the one ultimate creative purpose or will which is superconscient in character. Integralism stresses the need for contacting and co-operating with this superconscient Will or dynamic Divine through balanced self-development and self-perfection. Knowledge of this superconscient creative purpose would impose the ideal of being true to the kindred points of heaven and home, i.e. true to the reality and signifi-cance of material nature as also to the sublimity and grandeur of the spiritual ideal. It is such a balanced growth of personality and integral self-opening to the superconscient creative Will which alone can enable man to fulfil his destiny as a dynamic instrument of higher advancement in cosmic evolution. The more man can open himself without reserve to the evolutionary world-spirit, the more it would become possible for humanity to be the vehicle of higher patterns of perfection realizable in the world.

[1] Aurobindo, *The Life Divine*, p. 13.

THE CONCEPT OF EVOLUTION IN INTEGRAL PHILOSOPHY

It should be evident from the above that in integralism the traditional nondualistic outlook of the East is fruitfully combined with the concept of creative evolution and unlimited progress in the material world, which has been an essential factor in the growth of modern Western civilization. The notion of evolution has, however, been substantially modified and transformed in order to fit into the nondualistic picture, and harmonize with the central conception of reality as essentially beyond space, time and relativity. Or it may be said that Integralism carries the nondualistic outlook on life to its most comprehensive formulation such as entails an affirmation of the full reality and significance of material evolution and progress. According to integralism, evolution is not simply an increasingly complex configuration of matter and motion, presided over by chance. Nor is it 'the rattling-off of a chain forged innumerable years ago', presided over by an extra-cosmic divine mind. Nor is it the gradual emergence, in accidental fashion, of new qualities and superior values, all out of the void. In the view of Integralism, the evolutionary impetus is the superconscient power of creative self-expression of pure supra-evolutionary existence. The dynamism of time is the self-expansive urge of the timeless transcendence. The process of evolution is the infinitely diversified self-determination of the essentially indeterminable reality. Nondual reality is cosmically manifested as the one dynamic world-spirit, and evolution is the creative adventure of the world-spirit in the unchartered ocean of material inconscience, so that the infinite possibilities inherent in reality may be infinitely expressed in material conditions. The superconscient dynamism of the world-spirit is endlessly productive of fresh novelties, higher developments, and new emergent values in the course of cosmic evolution. Minerals, the vegetable kingdom, the animal creation, human rationality, etc., provide the concrete illustration of such emergence. But they do not emerge into being out of the void; they are precipitated in the space-time continuum out of the infinite riches of the creative world-spirit. At the human stage, the process of evolution is in travail with the production of still higher values, namely, the embodied supermind or supermanhood. Supermanhood would be the 'outflowering of the Divine in collective humanity', or the emergence of a new world-order characterized by peace, progress and unity.

INTEGRAL YOGA

Since creative evolution in the material medium is the diversified self-expression of the world-spirit, and since man is essentially a dynamic centre of operation of the latter, his highest destiny is fully to co-operate with the latter by way of advancing the cause of evolution. This is the practical bearing of integral nondualism. Sri Aurobindo has called it integral yoga. It is a dynamic spiritual ideal definable as the art of harmonious and creative living. The essence of integral yoga lies in free, active, and effective co-operation with the super-conscient force of evolution or the dynamic Divine. But how do you co-operate with the dynamic Divine, or the evolutionary world-spirit?

Broadly speaking, there are two essential factors in such co-operation, which constitute the distinctive features of integral yoga as a way of living. These are: first, the balanced unity of meditation and action; and secondly, an intelligent correlation of the ascending and descending movements of consciousness. By stressing the need for a balance between meditation and action, integral yoga points out that it is by harmonizing the introverted and extraverted tendencies of human nature that a person can attain self-perfection and fruitful self-fulfilment. Through meditation one more and more realizes one's true self as a free centre of self-expression of the dynamic world-spirit. Through action one more and more relates oneself to other fellow-beings in love, fruitful co-operation and constructive endeavour toward the fulfilment of the Divine in society. Through meditation one explores the inner regions of the unconscious, removes the internal conflicts and tensions, and acquires profound spiritual insights. Through action one keeps a firm hold on the concrete realities of the physical world, so that the glories of the spirit may be increasingly expressed in the material medium. Through meditation one tears the veil of ignorance (*māyā*), and removes those obstacles in the unconscious mind which hinder the right perspective, i.e. the vision of things as they are in their true proportions and in the context of the eternal. Through action one seeks to express that inner vision toward the fulfilment of the profoundest possibilities of human life and nature. Free and full co-operation with the dynamic Divine naturally assumes the form of *līlā*, i.e. divine play, because it is spontaneous and joyful, free of any sense of compulsion or any burden of anxiety. It is relaxed action, which combines the impulse of creative joy with the spirit of non-attachment to fixed forms and stubborn desires. It is illuminated action which combines the calmness of self-poise with the fullness of enthusiasm in the cause of truth and human welfare.

The second distinctive feature of integral yoga is, as has been stated above, an intelligent correlation between the ascending and descending movements of consciousness.[1] The ascending movement consists in the gradual broadening of spiritual outlook, in rising to higher levels of consciousness, and eventually in apprehending reality as at once the supra-cosmic silence and the cosmic manifestation, as the formless indeterminable (*Śiva*) and the power of infinite self-determination (*Śakti*), as timeless perfection and the evolutionary force of time. Integral experience of reality reveals the truth that spiritual ascent is an incomplete achievement without material descent. So the descending movement of integral yoga lies in bringing down the light and power of higher consciousness into all the strata of our material existence. It consists in transforming the physical, the vital and the mental into effective channels of expression of universal love and all-unifying truth, instead of rejecting them as an unreal superimposition upon the pure self. It consists in transmuting, and making constructive use of, such material forces as health, sex, money, social position, political power, etc., toward the higher ends of

---

[1] Aurobindo, *On Yoga* (Pondicherry: Sri Aurobindo Ashram, 1955), p. 292. See also Sri Aurobindo, *The Riddle of this World* (Pondicherry: Sri Aurobindo Ashram, 1951), pp. 16–22.

human unity and progress, instead of rejecting them as mundane, secular or undivine. Such a co-ordination of ascent and descent in the practice of integral yoga is broadbased upon the integral conception of evolution as the progressive self-manifestation of the superconscient world-spirit in material conditions. It is inspired by an 'awareness of the whole world as the expression, play, or *līlā*'[1] of the Divine.

[1] Sri Aurobindo, *The Yoga and Its Objects* (Pondicherry: Sri Aurobindo Ashram, 1952), p. 10.

2

S. CHATTERJEE

Mind and Supermind in Sri Aurobindo's Integralism

SRI AUROBINDO is one of those great Indian saints who have maintained the continuity of Indian culture through the ages. The foundation of this culture was laid in the Vedas and the Upaniṣads. Since then, there is an unbroken succession of different teachers and religious leaders at different times and places in this ancient land of India. They have infused new life into the body of Indian culture and saved it from the attacks of rival cultures by expanding and enlarging it, so that it might assimilate the best in them or absorb them altogether. There were certain periods of Indian history which presented a crisis in Indian culture and threatened it with disruption and disintegration. But Providence has so ordained it that at every such juncture, one or more of India's great teachers and reformers have sprung up and met the challenge effectively. The result is that although there have been ebb and tide, rise and fall in the stream of India's cultural life, it has maintained an unbroken continuity from the hoary past to the living present. Sri Aurobindo's life and philosophy constitute a golden link in the chain that connects the past with the present in India's cultural life.

THE CONFLICT OF PHILOSOPHIES

The world of philosophy, eastern as well as western, has been the scene of an ever-recurrent clash and conflict between two opposed camps, almost from the very beginning of its history down to the present day. These two are the camps of materialism and idealism, naturalism and spiritualism. The entire course of philosophical speculation from its inception up to this time oscillates between these two extremes in alternating rhythms. On the one hand, there appeared some thinkers who based their metaphysics on sense experience and accepted the physical world as the only real world, and regarded matter as the only ultimate reality. They are variously designated as materialists, physicalists, naturalists, panhylists, panobjectivists and positivists. Whatever may be the names given to them, they all agree in holding that only matter and the physical world are real, and in negating what is called mind, soul, spirit or God. These they look upon with suspicion and distrust, and reduce them either to certain epiphenomena arising out of matter and its complex organization or to illusions and fictions fabricated by the feverish brain and fear-stricken mind of man. On the other hand, there are the idealists and spiritualists, the panpsychists and subjectivists, who look upon mind, soul or spirit as the only reality, and negate matter and physical reality. These they reduce to ideas and thoughts of the mind, and disparage as products of the unregenerate mind and uncultured brain of man. Thus drawn up in battle array, the materialists and the idealists have gone on fighting with one another, and moved up and down in cycles, so to say, without either side being able to win a decisive and final victory over the other, or to achieve a peaceful and permanent reconciliation with each other.

SRI AUROBINDO'S RECONCILIATION OF THE CONFLICT

Sri Aurobindo's integral idealism is a monumental synthesis and happy reconciliation of ordinary, one-sided idealism and militant materialism. His idealism has its roots in the Vedas and Upaniṣads and the Bhagavad-gītā, and it thrives on the modern scientific and philosophical thought of the West. In speculative boldness it is almost unrivalled and unparalleled in the history of human thought. He draws to a focus divergent currents of thought—Vedic, Tāntric, Buddhist, Sāṅkhya,

Yoga, Viśistādvaita and Advaita, and modern western science and philosophy—and welds them into a synthetic philosophy through *sādhanā* (i.e. a course of arduous and strenuous spiritual training and discipline), and an intense life of continuous meditation.

REALITY AS OMNIPRESENT SAT-CIT-ĀNANDA

The central and basic concept of Sri Aurobindo's integral idealism is that 'All this is the Brahman', that 'An Omnipresent Reality is the Brahman, not an omnipotent cause of persistent illusions'.[1] Brahman being Reality omnipresent, everything—great or small, mental or physical, spiritual or material—is in Brahman, manifests Brahman and is Brahman. Sri Aurobindo starts with this conception of an omnipresent Reality of which neither the non-being at the one end nor the universe at the other are negations that annul; they are rather different states of the reality, obverse and reverse manifestations. This omnipresent Reality is the truth of all life and existence, whether absolute or relative, whether corporeal or incorporeal, whether animate or inanimate, whether intelligent or unintelligent. The reality is one in all its infinitely varying and even conflicting self-expressions. From that all variations begin, in that all variations consist, to that all variations return. The reality or Brahman is the *alpha* and *omega* of all existence. The Brahman is the One besides whom there is nothing else existent. In it all affirmations are denied only to lead to a wider affirmation, and all antinomies confront each other in order to recognize one truth in their opposed aspects and embrace by the way of conflict their mutual unity. This, Sri Aurobindo says, is 'The real Monism, the true Advaita . . . which admits all things as the one Brahman and does not seek to bisect Its existence into two incompatible entities, an eternal Truth and an eternal Falsehood, Brahman and non-Brahman, Self and not-Self, a real Self and an unreal, yet perpetual Māyā'.[2] 'The highest experience of this Reality in the universe shows it to be not only a conscious Existence, but a supreme Intelligence and Force and a self-existent Bliss, and

---

[1] Aurobindo, *The Life Divine*, p. 31. [2] *Ibid.*, p. 31.

beyond the universe it is still some other unknowable existence, some utter and ineffable Bliss.'[1]

When we look at the world around us in a calm and dispassionate spirit, what we observe is a boundless energy of infinite existence and infinite movement pouring itself out in infinite space and unlimited time. Modern science and some modern western thinkers like Samuel Alexander assure us that the universe is a play of this infinite energy and movement. But what is this all, this infinite and omnipotent energy? The Vedānta declares that this movement presupposes and is an aspect of a great timeless, spaceless, motionless existence which is immutable, inexhaustible, actionless, though containing all this action. This is pure existence—existence without quantity, without quality, without name and form, and so ineffable and indescribable. This is the nirguṇa Brahman of the original Vedānta, i.e. the Upaniṣads.

We have then two fundamental facts or realities, the fact of pure existence and the reality of energy or movement. We have to accept the double fact, admit both Śiva and Kālī, the motionless and the moving, and try to understand their relation. Is this universal energy an unintelligent power, an unconscious mechanical force, or is it a conscious energy, an intelligent power? Sri Aurobindo's answer is: 'It is really the power of cit, conscious force, in its nature of creative self-conscience.' This conscious force as inherent in pure, absolute existence—the dynamic principle at the root of the world process—is Kālī, the Mother. Behind the cosmic energy which we observe all around us, there is thus a cosmic consciousness of which cosmic energy is an outflow and manifestation.

The ultimate existence of the Vedāntins is not bare existence; it is a conscious existence or conscious energy, the very nature of which is bliss. An absolute existence which is infinite energy of consciousness is bliss itself. Absoluteness of conscious existence is illimitable bliss of conscious existence; the two are only different descriptions of the same thing. Brahman is thus infinite bliss or the infinite delight of the creative play of force. The self-delight of Brahman is not limited. Just as its energy of consciousness is capable of throwing itself into

[1] Aurobindo, *The Life Divine*, p. 32.

38

infinite forms, so also its self-delight is capable of movement and variation, of revelling in the infinite flux of innumerable universes. The one existence-consciousness that is Brahman manifests itself in numberless universes to enjoy the infinite movement and variation of its self-delight.

It should be noted here that although conscious energy or force presupposes and inheres in pure being or existence, yet it is not the essence of all existence, and does not bind it or constrain it to be always active and creative. If it were so, Brahman would be limited by *Sakti* as It seems to be in the Tantra and in Māyā-Vāda. Rather, we are to say that the conscious force inherent in the pure existent may be at rest or it may be in motion. But if the conscious force of Brahman, which may be at rest and remain equilibrated, is yet found to be active and creative, the only reason for creation is the delight of it. It is for the sheer joy of the thing that the Absolute creates and sustains the world. 'World-existence is the ecstatic dance of *Siva* . . . its sole absolute object is the joy of the dancing.'[1]

So far we have found that the omnipresent Reality is Sat-cit-ānanda and that all things are Saccidānanda. But how from Reality the phenomenal world arises requires explanation. That there is a process and a law guiding it is recognized by us when we study the history of the world. This law cannot be, as some thinkers suppose it to be, a blind mechanical law of the equilibrium of forces working by the accident of development and the influence of the past. Since force is a self-expression of conscious existence, the line of development which force has taken must correspond to a perception of some self-truth and the determination of the line must result from a power of self-directive knowledge inherent in consciousness which enables it to guide its own force along the chosen line. That is, evolution must proceed from God's self-determining power to think or perceive (ikṣaṇa) a certain truth in Himself and to guide His force of creation along the line of that truth. God as infinite consciousness can produce only infinite results. To settle upon a fixed truth or order of truths and build a world in conformity with that which is selected out of infinite

<hr>

[1] Aurobindo, *The Life Divine*, p. 74.

possibilities requires a selective faculty of knowledge commissioned to shape finite appearance out of the infinite Reality. This faculty or power was called māyā by the Vedic seers. Māyā meant for them the power of infinite consciousness to form name and shape out of the vast illimitable truth of infinite existence. It is by māyā that the Infinite finitizes, the static being becomes dynamic becoming, and out of the Absolute the world of phenomena emerges, for the play of one existent with another, of one self with others. The mental play or the *illusion* of māyā conceals the truth from man and misleads him into the belief that he is one against others and not inseparably one with the rest of existence. But he has to emerge from this error into the supramental play or the *truth* of māyā where the 'each' and the 'all' co-exist in the unity of the one truth and manifold symbol or appearance. We have first to embrace the lower or mental māyā and then transcend it; for it is God's play with division and limitation, strife and suffering. The other or higher māyā has to be overpassed, then embraced; for it is God's play of the infinities of existence, of the lights of knowledge and the ecstasies of love, that for which God's energy went out of Him at the first and in which she finds her fulfilment at the last.

There is, therefore, no ground for pessimism and illusionism in the Vedānta. Those who declare the world as full of misery and suffering, or disparage it as void of reality, miss the link between the lower and the higher māyā. To them the mental māyā is the creatrix of the world and a world constructed by the mental māyā is an inexplicable paradox, and a fixed yet floating apparition which can be called neither real nor unreal. But on Sri Aurobindo's interpretation of the Vedānta, there is a relation between reality and appearance, the truth behind and the conceptive phenomenon in front, a relation which is not merely that of an opposition. For him the creative Idea is the Real-Idea, that is to say, a power of conscious force expressive of real being, born out of real being and partaking of its nature. The world is, therefore, not a figment of conception in the universal mind, but a conscious birth of that which is beyond mind into forms of itself. A truth of conscious being supports these forms and expresses itself in them, and the knowledge corresponding to the truth thus expressed reigns as a supramental truth-consciousness (*ṛtacit*). To this supreme truth-consciousness, Sri Aurobindo has given the name 'Supermind'. It is the link between Saccidānanda and the finite world. The world thus expresses a foreseen truth, obeys a predetermining will, realizes an original formative self-vision—it is the growing image of a divine creation.

SUPERMIND

The supermind as an infinite principle of creative will and knowledge, organizing real ideas in a perfect harmony before they are cast into the mental-vital-material mould, is the creator of the worlds. But such an infinite, omniscient, omnipotent mind would be quite different from what we know as mind; it would not be mind at all, but the supramental truth. Yet it is not entirely alien to us. We can not only infer and glimpse that truth, but we are capable of realizing it. In fact, it is the truth which our gradual self-expression in the world aims at and is meant to achieve. In it the truth of being is luminously one with all its manifold expressions. It is the comprehensive and creative consciousness which by its power of pervading and comprehending knowledge is linked to that self-awareness by identity which is the poise of the Brahman, and by its power of projecting, confronting, apprehending knowledge is the parent of that awareness by distinction which is the process of the mind. It has the knowledge of the One, but is able to draw out of the One its hidden multitudes; it manifests the many, but does not lose itself in their differentiations. The supermind contains and upholds the diffusion of the One into the many and prevents it from being a real disintegration. It possesses the power of development, of evolution, of making explicit, and that power carries with it the other power of involution, of envelopment, of making implicit. In the divine and creative supermind all is one in being, consciousness, will and delight, yet with an infinite capacity of differentiation that deploys but does not destroy the unity. We have to regard the supermind as the nature of the Divine Being, not indeed in its absolute self-existence, but in its action as the lord and creator of its own worlds. This is the truth of what we call God, although it is not the too personal God of ordinary theism.

The supermind is the necessary intermediate link[1] between Saccidānanda—the one existence, consciousness and bliss—and the phenomenal world of the many—of mind, life and matter, of space, time and causality. For in itself Saccidānanda must be a spaceless and timeless absolute of conscious existence that is bliss; but the world is an extension in time and space and a movement, a development of relations and possibilities by causality. That which thus develops all things must be a knowledge-will or conscious-force which is the essential nature of existence. But the developing knowledge-will cannot be mental; for mind does not know and cannot control the divine law of development of all things out of conscious-force, but is governed by it, is one of its results and moves in the phenomena of the self-development and not at its roots. Further, the creative knowledge-will which develops all must be in possession of the unity of things and must out of it manifest their multiplicity; but mind is not in possession of that unity, it has only an imperfect possession of a part of the multiplicity. Therefore, there must be a principle superior to the mind which is adequate to explain the creation of worlds in time and space. The supermind is this principle. It is Saccidānanda itself, but Saccidānanda not resting in its pure infinite consciousness, but proceeding out of this primal poise into a movement which is its form of energy and instrument of cosmic creation.

In the principle of supermind there are three general poises or sessions of its world-founding consciousness.[2] The first founds the inalienable unity of things. It is not the pure unitarian consciousness of Saccidānanda in itself which is timeless and spaceless, and does not cast itself out in any kind of extension. On the contrary, it is an equal self-extension of Saccidānanda as it comprehends all, possesses all and constitutes all things. But this all is one, not many; there is no individualization. In it all is developed in unity and as one; all is held by this divine consciousness as forms of its existence, not in any degree as separate existences. It is the pure divine

---

[1] Aurobindo, *The Life Divine*, p. 133. [2] *Ibid.*, p. 135.

ideation and formation in the Infinite, not an unreal play of mental thought, but a real play of conscious being.

In the second poise of the supermind the divine conscious-ness stands back in the idea from the movement which it contains, realizing it by a sort of apprehending consciousness, following it, seeming to distribute itself in its forms. In each name and form it would realize itself as the stable conscious-self, the same in all; but also it would realize itself as a *concentration* of conscious-self following and supporting the individual play of movement and upholding its differentiation from other play or movement—the same everywhere in soul-essence, but varying in soul-form. This concentration supporting the soul-form would be the individual divine or jīvātman as distinguished from the universal divine or one all-constituting self. There would be no essential difference between them, but only a practical differentiation for the play which would not abrogate the real unity. The universal divine would know all soul-forms as itself and yet maintain a different relation with each separately and in each with all the others. The individual divine would know itself as a soul-form and soul-movement of the One, and by a comprehending action of consciousness enjoy its unity with the One and with all soul-forms, and by an apprehending act of consciousness support and enjoy its individual movement and its relations of a free difference in unity both with the One and with all its forms. It would maintain its individual existence and yet realize itself as the One that has become all, and enjoy even in its particular modification its unity with God and all its fellows.

The third poise of the supermind further modifies it so as to support the evolution of a diversified individuality which, by the action of Ignorance, becomes in us at a lower level the illusion of the separate ego. Here the individual divine would so predominantly make the play of relations with the universal and its other forms the practical field of its conscious experience that the realization of utter unity with them would be only the far-off end and culmination of all experience. This third poise would, therefore, be that of a sort of fundamental blissful dualism in unity between the individual divine and its universal source, i.e. Saccidānanda.

These three poises of the supermind involve no departure from the supreme truth-consciousness, no lapse into the falsehood and the ignorance. For the secondary and tertiary supermind would only develop and apply in the terms of the divine multiplicity what the primary supermind had held in the terms of the divine unity. The supermind is thus the creative idea which retains to the full the truth of the supreme Spirit. Mind, life and matter are an inferior expression of it and are inevitably drawn towards it and try to reach it as their final goal.

MIND AND SUPERMIND

Although mind is an expression of supermind and ever tries to reach and attain it, yet in its essence it is a consciousness which divides, limits, cuts out and separates forms of things from the indivisible whole of existence in which they really are and must always be. It is true that mind has a constant urge to go beyond the parts and grasp the whole. But by its inherent limitations it always fails in its attempts. If it goes beyond and tries to conceive a real whole, it loses itself in a foreign element; it falls from its own ground into the ocean of the intangible and the infinite where it can neither perceive, conceive, sense, nor deal with its subject for creation and enjoyment. 'Mind cannot possess the infinite, it can only suffer it or be possessed by it; it can only lie blissfully helpless under the luminous shadow of the Real cast down on it from planes of existence beyond its reach.'[1]

This essential faculty and the essential limitation that accompanies it are the truth of mind and fix its real nature and action, *svabhāva* and *svadharma*. Its function is to translate infinity into the terms of the finite, to limit, depiece. In our consciousness it actually does this to the exclusion of all true sense of the infinite. Thus mind is the nodus of the great ignorance, because it is that which originally divides and distributes the infinite into the terms of the finite. Since, however, the finite is only an appearance of the infinite, there must be an original consciousness which contains and views both at the same time and is conscious of all their relations. In that consciousness there is no ignorance, because in it the

[1] Aurobindo, *The Life Divine*, p. 151.

44

finite is not separated from the infinite as an independent reality; but still there is a subordinate process of delimitation—otherwise no world of finites could exist—a process by which mind, life and matter come into phenomenal being. This subordinate process of the eternal seer and thinker may be called the divine mind. And it must obviously be a subordinate and not really a separate working of the supermind, and must operate through the apprehending movement of the truth-consciousness. That apprehending consciousness, the Prajñāna, places the working of the indivisible all—the supermind—as an *object* of creative knowledge before the consciousness of the same all, somewhat as a poet views the creations of his own consciousness placed before him as if they were things other than himself, while really they are no more than formations of his own being and are indivisible from him. Thus Prajñāna makes the fundamental division which leads to all the rest, the division of the Puruṣa, the conscious soul, and the Prakṛti, the force-soul or nature-soul.[1]

Thus the elements of division have come into being, the infinity of the One has translated itself into an extension of conceptual time and space; the omnipresence of the One in that extension translates itself into a multiplicity of the conscious soul, the many puruṣas of the Sāṅkhya; the multiplicity of the soul-forms has translated itself into a divided habitation of the extended unity, their many mind-bodies. But there is as yet no real division and separation. It is as yet only 'as if', for the divine mind is not deluded, it is aware of all as phenomenon of being and keeps hold of its existence in the reality of being; it does not forfeit its unity. A new factor, a new action of conscious force is therefore needed to create the operation of a hopelessly limited mind as opposed to a freely limiting mind, of the creative mind as opposed to the divine. That new factor is avidyā, ignorance, the self-ignoring faculty which separates the action of mind from the action of the supermind that originated and still governs it from behind the veil. Thus separated mind perceives only the particular and not the universal, or conceives the particular in an unrelated universal and no longer both as phenomena of the infinite.

[1] Aurobindo, *The Life Divine*, pp. 152–3.

45

This limiting avidyā or ignorance which spells the fall of mind from supermind and gives rise to the idea of real division, proceeds from the individualized soul viewing everything from its own standpoint and excluding all others, concentrating itself upon itself and ignoring all others, forgetting the fact that all others are also itself. It is due to the individual souls losing sight of the obvious fact 'that all minds are One Mind taking many standpoints, all lives One Life developing many currents of activity, all body and form one substance of Force and Consciousness concentrating into many apparent stabilities of force and consciousness . . .'[1]

This ignorance is further deepened in man when he identifies his self with the body and wrongly thinks his mind to be determined by the body, especially the brain and the nervous system which it uses as the instrument of its conscious superficial action. But behind this corporeal mentality there is the subconscious or subliminal mind which knows itself to be more than the body and is capable of escaping from this absorption in body and life. This higher mind is able to perceive and deal with other souls as other forms of its pure self. But even the higher mind does not escape from the original error of mind. For there is still the veil of avidyā between the mental and the supramental action. It is only when the veil is rent and the mind becomes responsive to a supramental action that it gets back to the truth of things and becomes instrumental to the supermind. In truth mind is a subordinate action and instrument of supermind. It fulfils its function in the truth, which is to hold forms apart from each other by a phenomenal, a purely formal delimitation of their activity. It has to uphold an individualization of conscious force, delight, substance, which derives all its reality from the supreme universal behind. What we call the ignorance does not create a new thing and absolute falsehood, but only misrepresents the truth. The ignorance is the mind separated in knowledge from its source of knowledge and giving a false appearance of opposition and conflict to the harmonious play of the supreme truth in its universal manifestation, or of the truth of Saccidānanda as the manifest universe (viśva-rūpa).

[1] Aurobindo, The Life Divine, pp. 155-6.

46

3

FREDERIC SPIEGELBERG

Sri Aurobindo and Existentialism

THE spirit of Sri Aurobindo, of course, is alive, like the spirit of all great masters—is and remains alive. But after Sri Aurobindo is no longer with us for over seven years, it seems time now to review the situation and ask ourselves how Sri Aurobindo and his teaching fits into present-day thinking.

There are today a number of systems at work, particularly among western people, of which Sri Aurobindo was hardly aware, could hardly be aware, since they were only in the beginning stages developing in Europe. But in the meantime they have developed so strongly and quite independent from other systems, particularly from Indian systems, that we have to ask ourselves bluntly: Is there still a great message in Sri Aurobindo's system after we have studied existential philosophy?

What do we mean by the word 'existentialism'? I know that everybody who has read any newspapers in the last weeks will think of the 'Beatniks' of the North Beach gang of young artists or pseudo-artists in San Francisco, who all of them know a great deal more about existentialism than most of us do, because they use this word as a live slogan, as a new type of philosophy of life. Some of you, however, may think a little bit more deeply, of Sartre, and of the various novelists who have built on this French philosopher's ideas. Very few of us probably are aware of the longer historical background of this sweeping modern European movement, which actually should be followed down to the Middle Ages, to the thirteenth and fourteenth centuries, when a new movement in western thought, in the early scholastic time, took over: that is the philosophy of nominalism.

William of Occam and a number of his successors preached the philosophy of nominalism, which instantly became very questionable to the Church, and was ruled out later on as a heretic view. What was this bold new philosophy of nominalism in the Middle Ages? Well, to understand it we have first to realize what the prevailing philosophy of the time was. You might briefly say it was 'Platonism' with various derivations and changes. But it was Platonism in so far as one believed in the priority of the 'idea', of the pattern that stands behind events, behind everyday reality and of which this reality of ours, our living day, was only a shadow, a very doubtful imprint, not truly giving us the fullness of that greater power that stood above, below, or behind, or however you want to express it, outside the reality of our every day.

The nominalists were the first ones to challenge this Platonic thinking and thereby to become, to a certain extent, anti-Christian or at least suspicious to the straight line of orthodox fundamentalist Christianity of the time. Because Christianity, as one of the recent greatest existentialists, Martin Heidegger, has said—Christianity was really 'Platonism for the folks'. It was somehow whittled down Platonism that was not any more on the level of high understanding but Platonism for everybody, easy to grasp without containing, of course, the full essence of Platonism and of the Platonic idea doctrine. Nominalism stated what Sartre, the French philosopher, has repeated in our time—and this is probably the most frequently repeated sentence of all existentialist philosophers—Sartre says: 'Existence precedes essence', and that is the key message of existentialism. All philosophies before had said 'Essence precedes existence', that meant to say—to give an example—if we would speak of a man, a concrete man, a human being on the one hand and humanity on the other hand, the idea of Platonism and of Christianity would have been that humanity is the basic pattern, is the real creation of God. It is there in the beginning. A single man on earth today, here and now, is derived from that great idea of humanity, is a special case of it—a minor case of minor importance. The idea precedes what we would call the visible appearance behind it. But Sartre reverses this position when he claims just the other way around, 'Existence precedes essence'. Of course there are single men, many single men really around us, and we can see them with our eyes here and now. Therefore, we can secondarily arrive at the idea of mankind and of humanity, which in itself has not the same powerful, immediate existence value as the human being with whom I am here and now in contact. You, here in this room, obviously are a lot more important to me than the idea of mankind which is somewhere in the ether, vaguely overhead. What does it mean to me? But you mean a great deal to me, right here and now. So you precede whatever there may be as an idea of mankind.

William of Occam, the founder of this mediaeval nominalistic system, went so far as to say that an idea is merely a *flatus voci*, which means an exhalation. It is just a noise like 'blah, blah'. It is ruminating ether which we have set into motion; 'mankind', in other words—is just a word. It is not tangible. No one has ever touched or seen mankind. We can talk about it in mathematical, abstract ways. It is not a matter of direct experience. Ideas were ultimately dethroned from their high place of honour, on which Plato had put them, by the nominalists of the Middle Ages. This particular tradition has been very suspicious to Christians throughout the times, because they are clinging to popularized Platonism more and more.

This idea of nominalism has, as it were, a revival today in the philosophy of existentialism. This is not all that existentialism has to say, but it is one of its important aspects. Modern existentialism goes back to the Middle Ages, and even in our century, in its revived form, does not yet start with Sartre, but really with the Danish theologian Kierkegaard in the last century, and with Karl Jaspers, and finally comes to Sartre and to Madame Beanvoir, and to a long line of French literates who are now sitting in the various Boulevard cafés on the Left Bank discussing existentialism, almost in the style in which our 'Beatniks' in San Francisco have taken it up in their Co-Existence Bagel Shop and in the old Spaghetti Factory. We have in Paris and in San Francisco very, very related movements. However, the Sartre clan and related literary groups today do not represent the highest and best form of existentialist philosophy. And while Kierkegaard was not yet a systematic philosopher, and the 'Beatniks' are no more systematic philosophers, there is one man outstanding in the middle who has given the most illuminating expression to the ideas of existentialism—that is, Martin Heidegger. If Heidegger could only be translated into English, you would all agree with me that here are profound ideas. Unfortunately, Heidegger is not translatable into English. It has not been done and it probably cannot be done properly. I would not dare to do it and I do not know anyone who can, because Heidegger, like so many of the modern German philosophers, philosophizes partly by creating a new language—a new German—new words all along. He uses a great many terms, which, just as the famous Japanese terms of Zen-Buddhism are completely untranslatable, cannot be rendered into English. And many of his words, which are quite obvious and quite intelligible to a German, remain to us as vague and as strange as any Haiku, which also, of course, cannot be translated from the Japanese into English. It is a vague rendering of something that is in it, but you do not have the essence—you do not have the real life blood of it.

Martin Heidegger himself is a very extraordinary personality. He has a great deal of defeatism, a negativistic attitude to life that you also find in extremes in Sartre and the 'Beatnik' followers. This attitude came out in his personality in the way he talked. He always stood bent and he always talked, as it were, in a circle—back into himself. He did not project and he did not try to project, and 'death' was his third word. The second word was 'non-being'. Negative expressions were prevailing and had a definite preference over positive expressions. There were more expressions for the darkness and negativities of life—far more than ever for its possible, but very doubtful, brightnesses and positivities.

Martin Heidegger has never studied Indian philosophy. He remained and remains today, as far as I know, unaware of Sri Aurobindo, unaware of Vedānta even, though he has shown recently signs of becoming interested to start looking into this field, because it was too obvious to too many of his students that a certain amount of parallels were there which may be interesting to the creator of an existentialistic system itself further to investigate. Because, back of Heidegger's system in all of his many writings, you would find, if you could read it in its original, that there is a great deal of mysticism, of deepest metaphysical thought, of religion, of theology. Martin Heidegger himself would be the last one to admit that. In fact, he is highly insulted if anybody ever dares to suggest that some of his existentialist statements have a religious, mystical, theological implication. That is good so. Because Heidegger does not want to speak a religious theological language and so he deliberately keeps away from all kinds of old-fashioned expressions which, for many of us, would be dead. The expressions of traditional theology and even of traditional spiritism and mysticism have taken on with many of us, with many of our best searchers and experts, so much negative characteristics that it would only deflect our attention from Heidegger if he would use them. And, in the attempt to wrestle for entirely new expressions for an entirely new experience, we gain a great deal more by the novelty of words than if he would have used perfectly adequate and possible expressions of the past. Of course, there is a drawback in the fact that he, himself, remains unaware of his interrelation with the great thoughts of traditional metaphysics and religions, as well as with the great thoughts of Indian philosophy. He would reject any such analogy most sternly; this, of course, is a personal limitation which, however, I think is not so bad for us to bear as if he would instead have given us his experiences in an old language, which would not open our eyes and any windows to what is above us.

Now very briefly—what is this central message of Martin Heidegger as the most systematic of all the existentialists? In mediaeval Latin, one might call it the emphasis on the *hic* and *nunc*, the here and now. As I said, in relation to nominalism, not words, verbalization, not ideas, but the direct experience of the things is what matters, of things that touch us, that are around us. An ever repeated sentence of Martin Heidegger, and all of the followers in the existentialist group, is to say that nobody knows any reality at all until he is in it—until he has become a part of it. The standing over against, in objective witness-consciousness, does not give us any knowledge.

Heidegger, who usually dressed in a forester's coat and with wool socks to the knees, and was fond of hiking through the fields and forests of the Black Forest region in southern Germany, said again and again that a man who walks through the fields and admires the beautiful colour of the earth, of the grain, of the flowers (which are weeds), of the clouds, of the sunshine, does not know those fields; only the farmer does, because to him alone it is a life issue. A mere aesthetic appreciation or understanding is a misunderstanding. It does not go to the core. The man who takes a hike through the woods does not know these woods. It is only the forester who can tell what the woods are all about, when he with chalk marks the trees which are not so good and ought to go down soon. And so on in all other fields of life, any kind of science, any kind of knowledge means primarily and first of all leading experimentally into things, participation in them. If you do not become like the children, you will not understand the children. You will not know the children at all. As a foreign observer, as an adult, you will look at them in their cuteness, but you will know nothing truly about them.

In this respect I do feel there is a great deal of similarity between Heidegger's new existentialist emphasis on direct experience and direct participation with things, rather than on looking at them from outside, with traditional Indian philosophy, and with the traditional Indian epistemological approach which also rules out, like the existentialists, the only importance of reasoning and inference. It has its place but it will not ever get us to the full understanding of reality. You have to realize it. You have to open your eyes. It has to be right in front of you and you have to visualize it. It has to become an experience. This is the statement of Vedānta. This is the statement of Aurobindo. And this is also the statement of Heidegger, very much in contrast to the high esteem, sometimes the overestimation, in which reason and thinking is held among all other kinds of philosophers. There is a great deal of overemphasis and overestimation given to thinking. Herein, Heidegger and Aurobindo agree.

What is thinking, after all? Have you been thinking lately? Am I thinking at this moment? You are digesting my words and I let them come. Or, as Aurobindo says in answer to a letter of Dilip Kumar Roy when he asked him a by-the-way question like: 'Do you think, O Master, that it is this way or that way', Aurobindo does not answer this question itself, but he says instead: 'What you call thinking, I never do. I see or I don't see. That is all.' This is a word which Heidegger could very well make his own. He does not think. He does not believe in the importance of thinking, but rather in the importance of living, and of realizing, and of experiencing.

Heidegger has one word which is of foremost importance in his own system. That is the word, *Sein*. His first book was called *Sein Und Zeit*, 'Being and Time'. *Sein*, in German, is unfortunately mistranslated by calling it Being. It is the be-power itself. This particularly emphasized state of being, for which the Sanskrit language would use the word *sat* rather than the word *bhava*. It is the essence and the key word of Heidegger's existentialism. Everything is *Sein*. And there cannot be anything that is not ultimately a part of that all-comprising Beingness. Even becoming is an expression of Being. This statement can be found in Aurobindo. When am I an existentialist? The moment in which I abandon mere abstract thinking, because I am disgusted with it, because I feel that it does not get me anywhere. The moment that I get over the narrow limitations of my reasoning and feel driven instead to experience the bewildering, monstrous miracle of this our being here and now, in this moment on earth, I am an existentialist. When, instead of raising my eyes to nowhere beyond in order finally to hallucinate some Life Power there; if, instead of doing anything like that, I am puzzled, stimulated, enthused by the hardness of metal, by the clicking of time, by the warmth of your breath, by the sound of my own voice and the movement of my own fingers. The moment that I touch this bewildering, surprising, unexplainable, perfectly miraculous reality itself as an astounding mystery, I have become an existentialist. In this again, Heidegger and Aurobindo, without knowing of the existence of each other, agree at depths.

The subjectivity of man, his thinking, his reasoning, has

unfortunately replaced the reality of his *Sein*, of his being itself. We put up a veil ourselves. It is not a veil of māyā. It is a veil of our own making. It is a veil of my own subjectivity with which I cloak the wonderful, bewildering reality before my eyes all the time and which I make the standard for the evaluation of even the divine powers. They become subject to man's standards. God becomes the highest value and what replaces the Divine is not superman. It is not as it should be—the gnostic being—but my own limited personal subjectivity.

Even philosophy, so says Heidegger, will eventually disappear; so will religion; because they are too rational, because they are too far-fetched. They are not existentialist as they should be. They will lose their appeal. Sri Aurobindo says in one of his letters, 'it seems today that all religions are somehow "off shade".' They do not hit any more. You can't select any one of them as primary and as true nor can you make a mixture out of all of them in order to have a true religion. This statement can be found in Aurobindo's *The Life Divine*, as well as in a number of articles of Martin Heidegger. Here they agree completely. Man, it seems, through his stressed rationality has disposed of the miracle of Being and of the Divine. The only hope lies in an approach beyond man. Heidegger quotes Nietzsche and his idea of superman. So does Aurobindo. When it comes to testify to a mentality that is greater than the degenerated mentality in which we find ourselves as a whole in this century, superman is called for, and to characterize him we must say he will have true existentialist mentality, which looks for the direct experience rather than for the taming of reality by our mentality. This superman will have to be more daring than any man who ever walked. And therefore, because he is more daring, he will be able to say more.

Our task is beyond us. Aurobindo says there has been too much SOS crying of the soul in recent centuries in all religions, as if to save our souls were the highest goal to be achieved by man. Salvation is only a side line, something that comes out anyway if we are going after a great task, which is more important than to save our little and precious souls. Therefore, we should stretch beyond this mortifying drive toward redemption and atonement toward the real task over which we can forget the necessity of redemption and atonement and all such minor things. What is the task then, if it is not man? Aurobindo and Heidegger have both the same answer: the earth. That does not mean just this little planet in the solar system in contrast to saturn and venus and other planets, but it means matter. Earth is almost identical in Aurobindo's language with *Prakṛti*, with matter itself.

Heidegger proclaims these things by quoting poetry. He does not quote the saints of the Church, he does not quote the Bible, and he does not quote theological doctrines: he quotes poetry. And his most famous poet is one who ended in insanity, naturally, because he could not be sane and still be appreciated by the entire rational existentialists. I translate the poem of Hölderlin that Heidegger puts into the centre of his discussions of man's task to transform earth:

> Earth. Is not this what you long for?
> To be resurrected invisibly in us.
> Is it not your dream one day to become invisible?
> Earth invisible.
> What, if not transformation
>   Would be your urgent task?
> Earth—O you Beloved One,
> I will.

With this Heidegger agrees and with this Aurobindo agrees. Many of you, who have read the gigantic epic of our time, Aurobindo's *Sāvitrī*, will agree with me that but for the rhythm, this could be almost a quotation from one of the chapters of that epic, wherein Aurobindo speaks so often of 'this green, dangerous, wonderful earth'. Earth needs man to liberate her—maybe even Being itself. *Das Sein* needs man.

It has not been a very popular trend in the great world religions for several centuries to speak of God's need for man. One has concentrated on emphasizing man's need for God. Is it not just about time to reverse the position now? I know many men who today would not be satisfied if they were told that their need for the Divine would be satisfied and everything will come out fine in the end. We want more than that. I have heard such seemingly blasphemous statements as: 'I don't care whether I be damned or saved, as long as I know I have done the work that matters.' This is, of course, logical nonsense, because nobody who has done the work that matters can ever truly be called damned in any real sense, and if God would damn such a man, he would not be a God but a demon—a devil, actually. So we meet here an utter confusion of terms. It is interesting to note that Aurobindo is not alone in emphasizing once more the necessity of man to work for Being, for Saccidānanda, for the Ultimate, rather than to be comforted only by it. For this also is emphasized in existentialist philosophy, particularly in Heidegger, but also in many of his followers. Man feels himself once more as a crusader, as a fighter, as a knight with a great task which is foremost, and over which he can almost forget the divinities around him. He fights the fight for its own sake rather than to please anybody who dishes out a reward to him afterwards. Foremost among these existentialist poets is Rainer M. Rilke, the great Swiss-Austrian mystic, who, in his many poems of *The Book of Hours*, and in his later poems, emphasizes again and again how God is in need of man, how He waits for man, longingly, to do His work. How pitiful God is, if He is left alone, and man does not care for Him any more!

In one of these poems God is called the Great Neighbour. I shall try to paraphrase it.

O Neighbour God
You live up on the mountain in your little old cottage
All by yourself alone.
I wish I could go and keep you company.
But it is not easy to find your place
Because for such a long time
Nobody has walked the path that was leading up there
And the sands of time
And the winds, have blown the path over.
One can hardly find it any more.
But, if I should manage to find the way
And knock at your door,
I know I would be awfully welcome.
O Neighbour God,
So few have called on you lately.

This, probably, in the eyes of an orthodox Christian, would sound like impious blasphemy. But, of course, it is not to be taken as such. Here is the same spirit at work as we find in Aurobindo's emphasis that whatever is, is ultimately a reflex of Saccidānanda, the supreme Reality, be it ever so dark. Also becoming is ultimately a kind of being. That means that the higher philosophy, as Heidegger says, does not have to deny the lower ways of thinking, the lower ways of serving; only the higher philosophy has to deny the stubbornness of the claim of the lower thinking to be everything—to be the highest.

All ways of life, even the lowest ones, can be accepted by the existentialists in so far as they express one aspect of *Das Sein*, of this being power. Aurobindo says all has to be accepted, but all has to be transformed. In the transformed, in the newly visualized state, all has its meaning, all has its place. Nothing should be repressed, rejected, thrown out, denied, destroyed.

Heidegger says a philosophy of ultimate being cannot exist. Why not? Because we, men, are ourselves the philosophy of higher being. God philosophizes, but He does not do that by sitting down and thinking out thoughts, but by creating men. They are His thoughts. So therefore, we men cannot now pretend to have a philosophy of higher being, because we are ourselves the philosophy of higher being. This idea is very related to the greatest of our living theologians—Paul Tillich—who has said, that what we need today is not what all these dialectical theologians have said, a philosophy of broken thinking, because we are living in a poor time where everything is broken. We do not need 'a philosophy of broken thinking', but we need 'broken thinking'. In other words: only in the acceptance of this brokenness can we find meaning.

There is in all our wildest drives, whether they are sexual or artistic or power drives, an element of urgency. This bursting power within us drives us on to live and to die—to do anything —to have goals and to look forward—to press on: it is the greater being that works through me. It is the Ultimate itself, searching itself through us because without us, it could not find itself. This again is an idea which is related to the Indian doctrine of *līlā*, the playfulness of Brahman, who hides like a mother does—playfully behind the main pillar of the house so that the child can find her again. Joy is in the re-finding, in the renewed acquaintance, rather than in the steady staying of it. This is very much what Heidegger expresses and what is traditionally known also in the history of Christian theology. We find it in St Augustine's Confessions. In the very first chapter, St Augustine starts to speculate about God and he says, 'O God, do I know You or do I not know You? If I would know You, I would not search for You because I would have You. If I did not know You at all, I could not possibly search for You, because I would not know what to search for. So, this power in me that strives and longs and looks upward— this is You. I don't find You behind the stars or above the mountains; but in my own striving, in my own longing, You live.'

This is very much what Heidegger expresses when he says that our looking up longingly, that striving, that urgent searching, which is so familiar to man, is that very thing that is not familiar at all to God. Because He does not look up longingly and yet He does, because we are His looking up longingly. Heidegger insists that he is not a theologian, not a religious man, not a mystic—by no means—yet he happens to say that *Das Sein*—Being itself—comes to self-consciousness in our own longing. We, in our poverty, in the time of scarcity, give in this expression of searching and urgent longing a form to that tendency, that life blood, which circulates in Being itself as its major characteristic. The world of science and technique does not at all preclude a jump beyond itself, says Heidegger. We do not have to get away from civilization, to do away with all our gadgets and with the all-too-fast progress of technique and science. Rather, the more you go into science, the more you talk to the great men of science, the more you meet an awareness of the mystery, the more it becomes possible to take science itself as a jumping board. It does not any more today seem that science would drive us away from the opening of greater gates toward higher realization. Aurobindo in his *Sāvitrī* has said that many times. He agrees completely with the existentialist message as Heidegger presents it.

'The beginning is the result.' Whom do I quote, Heidegger or Aurobindo? Both. They both say the beginning is the result.

And, only in so far as *Das Sein* has shadowed itself down into our scarcity and poor existential being today, is it possible for us to live—to live upward again to that from where we come. Involution precedes evolution because, so says Aurobindo, Saccidānanda, the Ultimate itself, has shadowed itself down into the lowest level of the unconscious, of the atom itself, and of the lowliness and forgetfulness in our life; therefore we can remember again; therefore we can awaken. We can turn and grow upwards again. That is, you might call it, the ricochet of the ultimate Being and of the rotating movement of Brahman, that in a cosmic breathing exhales and inhales. And we ourselves are both the exhaling as well as the inhaling of Brahman.

4

S. K. MAITRA

Sri Aurobindo and Spengler:
Comparison between The Integral and
The Pluralistic Philosophy of History

I WELCOME heartily the idea which the sponsors of this volume have of publishing a collection of essays on different aspects of the integral philosophy of Sri Aurobindo, and thank them for the opportunity they have given me of making my humble contribution to it. As for the subject of my contribution, I feel that as I have written on various other aspects of this integral philosophy in other places, it will be most fitting if I write for this volume on his integral philosophy of history, especially as the West has thrown in the person of Oswald Spengler a serious challenge to this philosophy from the side of the pluralistic interpretation of history. This is my apology for the present paper, which makes a brief comparison between Sri Aurobindo's integral philosophy of history and Spengler's pluralistic philosophy of history.

SPENGLER'S 'THE DECLINE OF THE WEST'

Spengler has stated his philosophy of history in his great work, *Der Untergang des Abendlades* ('The Decline of the West'). It is a remarkable book from more than one point of view. It created quite a sensation when it appeared in Germany, and it had a phenomenal reception, for we are told that 90,000 copies of it were sold in the course of a few months. Considering that the book is a difficult philosophical work, this is really very remarkable. The only book of its kind with which it can be compared, so far as its phenomenal success is concerned, is Houston Stewart Chamberlain's book *Die Grundlagen des Neunzehnten Jahrhunderts* ('Foundations of the Nineteenth Century'). It is one of the most outstanding books of the present century. Not only is its theme very grand, but its style also is quite in keeping with the grandeur of its theme. Every word of this great book tells, and there are hundreds of thousands of them. The reader, in fact, is simply bewildered by the grandeur of its theme, the mass of imposing words, each one of which gives him a thrill, and also the marvellous scholarship which it exhibits. Philosophy, history, poetry, drama, and even mythology have been laid under contribution in order to find materials for constructing the grand edifice of the philosophy of history which this book represents. Science has also not been forgotten as a source from which to draw materials for this mighty structure. And although the sources from which the materials have been collected have been so varied and so multifarious, yet the edifice built with them shows a wonderful unity.

Such is the general character of what we may call the external side of this book. But it is only when we come to grips with the contents of this book that the marvellous genius of the author comes fully into view.

DESTINY AS THE MOVING PRINCIPLE OF HISTORY

The moving force behind history Spengler calls 'Schicksal' or 'Destiny'. This term plays a very important part in Spengler's philosophy, and it is therefore very necessary to understand its meaning. Spengler uses this term mainly on account of its freedom from all traces of teleology, much as Bergson uses the terms 'creative evolution' and *'élan vital'* to indicate that the principle behind the movement of evolution is a pure spontaneity, completely free from all determination by any purpose or design. Destiny, in fact, in Spengler's philosophy, has almost the same significance as Bergson's *élan vital*. Only, he will not use the word 'vital' because of its association with life. His object is to employ a term which is free from all association with matter or life or mind. Destiny in his view is precisely the word which serves this purpose, for it cannot be identified with a material or a vital or a mental process. Its absolutely indeterminate character is a sufficient guarantee of its freedom from all material or vital or mental leanings. Perhaps he got this idea of a pure driving force untrammelled by any leanings towards a material, vital or mental force, from Goethe's comparison of it with the wind, as we have in his well-known lines:

> *Seele des Menschen wie gleichst du dem Wasser*
> *Schicksal des Menschen wie gleichst du dem Wind*
> ('Soul of Man, how thou resemblest water!
> Destiny of Man, how thou resemblest the wind!')

DESTINY AND CAUSALITY

He puts it in sharp contrast to the principle of Causality. In fact, the opposition between Destiny and Causality is the main theme of his book. He sees in this opposition the key to the understanding of the problem of history. He explains its nature as follows:

The Destiny-Idea demands life-experience and not scientific experience, the power of seeing and not that of calculating, depth and not intellect. There is an organic life, an instinctive, dream-sure logic of all existence as opposed to the logic of the inorganic, the logic of understanding and of things understood—a logic of direction as against a logic of extension—and no systematist, no Aristotle or Kant has known how to deal with it.[1]

From this paragraph we see that not only the idea of Destiny but even the words which he uses to show its difference from that of Causality, for instance, 'a logic of direction, as against a logic of extension', 'organic life, . . . as opposed to . . . the logic of understanding and of things understood', 'life-experience and not scientific experience', 'the power of seeing and not that of calculating', 'depth and not intellect', suggest very strongly the influence of Bergson.

[1] *The Decline of the West*, Vol. I (London: Allen & Unwin Ltd., 1932), p. 117 authorized English translation by Charles Francis Atkinson.

In the further development of the principle of destiny also we notice very clearly the same influence. In the following passages, for example, where he speaks of the necessity of keeping the process of thinking in abeyance, in order to grasp the nature of the working of destiny, he comes very close to Bergson's view that to know the nature of the creative force or the *élan vital*, one has to give up the guidance of intellect or reason and have recourse to intuition:

He who comprehends the light-world that is before his eyes, not physiognomically but systematically, and makes it intellectually his own by the methods of *causal experience*, must necessarily in the end believe that every living thing can be understood by reference to cause and effect, that there is no secret and no inner directedness. He, on the other hand, who, as Goethe did, and for that matter as everyone does in nine out of ten of his working moments, lets the impression of the world about him work merely upon his senses, absorbing these impressions as a whole, feels the become in its becoming. The stiff neck of causality is lifted by mere *ceasing to think*. Suddenly, Time is no more a riddle, a notion, a 'form' or 'dimension' but becomes an inner certainty, *destiny itself*; and in its directedness, its irreversibility, its livingness, is disclosed the very meaning of the historical world-picture. Destiny and Causality are related as Time and Space.[1]

These words could very well have been put into the mouth of Bergson. Bergson's Time as pure flow is Reality, and all intellectual apprehension of Reality, including the viewing of it from the standpoint of causality, is a spatialization of it. To escape from spatialization it is therefore necessary, says Bergson, to discard the intellect and take recourse to intuition. Exactly similarly Spengler says that to give up the spatial view of things which the intellect brings with it, all that is necessary is to have recourse to pure feeling. Feeling, in fact, in Spengler takes the place of intuition in Bergson.

OPPOSITION BETWEEN CULTURE AND CIVILIZATION

The free movement of destiny is checked in the course of time, and thus there arises the rigid condition which is called civiliza-

[1] *The Decline of the West*, Vol. I, p. 118.

tion. Opposed to civilization is culture, where the free flow of destiny is preserved. The present state of human evolution in the West, in Spengler's view, is a civilization and not a culture. It is therefore a sign of degeneration, and for this reason Spengler gives his great work the title *The Decline of the West*, as its object is to show how in the course of centuries, culture in the West has lost its elasticity and become rigid—a sure indication of its degeneration.

Civilization is soulless, whereas culture is soul itself. As Spengler puts it, 'A Culture is Soul that has arrived at self-expression in sensible forms, but these forms are living and evolving. . . . This Culture is not only a grand thing but wholly unlike any other thing in the organic world. It is the one point at which man lifts himself above the powers of Nature and becomes himself a Creator.'[1] Creativity in its intensest form, therefore, is what expresses itself in Culture. With the gradual loss of creativity, due to regard for stereotyped laws and conventions, Culture slowly merges into Civilization, which represents man's loss of his soul in his infatuation for rigid forms. This change may be characterized as one from Time to Space. Culture which is pure Time slowly decays and hardens into Space, when it passes into Civilization.

FOR SPENGLER THERE IS NOT ONE CULTURE BUT SEVERAL

From what we have said above, it is clear that for Spengler there is not one culture but a number of cultures, not one history but a number of histories. Each culture is distinct from the others; each has its own morphology, its own self-expression which is rooted to the soil on which it grows. There is not one sculpture, one painting, one mathematics, one physics, but many, each in its deepest essence different from the others. Every truth has reference to its age. There are no eternal truths. Every philosophy is an expression of its age and its age alone. There is no universal system of philosophy for all ages.

[1] *The Decline of the West*, Vol. II, p. 331.

This view of the multiplicity of cultures is an off-shoot of the principle of destiny, which is the root idea of the whole book. Destiny precludes the idea of any fixed course; it treats everything as unique and irrepeatable.

Spengler, however, has not been able to keep strictly to this watertight-compartment view of culture. Otherwise he could not have spoken of the blending of three different cultures in the culture of the West. Nor could he have spoken of the parallelisms of different cultures.

This view of the multiplicity of cultures has been severely criticized by Toynbee, Sorokin and others, and rightly so. It is another evidence of the fundamental weakness of his initial standpoint of a purposeless, unconscious destiny as the moving force in history.

DIFFERENT TYPES OF CULTURE DUE TO THE DIFFERENT TYPES OF SOUL REPRESENTED BY THEM

The soul being the essence of culture, it follows that the different types of culture that have evolved historically are due to the different types of soul of which they are the expression. Nine main types he has recognized, of which three have played an important part in the shaping of Western culture, namely, the Apollinian, the Faustian and the Magian. There are, consequently, three different types of culture which western history has exhibited. The characteristics of these three different types have been clearly shown by Spengler. In fact, one of the chief merits of the book is in his wonderful delineation of the characteristics of these three different types of soul. European history, according to Spengler, is the result of the mixing of these three types. The Faustian is the most dynamic of these three types, and the Apollinian the most graceful. The Magian soul differs from both in being more inclined towards mysticism. Each of these types of soul has left its mark upon European history, and it is the commingling of these different types that has given us the European culture as we find it today.

CHARACTERISTICS OF THESE THREE TYPES OF SOUL

We now propose very briefly to deal with the characteristics of these three types of soul. The Apollinian soul is the soul that is responsible for classical culture. Its chief characteristic is its fondness for grace and symmetry and love of order and harmony. The Apollinian soul takes the individual body fixed in all directions as the ideal type of the extended. Examples of the product of the Apollinian soul are: 'mechanical statics, the sensuous cult of the Olympian gods, the politically individual city-States of Greece, the doom of Oedipus and the phallus-symbol'. Opposed to the Apollinian is the Faustian soul, whose prime symbol is pure and limitless space, and whose 'body' is the Western culture that blossomed forth with the truth of the Romanesque style in the tenth century, in the northern plain between the Elbe and the Tagus. The main features of the Faustian soul are thus indicated by the author:

To battle against the comfortable foregrounds of life, against the impressions of the moment, against what is near, tangible and easy, to win through to that which has generality and duration and links past and future—these are the sum of all Faustian imperatives from earliest Gothic to Kant and Fichte, and far beyond them again to the Ethos of immense power and will exhibited in our States, our economic systems and our technics.[1]

The contrast between the Apollinian and the Faustian soul he further indicates as follows: 'The *carpe diem*, the saturated being of the classical standpoint, is the most direct contrary of that which is felt by Goethe and Kant and Pascal, by Church and freethinkers, as alone possessing value—active, fighting and victorious being.'[2] The Apollinian soul is statically poised within fixed limits, whereas the Faustian soul craves for unlimited expansion. The Apollinian soul can therefore be called a soul-body, whereas the Faustian soul is soul-space.

Opposed to both the Apollinian and the Faustian soul is the Magian soul. It is bodyless as well as spaceless. It cannot therefore be represented by a statue. It is iconoclastic. It is, however, dualistic. For it there is the good soul and the bad

[1] *The Decline of the West*, Vol. I, p. 315.   [2] *Ibid.*

soul in eternal conflict with each other. But neither of these souls has a body or dwells in space. This dualism takes the form of the recognition of two substances, called respectively, the spirit and the soul, the falling from the world-cavern into humanity, abstract and divine, and the other a substance permeating the body. In the Magian conception it is the spirit which evokes the higher world, and through this creation, triumphs over mere life, the 'flesh' and nature. There thus runs through the Magian conception the distinction between the flesh and the spirit. There is also clearly evident the cavern idea, the idea of everything being topped by the All-Highest, which is symbolized in all Magian culture by the dome. The idea of the dome or of everything being under a Divine Principle, and the dualism of flesh and the spirit are the characteristic features of all Magian culture. In the impact of the Magian culture with the Faustian, the dualism of flesh and the spirit is often toned down, but not the idea of the dome, which is a perpetual reminder that everything is under a Divine Order or Principle.

CAUSES OF THE DECLINE OF WESTERN CULTURE, ACCORDING TO SPENGLER

All these types of culture—the Apollinian, the Faustian and the Magian—have combined to produce the culture which goes by the name of the Western. Its beginnings are no doubt to be traced to the Apollinian culture, but as it evolved, it developed the characteristics of the Faustian culture, distinguished by their greater dynamic power and urge towards spatial expansion. Afterwards Christianity brought with it the Magian characteristics, the notion of God and the Devil and the cavern idea. The Faustian characteristics are, however, gradually slowing down, and this is causing a steady decline in Western culture. Culture becomes ossified into civilization when it loses its dynamic character. This is, according to Spengler, what is rapidly happening in the West.

The rapid advance of science is one of the contributory causes of this decline, for it has led to the apotheosis of law as the chief guiding principle of the universe. But respect for law runs counter to the spirit of adventure and conquest which supplies the chief dynamic element in culture. Certain social changes, such as the abolition of nobility and rapid industrialization, have also furthered the process of the decline of the dynamic element in culture. The result is, Western culture is fast losing its inward ballast of dynamic power.

It is curious that Spengler looks upon nobility as the chief reservoir of the dynamic power of a nation. Thus, he says:

Culture and class are interchangeable expressions; they arise together, and they vanish together. For that very reason there is found in every culture a sharp sense of whether this or that man belongs thereto or not. The classical notion of the Barbarian, the Arabian, of the Unbeliever (Amhaarez, Giaour), the Indian, of the Sudra—however differently the lines of cleavage were arrived at—are alike in that the words do not primarily express contempt or hatred but establish that there are differences in pulse of Being which set an impassable barrier against all contacts on the deeper levels.[1]

He further makes clear the superiority of the nobility over the other classes from the point of culture by contrasting it with priesthood:

Every nobility is a living symbol of *Time*, every priesthood of *Space*. Destiny and second Causality, History and Nature, the When and the Where, race and language, sex-life and feeling-life—all these attain in them to their highest possible expression. The noble lives in a world of facts, the priest in one of truths, the one has shrewdness, the other knowledge, the one is a doer, the other a thinker.[2]

This adoration of nobility at the expense of the other classes seems rather strange in these days, for nobility is nowadays associated with conservatism, with a tendency to stick to traditional laws and customs and possesses therefore less dynamic power than the other classes. Moreover, the qualities which Spengler finds in nobility, namely, that it lives in a world of facts, rather than in a world of truths, that it has shrewdness and not knowledge, that it is associated with doing and not

[1] *The Decline of the West*, Vol. II, p. 332.   [2] *Ibid.*, p. 335.

with thinking, do not to modern eyes seem to be qualities suggesting greater dynamic power, for truth is certainly more dynamic than facts. Moreover, how can shrewdness be supposed to have more dynamic power than knowledge? Knowledge by common consent has enormous driving force, whereas shrewdness by itself has no dynamic quality and gets whatever dynamism it possesses through association with the knowledge which it helps to acquire. It is knowledge which is the cause of the most revolutionary changes in the social as well as in other spheres, whereas mere shrewdness is a quality of doubtful value, unless combined with knowledge.

Priesthood may deserve all the hard things that Spengler has said about it, though in our country it must be remembered that the Brahmanas who represent the priestly class were always in the vanguard of progress. Spengler has evidently in mind the Christian Church in the Middle Ages, which was of course an incarnation of orthodoxy and prejudice. But nobility is also not free from these. It believes in an inflexible code of morality and further regards it as the privilege of its own class to follow it. Nobility signifies the possession of certain qualities, such as courage, whereas priesthood represents other qualities, such as greater love for knowledge, and by no stretch of imagination can it be said that the former are more dynamic than the latter.

'MAN MAKES HISTORY, WOMAN IS HISTORY'

But nowhere perhaps does Spengler's fondness for the division of human beings into different classes and his love for a pluralistic view of history find better expression than in his famous statement: 'Man makes history, woman is history.'[1] What exactly does Spengler mean by it? Evidently it brings women much nearer to the general direction of the historical process than men. He seems to have gone here much further than Goethe has done in the last line of Faust: 'Das Ewig-Weibliche zieht uns hinan' ('The Eternal-Feminine draws us on and upwards'). Woman here for Goethe represents the supra-rational factor, which is the driving principle in evolution.

---

[1] *The Decline of the West*, Vol. II, p. 327.

Spengler's idea, however, is somewhat different. True to his love for division and pluralism, he wants to divide history into two types—history as it is in itself, which is woman, and history as it is made, which is the role of man. Thus, after saying that man makes history and woman is history, he continues:

Here, strangely clear and yet enigmatic still, we have a dual significance of all living happenings—on the one hand, we sense cosmic flow as such, and on the other hand, the chain and train of successive individuals brings us back to the microcosms themselves as the recipients, containers and preservers of the flowing. It is the 'second' history that is characteristically masculine—political, social, more conscious, freer and more agitated than the other. Feminine, on the contrary, is the eternal, the maternal, the plantlike (for the plant has ever something female in it), the cultureless history of the generation-sequence, which never alters but uniformly and stilly passes through the being of all animal and human species through all short-lived individual cultures. In retrospect it is synonymous with Life itself.[1]

Woman, therefore, for Spengler stands for life itself, what is not subject to any regulation. For man, on the other hand, there is a certain contradiction. As he puts it, 'he is this man, and he is something else besides'. This something else woman neither admits nor understands, but 'feels it to be a robbery and violence upon that which is holiest'. There is thus, according to Spengler, an eternal war going on between the two sexes, which will continue as long as the human race continues.

Thus there are two kinds of history—woman's history and man's history. Woman's history is destiny itself. It is cosmic. Man's history, on the other hand, is political. This is a fundamental dualism which nothing can remove. 'There are public life and private life, public law and private law, communal cults and domestic cults. . . . This double significance of directional Time finds its highest expression in the idea of the State and the Family.'[2]

There is no escape, according to Spengler, from this fundamental dualism. It belongs to the essential nature of time, that

[1] *The Decline of the West*, Vol. II, pp. 327-8.   [2] *Ibid.*, p. 329.

70

is, of the life-process itself. It represents, in fact, two aspects of the life-process, as pure flow and as concretization into definite objects. This double aspect of the life-current is very similar to the double movement of the *élan vital* in Bergson. In fact, as we have seen already, Spengler's whole conception of history is thoroughly Bergsonian.

THE CRISIS OF HISTORY: CULTURE CRYSTALLIZES INTO CIVILIZATION

It is a natural consequence of this view of the double aspect of the life-current that as it proceeds, it goes on hardening, until it loses its original elasticity. This is what happens to all culture, sooner or later. The elasticity of the life-current goes on slowly diminishing, until it is lost entirely. This is what Spengler calls the change from culture to civilization. Culture represents the free untrammelled flow of the life-current; civilization its hardening into rigid forms. This is what has happened already to Western culture. It is bound to happen to other cultures also, according to Spengler, for it is the fundamental process of evolution. Of course, it is a sign of decay, and the object of his great work, *The Decline of the West*, is to show how and why this decay has set in in Western culture.

The resemblance with Bergson's philosophy here is also very striking. Just as Bergson says that when the life-current slows down, matter emerges, so also Spengler asserts that with the gradual hardening up of the life-force, civilization results. Matter in Bergson, and civilization in Spengler, though themselves the product of the life-force, yet have this as their main characteristic, that they impede the flow of it. But whereas in Bergson the impediment is only temporary and the life-current is in a position to chalk out a path for itself in another direction when it is obstructed, in Spengler this obstruction is more permanent and only ceases when a new culture emerges on the complete disappearance of the old. And there is no knowing when it will emerge and whether it will emerge in the same place. And what is worse, there is no guarantee that it will be an improvement upon the old.

71

DENOUEMENT OF PLURALISTIC PHILOSOPHY OF HISTORY: SRI AUROBINDO COMES TO OUR RESCUE HERE

This is the sad denouement of Spengler's pluralistic philosophy of history. And our disappointment is all the greater because of the grandeur of Spengler's work. This disappointment I expressed in another connection some years ago; and I cannot do better than quote the words which I used then:

I ask in all seriousness: Is this to be the fate of history? Is history to be a destiny without a destination? Is the end of man, with his Apollinian, Faustian and Magian soul, to be 'swallowed up and lost in the wide womb of uncreated Night'? It is clear a reorientation of the philosophy of history is absolutely needed if it is to be saved from this fate. Fortunately for us there has emerged in the person of Sri Aurobindo a philosopher who has rescued history from this fate. History, he says, is no doubt the expression of man's destiny. But this destiny is not something indefinite and inchoate. On the contrary, it is another name for the Spiritual Principle which is involved in, and towards which is moving, the universe. It is not mere drifting, it is not mere flow, but it is movement towards a definite goal. Destiny without destination is absolutely meaningless.[1]

Indeed, the conception of destiny of Spengler, with its absolutely indeterminate character, is the root-cause of all the difficulties that one notices in his philosophy of history. Its pluralism is also a direct consequence of it. It is because the process of history, as conceived by him, has no definite goal before it, that the directions along which it moves are multifarious. The difficulty is the same here as in Bergson's creative evolution. Just as creativity with Bergson means only absolute arbitrariness, so here also destiny introduces us to the idea of complete indeterminateness, leading to hopeless pluralism. For as there is no directive principle guiding the march of history, its paths must necessarily be infinitely multifarious.

It is a fear complex that is at the root of this resort to indeterminateness. This is the fear of falling into the meshes of reason with its principle of causality. Here Sri Aurobindo

[1] 'The Philosophical Interpretation of History' (*Bulletin of the Ramakrishna Mission Institute of Culture*, February 1954).

will join Spengler in resisting the tendency to fall into the
snares of the causal or rational explanation of history. Nobody
has more clearly pointed out than he the defects of the causal
interpretation of history, which is a product of the apotheosis
of reason. Every page not only of *The Life Divine* but also of
his other books is a repudiation of the idea that man's greatest
gift is reason and that all his activities are to be judged by the
measuring rod of reason or intellect. Innumerable quotations
can be made from his writings to prove this. We give below
as a sample a quotation from *The Human Cycle* to prove this:

Therefore, too, this perfection cannot come by the mental idea
dealing with the Spirit as it deals with Life. The idea in mind
seizing upon the central will in Spirit and trying to give this higher
force a conscious orientation and method in accordance with the
ideas of the intellect is too limited, too darkened, too poor a force
to work this miracle. Still less can it come if we chain the spirit to
some fixed mental idea or system of religious cult, intellectual truth,
aesthetic norm, ethical rule, practical action, way of vital and
physical life, to a particular arrangement of forms and actions and
declare all departure from that a peril and a disturbance or a devia-
tion from spiritual living. . . . In fact, as we have seen, the mind and
the intellect are not the key-power of our existence. For they can
only trace out a round of half-truths and uncertainties and revolve
in that unsatisfying circle.[1]

In the same strain Sri Aurobindo speaks also in another
passage of this book:

The ultimates of life are spiritual and only in the full light of the
liberated self and spirit can it achieve them. That full light is not
intellect or reason, but a knowledge by inner unity and identity
which is the native self-light of the fully developed spiritual consciousness—and, preparing that, on the way to it, a knowledge by
intimate inner contact with the truth of things and beings which is
intuitive and born of a secret oneness.[2]

We need not make further quotations. It is perfectly clear
from the whole trend of Sri Aurobindo's philosophy that he is

[1] *The Human Cycle* (Pondicherry: Sri Aurobindo Ashram Press, 1949),
p. 303.   [2] *Ibid.*, pp. 211–12.

opposed to the view which looks upon reason with its principle of causality as the determining factor of the historical process. He is, therefore, perfectly in agreement with Spengler in the latter's revolt against the determinism of reason. But while Spengler thinks that the only way to escape from this determinism is to pass into complete indeterminism, Sri Aurobindo expresses in clear and unambiguous terms that to get rid of the determinism of reason it is not at all necessary to pass into complete indeterminism. In fact, complete indeterminism is the negation of all philosophy. There is a higher determinism and a lower determinism. Evolution, in fact, is a passage from a lower to a higher determinism. What is wrong with causal determination is not that it is determination, but that it is determination by an outside agency. The cause is never perfectly united with the effect, so that causal determination never loses the character of an imposition by an outside agency.

In the higher determinism there is the complete disappearance of this sense of an imposition by an outside agency. Determination then becomes completely self-determination. But can one say that what is self-determined is less determinate than what is determined by an outside agency? Rather it is more determinate. This will enable us to understand the difference between the determinacy of our mental consciousness and that of the supramental consciousness. In the following passage from *The Life Divine*, Sri Aurobindo explains this difference very clearly:

But the being and action of the Infinite must not be therefore regarded as if it were a magic void of all reason; there is, on the contrary, a greater reason in all the operations of the Infinite, but it is not a mental or intellectual, it is a spiritual and supramental reason; there is a logic in it, because there are relations and connections infallibly seen and executed; what is magic to our finite reason is the logic of the Infinite. It is a greater reason, a greater logic because it is more vast, subtle, complex in its operations; it comprehends all the data which our observation fails to seize, it deduces from them results which neither our deduction nor induction can anticipate, because our conclusions and inferences have a meagre foundation and are fallible and brittle.[1]

[1] Aurobindo, *The Life Divine*, p. 298.

74

The mode of working of the higher consciousness is no doubt very different from the mode of working of our ordinary mental consciousness. It may even be quite unintelligible to this consciousness, and not only unintelligible but even contrary to the logic of this consciousness; but far from this proving that it has no logic or method, it proves just the opposite. Sri Aurobindo, therefore, warns us against the facile conclusion that because its mode of working is very different from that of our mental consciousness, therefore, there is no method in its working and it operates absolutely arbitrarily:

It is evident that such a Consciousness and Will need not act in harmony with the conclusions of our limited reason or according to a procedure familiar to it and approved by our constructed notions or in subjection to an ethical reason working for a limited and fragmentary good; it might and does admit things deemed by our reason irrational and unethical because that was necessary for the final and total Good and for the working out of a cosmic purpose. What seems to us irrational and reprehensible in relation to a partial set of facts, motives, desiderata, might be perfectly rational and approvable in relation to a much vaster motive and totality of data and desiderata. Reason with its partial vision sets up constructed conclusions which it strives to turn into general rules of knowledge and action and it compels into its rule by some mental device or gets rid of what does not suit with it: an infinite Consciousness would have no such rules, it would have instead large intrinsic truths governing automatically conclusion and result, but adapting them differently and spontaneously to a different total of circumstances, so that by this pliability and free adaptation it might seem to the narrower faculty to have no standards whatever.[1]

But once we root out this foundational idea of Spengler upon which his whole view of history is based, which is a legacy from Bergson, namely, that the historical process is a pure flow which does not know towards what it is flowing, and which is absolutely undetermined by any goal or destination, the rest of the Spenglerian edifice crumbles very quickly. For then it cannot be maintained that civilization will make an end of all culture, for if culture (which is another name for the historical

[1] Aurobindo, *The Life Divine*, p. 299.

process) has a definite goal before it, then it cannot be stopped before it reaches this goal. Sri Aurobindo has also pointed out very clearly that hardening or crystallization is not the last word about a culture, but that after this hardening, a fresh wave sets in to save it. As he puts it: 'Each movement indeed tends to petrify after a shorter or longer activity, but a fresh shock, a new wave arrives in time to save and regenerate.'[1]

WHAT IS TRUE, FROM SRI AUROBINDO'S POINT OF VIEW, IN SPENGLER'S VIEW OF THE CRYSTALLIZATION OF CULTURE INTO CIVILIZATION

To do Spengler justice, however, it must be said that he has done great service in pointing out the danger which threatens Western civilization at the present moment. If he had lived in the present atomic age, he would surely have painted in his own inimitable way an even darker picture of the dangers which lurk in that civilization today. Sri Aurobindo would heartily have joined him in this task—which is undoubtedly a very important one—of warning us of the terrible fate which awaits this civilization if it goes on in the way in which it has proceeded during the last few centuries. As Sri Aurobindo has repeatedly pointed out, the crisis which threatens human—and not merely Western—civilization at the present moment is the apotheosis of science, to the neglect of the other and greater values, that has gone on unchecked for so many centuries. But Sri Aurobindo does not stop by merely pointing out the danger. He shows also the way in which the danger can be averted. It is, he points out, the inevitable result of the growth of mental evolution, and the remedy therefore lies in creating an atmosphere favourable for the appearance of a consciousness higher than the mental which will slowly but surely change the present civilization into something higher.

Unfortunately, Spengler, while he points out very clearly the danger, does not suggest any remedy. In fact, according to him, there is no remedy. The present Western civilization is doomed, and nothing can save it. This is, however, totally

[1] Sri Aurobindo, *The Human Cycle*, p. 237.

opposed to Sri Aurobindo's view, according to which the process of evolution can never stop, and that it is bound to reach its goal, which is nothing less than the complete divinization of man. It is something even more: it is also the transformation of nature into supernature. This is very beautifully expressed in the following concluding passage of *The Life Divine*:

If there is an evolution in material Nature and if it is an evolution of being with consciousness and life as its two key-terms and powers, this fullness of being, fullness of consciousness, fullness of life must be the goal of development towards which we are tending and which will manifest at an early or later stage of our destiny. The self, the spirit, the reality that is disclosing itself out of the first inconscience of life and matter, would evolve its complete truth of being and consciousness in that life and matter. It would return to itself—or, if its end as an individual is to return into its Absolute, it could make that return also—not through a frustration of life but through a spiritual completeness of itself in life. Our evolution in the Ignorance with its chequered joy and pain of self-discovery, its half fulfilments, its constant finding and missing, is only our first state. It must lead inevitably towards an evolution in the knowledge, a self-finding and self-unfolding of the Spirit, a self-revelation of the Divinity in things in that true power of itself in Nature which is to us still a Supernature.[1]

SRI AUROBINDO'S DISSENT FROM THE CYCLIC VIEW OF THE HISTORICAL PROCESS

Another important point where Sri Aurobindo differs from Spengler is on the question of the cyclical view of the historical process. Spengler, as we have seen, is an advocate of the cyclical view. Each culture, according to him, has got its four epochs, spring, summer, autumn and winter, indicating respectively growth, maturity, decline and final fall. There is some resemblance here with our Indian conception of the four *yugas*, but there are great differences also. For one thing, all the four epochs exist in every culture. It is not that one culture succeeds another culture as one *yuga* succeeds another. In fact, so far as the different cultures are concerned, Spengler has not

---

[1] Aurobindo, *The Life Divine*, p. 947.

placed them in an ascending or descending scale. He has, on the contrary, shown their parallelisms.

Sri Aurobindo is definitely of opinion that the process of history is not cyclical. In fact, in his view, the cyclical view of evolution will make evolution a farce, for if one epoch takes it upward, another epoch will bring it down, and the net result will be a big cipher. This is as true of our Indian conception of evolution characterized by the four *yugas*, as of Spengler's conception of it characterized by his theory of the four epochs. For Sri Aurobindo evolution is an onward march from lower to higher levels, and ultimately, to the highest level, namely, Saccidānanda or the Absolute. It is progress all through, not progress followed by regress and vice versa. There may be, and indeed there are, occasional setbacks, but they cannot impede the onward march of evolution. Even in the case of rebirth in the present state of our evolution, Sri Aurobindo does not accept the traditional view of our country, namely, that the fate of the soul after death is determined by the law of Karma. For him the law of Karma is to yield to the higher principle of the evolution of the Spirit, and therefore there is no lapse into a lower state.[1]

Apart from this, there is another reason why, from the standpoint of his integral philosophy, it is not possible for Sri Aurobindo to accept the cyclical view of the historical process. The cyclical view believes in the emergence of a new epoch on the total extinction of the previous one. From the point of view of integral philosophy, the new epoch does not emerge on the extinction of the previous one, but by transforming it. There is no wiping out of any previous stage when evolution passes to a higher stage, but the previous stages exist though in a changed form, in which the principle of the lower stages is more integrated with that of the higher stage than before. This is known as the principle of transformation and is an important principle in Sri Aurobindo's philosophy of history.

[1] Aurobindo, *The Life Divine*, p. 725.

SRI AUROBINDO'S OBJECTION TO SPENGLER'S THEORY
OF A BIPARTITE DIVISION OF HISTORY INTO
A WOMAN'S HISTORY AND A MAN'S HISTORY

From the point of view of integral philosophy, history is one, and therefore there cannot be a division of history into a woman's history, which is cosmic, and a man's history, which is political. One is called by Spengler 'history as flow', and the other, 'history as made'. History as made is also as much a part of cosmic history as history as flow, for the persons who 'make' history are themselves products of cosmic history.

Spengler here in this bipartite division of history has gone much beyond where Goethe would have liked us to go. For the closing line of Goethe's *Faust*[1] only speaks of the Feminine Principle, which is nothing else than the suprarational principle, as the ultimate directive force of the universe.[2] There is nothing in it to suggest a bipartite division of history into a woman's history and a man's history, far less any conflict between the two.

What we have said above about Spengler's division of history into a woman's history and a man's history applies equally to his division of human culture into Apollinian, Faustian, Magian, etc., though here we must say Spengler is less inclined to keep the different cultures completely apart as he is in his bipartite division of history, for he speaks of a mingling of these cultures to form the Western culture of the present day.

The great need of the day is to realize the fundamental unity of the human race. Here nobody has done greater service than Sri Aurobindo. But the way in which he has done it is very different from the way in which the nineteenth-century humanists in the West tried to do it. Their view of man was confined to what man is at the present moment, that is to say, a mental man full of egoism and other limitations incidental to the mental stage of evolution. But Sri Aurobindo is definite

---

[1] 'Das Ewig-Weibliche zieht uns hinan' ('The Eternal Feminine draws us on and upwards').

[2] S. K. Maitra, *The Meeting of the East and the West in Sri Aurobindo's Philosophy* (London: Luzae & Co. Ltd.), 1956, p. 381.

that with this view of man, it is impossible to think of effecting any real human unity. Unless we look upon man's present stage as a temporary stage which he is bound to transcend in his march to his ultimate goal, the idea of human unity is absolutely chimerical. In fact, the unity of man can only be realized through the idea of the divinity of man, as Sri Aurobindo has very clearly and very forcibly stated in the following passage:

A spiritual religion of humanity is the hope of the future. By this is not meant what is ordinarily called a universal religion, a system, a thing of creed and intellectual belief and dogma and outward rite. Mankind has tried unity by that means; it has failed and deserved to fail, because there can be no universal religious system, one in mental creed and vital form. The inner spirit is indeed one, but more than any other the spiritual life insists on freedom and variation in its self-expression and means of self-development. A religion of humanity[1] means the growing realization that there is a secret Spirit, a divine Reality, in which we are all one, that humanity is its highest present vehicle on earth, that the human race and the human being are the means by which it will progressively reveal itself here. It implies a growing attempt to live out this knowledge and bring about a kingdom of this divine Spirit upon earth. By its growth within us oneness with our fellowmen will become the leading principle of our life, not merely a principle of co-operation but a deeper brotherhood, a real and an inner sense of unity and equality and a common life. There must be the realization by the individual that only in the life of his fellowmen is his own life complete. There must be the realization by the race that only on the free and full life of the individual can its own perfection and permanent happiness be founded.[2]

This is Sri Aurobindo's conception of the ideal of human unity—an ideal towards which human evolution is moving and which it is bound to realize.

[1] We need hardly point out that this 'religion of humanity' is very different from the 'religion of humanity' as conceived by Auguste Comte.

[2] Sri Aurobindo, *The Ideal of Human Unity* (Pondicherry: Sri Aurobindo Ashram Press, 1949), p. 378.

5

CHARLES A. MOORE

Sri Aurobindo on East and West

AT this time of great concern about mutual understanding
between Asia and the West and of a recognition of the potential
fruitfulness of an East-West cross-fertilization of ideas, just
where does Sri Aurobindo stand on these matters? Because of
his overall point of view, it is very easy to think of Sri Aurobindo
as promoting and even employing a synthesis of East and West,
as will be indicated in detail later in this paper. It is easy for
a Westerner to understand and appreciate the appeal which
Sri Aurobindo has to many thinkers in modern India because
the modern Indian thinker has had intellectual contact with
the West and has almost inevitably been influenced by that
contact. It is also easy to understand Sri Aurobindo's unpopu-
larity among some Indians because there seems to be a high
degree of Westernization or at least influence from the West in
his work which can easily make it unacceptable to thoroughly
traditional—and especially nationalistic-minded Indians. It is
easy, further, for the Westerner himself to appreciate the
philosophy of Sri Aurobindo, because, although it is an Indian
philosophy and although it depends fundamentally upon
traditional Hindu thought—the Vedas, the Upaniṣads, the
Gītā, and the Vedānta—nevertheless there are very many
elements within the complex of Sri Aurobindo's thought which
strike a familiar note to the Westerner and which he therefore
welcomes. There is an apparent inclusion in the totality of
Sri Aurobindo's system of many ideas which are fundamentally
indigenous and perhaps unique to the West. All of these factors
make for a welcome impression that Sri Aurobindo has achieved
the goal of the modern world—a synthesis and harmony of

East and West in basic ideas and ideals. And when we add to this the fact that Sri Aurobindo is rather highly critical in his own tradition of some of the extremes in terms of which the West (and many in the East, too) has generally interpreted and understood the East (especially India), his appeal to the Westerner becomes even stronger. It would seem that he has thereby furthered the cause of synthesis by injecting Western ideas into the Indian tradition and by removing from the Indian tradition those special features which through the ages have made Hinduism unappealing to the West generally and unacceptable to Westerners—except for some extreme idealists.

This is the impression which one draws from a general—and possibly from a comprehensively detailed—study of Sri Aurobindo's writings. However, the matter is not so simple. Sri Aurobindo's philosophical relation to the West seems to be, instead, extremely complex and difficult to understand. Simply for the sake of identifying his true point of view and attitude, it is worth while to examine the question.[1] And, more important, since the achievement of philosophical synthesis between East and West is an ideal, if not a necessity, of the modern world, it is essential that we determine how far in this direction Sri Aurobindo has travelled and to what extent he has succeeded— to determine both the degree of success and the manner in which he has achieved this success.

As one studies Sri Aurobindo's basic writings in detail, one discovers many attitudes and many relationships, compatibilities and incompatibilities, opposition and cordiality, deliberate rejection and deliberate or veiled acceptance, etc. To summarize these various relationships in order to point out the complexity of the problem, we find: (1) strong contrasts of East and West; (2) general and detailed criticisms (expressed or implied) of the West in view of its falsities, its inadequacies, its limitations; (3) the acceptance of many general attitudes of the West as far as they go, but the necessity of going beyond

[1] This paper is not to concern itself with the deeper and more philosophical phases of Sri Aurobindo's doctrines or the detailed ways in which he harmonizes or reconciles theories of East and West. Much has been done on this aspect of the problem by scholars much more qualified than the present writer. Nor are we concerned here with political issues.

the Western points of view in line with the wisdom of traditional Indian Vedānta; (4) suggestions of significant contributions of the West to the East, perhaps especially in the areas of
social philosophy, but even in the area of methodology and,
possibly, in metaphysics; (5) a decided emphasis upon the
East's superiority to the West[1] in terms of replacing Western
doctrines, or modifying them, or demanding their development
into higher and farther reaches; (6) a distinct impression (by
the reader) that Sri Aurobindo's philosophy does *in fact* consist
of a synthesis of ideas from the West and ideas from the East;
(7) an insistence throughout that ideas or ideals of merit in the
West which seem to be implied in the development of his
thought are not Western in origin but are derived from an
accurate understanding and correct interpretation of the
traditional Vedāntic philosophy of India; and (8) criticism of
certain basic popular or traditional interpretations of Indian
thought in terms of attitudes or ideas that seem to be Western
but which are not accepted as such.

Clearly, then, the complexity and difficulty of the problem
with which we are concerned cannot be denied or ignored.

The situation is further complicated by what might be called
psychological factors which defy adequate analysis or exact
determination of their significance. Such factors are the typical
Indian respect for tradition, the modern Indian sense of
nationalism, the almost inevitable psychological influence of
his thorough acquaintance with Western thought (and his long
residence in the West); and the inevitable intermingling of the
two bases of knowledge, one Indian, the other Western. These—
and perhaps other—psychological considerations complicate
the question and probably doom any investigation to failure.

This situation strikes one as very similar to the Socrates-
Plato problem, one of the famous 'Platonic questions', as to
where in Plato's philosophy or in the Dialogues Socrates stops
and Plato begins. What is Platonic and what is Socratic in the
Dialogues? I tend to agree with one of my revered professors

---

[1] 'India has got to get back *entirely* to the native power of its own spirit'
(*The Renaissance in India*) (Calcutta; Arya Publishing House, 1946), p. 43
(italics are mine). Also, he says she must so transmute and indianize whatever
the West offers, so absorb it and so transform it *entirely* into itself that its
foreign character disappears. *Ibid.*, p. 33 (italics are mine).

who held that not even Plato could answer this question. I suspect that Sri Aurobindo would face the same difficulty.

Be all this as it may, there is one seemingly indubitable fact, and that is that in the essential substance of this metaphysics and in the method by which he achieves his conclusions—omitting in this consideration the mystical approach—the basic ideas of East and West do in fact come together in a synthesis or harmony, regardless of psychological difficulties of interpretation and other complexities of the ways and means by which this synthesis has been achieved. Regardless of the origin or basis of this synthesis, there is no denying the fact that in his overall point of view East meets West and West meets East in one of the most attractive syntheses the mind of man has ever achieved. In fact, one may even this early in this study venture the opinion that his method of synthesis is the only one which holds any promise of success, namely, by way of evolution, development, ascent, actuated or implemented by involution and directed toward spiritual fulfilment and perfection.

Before citing specific ideas or doctrines which seem especially compatible with the West as well as the East, let us note the simple and obvious fact that his entire point of view—the integral point of view—would almost automatically dispose his mind toward a synthesis of ideas drawn from various sources, Eastern and Western, with constant emphasis upon synthesis in general, as well as in innumerable instances dealing with specific philosophical problems. His integral point of view is inevitably open to all evidence, all suggestions, and the full range of his experience. His is essentially a synthetic mind. His genius consists in finding synthesis or harmony where others find only contrast, opposition, divisive distinction. It seems inevitable that a synthesis of East and West should be part of the approach and result of a thinker who appeals for 'an integral human experience'[1] or 'the all-view of the Absolute'.[2] The whole tenor of his thought and work is that of synthesis and integration of those ideas and ideals which by themselves are guilty of the sin of divisiveness but which as parts of an ever-growing or developing whole become significant and true.

[1] Aurobindo, *The Life Divine*, p. 11.   [2] *Ibid.*, p. 347.

Sri Aurobindo wants 'a larger and completer affirmation'.[1] He
wants 'the rich totality of a supreme and integral realization of
eternal Being'.[2] This is the language of totality, which, in a
sense, probably knows no East and West in the deeper resources
of his mind, and can (and does) draw from the entire storehouse
of resources of his rich and full mind to bring about the complete
affirmation he considers the only ultimate truth.

In addition to this overall point of view, there are, as has
been said, almost innumerable specific instances of ideas,
ideals, doctrines, and methods, in which a synthesis has been
achieved between typical Eastern and typical Western tendencies. Among these are many ideas or attitudes which
Westerners recognize, which appeal to Westerners, and which
therefore make them see in Sri Aurobindo's thought a synthesis
of their Western points of view with the Eastern, specifically
the Indian. Among these may simply be listed,[3] without any
elaboration whatsoever, the following: the idea and method of
evolution and development from the more material to the
highest spiritual; possibly the idea of involution (as perhaps in
Aristotle, Hegel, Leibniz, and others); possibly even the idea
of the necessity of the expression of the Absolute in the non-
Absolute;[4] a demand for realism as opposed to the alleged
illusionism of Hinduism;[5] the reality of the individual as well
as the overall One, or at least the significance of the individual
properly understood;[6] the demand for the active as well as the
passive;[7] an insistence on the importance of the outer man as

[1] Aurobindo, *The Life Divine*, p. 24. See also *ibid.*, Chapters II and III
together.   [2] *Ibid.*, p. 210.

[3] See note, p. 82. The writer deliberately (and wisely) leaves detailed
analyses to others.

[4] This topic (or question) could well be the subject of a very important
study. It is rather crucial in comparing Sri Aurobindo's view of the Absolute
with the views of Western Absolutists. References to the point are very
numerous in *The Life Divine*, with seemingly different possibilities of interpretation. See, e.g., pp. 103, 105, 163, 217, 284–6, 310, 411, 416, and 432.

[5] E.g., see *ibid.*, pp. 95, 393, 396, 405, 417, 419, 427, 569, 604–5, 782; also
Book I, Chapters XIII and XXVIII.

[6] See, e.g., *ibid.*, pp. 35–41, 117, 142, 147, 291, 330 ff., 516, 570, 589. See
also, for contrary view, *ibid.*, p. 323.

[7] E.g., see *ibid.*, p. 753; also *ibid.*, Chapters II and III, especially the latter.
See also, perhaps especially, *The Renaissance in India*, pp. 65–7, quoted
in part below, note 3, p. 86. He speaks disapprovingly of 'the loss of the gust of
life', *ibid.*, p. 80.

well as the inner man;[1] the demand for the living, dynamic life as well as the life of asceticism;[2] the compatibility of spirituality and life as we know it in the here and now;[3] the contention that truth of life and truth of spirit are to be united;[4] the belief that matter has a part to play in the universal scheme, that it is 'fit and noble';[5] that *māyā* does not mean illusion but energy, force, the dynamic element in reality;[6] that reason and intellect are not only useful up to a point but indispensable;[7] that even ignorance is essential, toward the development of complete insight, knowledge and spirituality;[8] that 'The Indeterminates, Cosmic Determinations, and the Indeterminable' are all real and necessary;[9] that 'Brahman, Purusha, Ishwara—Maya, Prakriti, Shakti' are all real and essential;[10] that both the personal and the impersonal are indispensable parts or aspects of reality.[11]

At times Sri Aurobindo does not seem to be opposed at all to the recognition of a synthesis of East and West. He says in so many words: 'To this mutual self-discovery and self-illumination by the fusion of the old Eastern and the new Western knowledge the thought of the world is already turning.'[12] He distinctly opposes, however, any artificial addition of the two traditions and a distortion of Eastern wisdom through modification by the West.[13] He wants 'no mere Asiatic

---

[1] Aurobindo, *The Life Divine*, p. 366.

[2] See above, note 7, p. 85; see especially *ibid.*, Chapter III. See also note 3, below.

[3] See, e.g., *The Renaissance in India*, pp. 46, 77–8. He does not 'regard earthly life as a temporal vanity'. Nor does he, in his ideal, 'mean the exclusion of anything whatsoever from our scope, of any of the great aims of human life, any of the great problems of our modern world, any form of human activity. . . .', *ibid.*, pp. 65–68. [4] See, e.g., *The Life Divine*, p. 890.

[5] *The Renaissance in India*, pp. 8–9. See also *The Life Divine*, pp. 431, 876, and Chapter XXV. See also Sri Aurobindo, *Evolution* (Pondicherry: Sri Aurobindo Ashram, 1950), Chapter III, especially pp. 30–33.

[6] See above, note 5, p. 85; also *The Life Divine*, Book II, Part I, Chapters II, V, VI.

[7] See *ibid.*, pp. 12–13, 20, 33, 65–6, 331, 780, 782. See also *Evolution*, p. 34.

[8] See, e.g., *The Life Divine*, pp. 446, 504, 505–7, 549. Also, of course, *ibid.*, Book II, Part I, Chapters VII, VIII, XI, XII, XIII.

[9] *Ibid.*, Book II, Part I, Chapter I. [10] *Ibid.*, Book II, Part I, Chapter II. [11] See above, note 10; also, e.g. *ibid.*, pp. 880–2. [12] *Ibid.*, p. 107. [13] *The Renaissance in India*, pp. 33, 38–43, 77–8.

modification of the West',[1] no 'incongruous assimilation',[2] but a 'subtle fusing'[3] seems to meet with his approval. He speaks of the period of Western influence upon Indian thought as a period of 'crude reception'[4] but also says that it '. . . left behind it results that were of value and indeed indispensable to a powerful renaissance'.[5] Without belabouring the point, then, there is over-abundant evidence of what amounts to a synthesis of East and West in the philosophy and writings of Sri Aurobindo.

Very tellingly Sri Aurobindo says: 'We have both made mistakes, faltered in the true application of our ideals, been misled into unhealthy exaggeration. Europe has understood the lesson, she is striving to correct herself; but she does not for this reason forswear science, democracy, progress, but purposes to complete and perfect them, to use them better, to give them a sounder direction. She is admitting the light of the East, but on the basis of her own way of thinking and living, opening herself to the truth of spirit but not abandoning her own truth of life and science and social ideals. We should be as faithful, as free in our dealings with the Indian spirit and modern influences; correct what was wrong with us; apply our spirituality on broader and freer lines, be if possible not less but more spiritual than were our forefathers; admit Western science, reason, progressiveness, the essential modern ideas, but on the basis of our own way of life and assimilated to our spiritual aim and ideal; open ourselves to the throb of life, the pragmatic activity, the great modern endeavour, but not therefore abandon our fundamental view of God and man and Nature. There is no real quarrel between them' (East and West); 'for rather these two things need each other to fill themselves in, to discover all their own implications, to awaken to their own richest and completest significance'.[6]

This is not to deny, however, that Sri Aurobindo sets up oppositions between East and West on many points, that he is highly critical of many of the West's points of view, methods, and goals (especially its alleged goal) and that he insists rather constantly that the true view—that derived from Indian

[1] *The Renaissance in India*, p. 35.   [2] *Ibid.*, p. 43.   [3] *Ibid.* p. 42.
[4] *Ibid.*, p. 38.   [5] *Ibid.*, p. 38.   [6] *Ibid.*, pp. 77–8.

tradition—transcends or goes beyond the range of the Western mind.

The interpretation that Sri Aurobindo is consciously seeking a synthesis of East and West is strongly brought into doubt by the fact that he is constantly setting East and West against each other, almost always, though not without exception, to the discredit of the West. It is this rather constant criticism of the West as West which makes it difficult to believe that he is thinking in terms of East and West as a partnership in ideas. However, his criticisms of the West are of the West as the West in its exclusive and one-sided perspective. This criticism of Western ideas is criticism of those ideas by themselves and in abstraction from the total perspective which he requires and in which many of these Western ideas can find a sound and important place. The criticism consists largely in the fact that these ideas are wrong because they are isolated, partial points of view; the West is wrong because it takes these one-sided points of view to be the ultimate and complete truth. There is no question that he places higher value on the contrasting Indian points of view in just about every case, but this is because he is thinking of these Indian ideas in the larger perspective, in the totality of view which in his interpretation represents the true meaning and essence of Indian-Vedānta philosophy. Indian ideas are truer because they are inclusive; the West's are unsound because they are exclusive. Although he recognizes the partial significance of practically all of the major Western points of view, he is highly critical of what he considers to be characteristic Western points of view. If one were to compile a list of characteristics which he applies to the East and another of those which he applies to the West, one would find them in sharp contrast almost item by item. Anyone who is acquainted with Indian philosophy or with the philosophy of Sri Aurobindo—or of any Vedāntin for that matter—will find nothing surprising in the following list of criticized concepts and attitudes, but it is significant that these contrasts and criticisms represent a major phase of his overall attitude on East and West. This is found in his specific criticisms of Western ideas and also in his comparative description of the Western and Indian points of view.

The major point at issue here is, of course, the lack or inadequacy of spirituality in the West or the impossibility of achieving full spirituality through the attitudes and methods of the Western mind. This is expressed many times in the works by Sri Aurobindo[1] and constitutes the basic motif of his entire criticism, of course, because the achievement of complete or full spirituality is the goal of Sri Aurobindo's life and teachings. In detail, Sri Aurobindo is critical of the West's exaggerated emphasis upon life;[2] its 'value of life' as opposed to 'truth of spirit'; its 'intellectual, rationalistic, . . . anti-religious' point of view;[3] its excessive or exclusive use of logic, science, reason;[4] its materialism, coupled with reason, to such an extent that the West seems to be identified in his mind with 'rationalistic Materialism'.[5] He feels that pure reason, the method of Western philosophy, may reach metaphysical principles, but it cannot reach 'integral being', which is achievable only by intuition and direct insight.[6] Reason accepts and rejects, whereas integral knowledge is not guilty of such unsound (untrue) divisiveness and abstraction.[7] He opposes its seemingly complete separation of religion and spirituality, on the one hand, and intellectuality and practical life, on the other, as 'two entirely different things';[8] its inade-

---

[1] See below, notes 6, 7; also *The Renaissance in India*, pp. 31, 45, 65. See also *The Human Cycle*, pp. 275, 277-8.

[2] *The Renaissance in India*, p. 30.   [3] *Ibid.*, p. 46.

[4] This point is made constantly and repeatedly, in practically every reference to the West as compared with the East, e.g. *The Life Divine*, Chapter II.

[5] At many places in Sri Aurobindo's writings, e.g. *ibid.*, p. 12.

[6] *Ibid.*, pp. 58 ff., 63, 67, 118, 119, 121, 128-9, 156, 165, 166, 184-7, 304, 323, 347, 415, 440, 493, 781, 827, 842, 910-11, 926, as examples of very many references.

[7] 'What to the mental reason are irreconcilable differences present themselves to the Overmind intelligence as coexistent correlations; what to the mental reason are contraries to the Overmind intelligence complementaries', *The Life Divine*, p. 258. Elsewhere he speaks of 'supramental rationality', *ibid.*, p. 341. This is the process by which he achieves the integral philosophy and its synthesis of Western incompatibles, such as the one and the many, the Absolute and the empirical, reason and intuition, spiritual and worldly or material, finite and infinite, inner and outer, form and formlessness, personal and impersonal, etc. See, e.g., *ibid.*, pp. 304-5.

[8] *The Renaissance in India*, p. 65.

quate concept of the very meaning of religion or spirituality.[1] He finds fault with the West's concept of religion and with its achievement merely of a personal God as contrasted with the Indian Supermind.[2] He condemns its interest in the outer man and the outer approach to truth rather than the indispensable inner way.[3] He finds Western philosophy of little value as in sharp contrast with Eastern philosophy since it has produced 'nothing of the first importance in fact which India has not already stated in forms better suited to her own spiritual temper and genius. . . .'[4] He is critical of Western philosophy also in its status as 'a dispassionate enquiry by the light of the reason into the first truths of existence, which we shall get at either by observing the facts science places at our disposal or by a careful dialectical scrutiny of the concepts of the reason or a mixture of the two methods.'[5] While he is also critical of the alleged but not intrinsic asceticism of India, which he calls 'bankruptcy of life', he is even more strongly critical of what he considers to be the materialistic point of view of the West, which amounts to 'bankruptcy in the things of the Spirit'.[6] He finds the greatest possible achievement in the West to be an overall agnosticism[7] as contrasted with the possibility of the achievement of absolute truth in and through the methods of Indian thought—inner search and intuition. He is critical of the West because of its limited perspective in terms of man as mere humanity.[8] He thinks of the West as dominated by the material, the vital, and the mental, which attitude falls short of the range and heights of true spirituality.[9] He criticizes the West for concern, at best, for things of the mind, as contrasted with the East's concern for the soul.[10] The West concerns itself with ethical evaluation and practice as of ultimate importance and therefore does not reach the truly

[1] Aurobindo, *The Life Divine*, pp. 782–3, 937; also *The Renaissance in India,* p. 65; also *The Human Cycle*, Chapter XXI; also *The Ideal of Human Unity*, Chapter XXXIV, especially pp. 361–2.   [2] *The Life Divine*, p. 123.

[3] See above, note 6, p. 89, for some references. See also *The Renaissance in India*, pp. 72–3.   [4] *Ibid.*, pp. 52–53, 72–73.   [5] *Ibid.*, pp. 72–3. [6] *The Life Divine*, Chapters II and III. See especially p. 11.

[7] *Ibid.*, pp. 11–13, 373.

[8] *Ibid.*, pp. 929, 938, as examples of many references, including those referring to reality as beyond matter, life, and mind, for example, *ibid.*, p. 130.

[9] See preceding note.   [10] *Ibid.*, p. 157.

spiritual or the higher point of view, which transcends the ethical and all similar values and levels of so-called spirituality.[1] The concept of individuality and even the concept of personality as emphasized so strongly in Western philosophy and religion are subjected to criticism as being the result of the intellectual approach, which is incapable of reaching 'the original undifferentiated truth of things',[2] in which individuality and personality are seen to represent a partial and limited point of view and of limited reality. He constantly contrasts the purpose or goal of the West, which he always interprets as worldly or even materialistic in a narrow or broad sense, with the profound spiritual goal of the East.

Such a detailed and item-by-item listing of the points of criticism of the West or of distinct opposition or difference between East and West, to the disparagement of the West, could continue indefinitely, so as to include practically all of the major ideas and ideals which the Western mind has developed as its fundamental points of view. Such more extensive elaboration is unnecessary here, however. It is much more significant to note only fundamentals. At two or three places in his writings,[3] Sri Aurobindo has concentrated his attention on this contrast and criticism and, despite the space involved, it seems wise to quote one long key passage to bring his overall point of view into clear and unmistakable focus. The following major passage, in his chapter on 'The Evolution of the Spiritual Man' in *The Life Divine*,[4] may be considered the most important comprehensive statement of his attitude on the subject under discussion, because it indicates both his recognition, within limits, of the value and significance of Western points of view, and also their inadequacies and the necessity of going beyond them or rejecting them if we are to

[1] Aurobindo, *The Life Divine*, pp. 884–7, 907. See also *ibid.*, Book II, Part I, Chapter XIV in its entirety. [2] *Ibid.*, p. 881.

[3] Of course, comparison and contrast of East and West are referred to many times and in many of Sri Aurobindo's works. I find especially helpful *The Renaissance in India* (in its entirety), *The Life Divine*, Chapters II and III. Other specific and somewhat concentrated treatments may be found in his *The Significance of Indian Art* (Pondicherry: Sri Aurobindo Ashram Press, 1953); *Evolution, The Human Cycle, The Ideal of Human Unity*, and, I understand, *Foundations of Indian Culture*, etc.

[4] *The Life Divine*, pp. 780–3.

reach true spirituality, which, of course, is Aurobindo's basic goal.

This key passage says in part:

An intellectual approach to the highest knowledge, the mind's possession of it, is an indispensable aid to this movement of Nature in the human being. Ordinarily, on our surface, man's chief instrument of thought and action is the reason, the observing, understanding and arranging intellect. In any total advance or evolution of the spirit, not only the intuition, insight, inner sense, the heart's devotion, a deep and direct life-experience of the things of the spirit have to be developed, but the intellect also must be enlightened and satisfied; our thinking and reflecting mind must be helped to understand, to form a reasoned and systematized idea of the goal, the method, the principles of this highest development and activity of our nature and the truth of all that lies behind it. Spiritual realization and experience, an intuitive and direct knowledge, a growth of inner consciousness, a growth of the soul and of an intimate soul perception, soul vision and a soul sense, are indeed the proper means of this evolution: but the support of the reflective and critical reason is also of great importance; if many can dispense with it, because they have a vivid and direct contact with inner realities and are satisfied with experience and insight, yet in the whole movement it is indispensable. If the supreme truth is a spiritual Reality, then the intellect of man needs to know what is the nature of that original Truth and the principle of its relations to the rest of existence, to ourselves and the universe. The intellect is not capable by itself of bringing us into touth with the concrete spiritual reality, but it can help by a mental formulation of the truth of the Spirit which explains it to the mind and can be applied even in the more direct seeking: this help is of a capital importance. . . . For the action of our intellect is primarily the function of understanding, but secondarily critical and finally organizing, controlling and formative.

The means by which this need can be satisfied and with which our nature of mind has provided us is philosophy, and in this field it must be a spiritual philosophy. Such systems have arisen in numbers in the East; for almost always, wherever there has been a considerable spiritual development, there has arisen from it a philosophy justifying it to the intellect. The method was at first an intuitive seeing and an intuitive expression, as in the fathomless thought and profound language of the Upaniṣads, but afterwards there was developed a critical method, a firm system of dialectics, a logical organization. The later philosophies were an intellectual account[1] or a logical justification of what had been found by inner realization; or they provided themselves a mental ground or a systematized method for realization and experience.[2] In the West where the syncretic tendency of the consciousness was replaced by the analytic and separative, the spiritual urge and the intellectual reason parted company almost at the outset; philosophy took from the first a turn towards a purely intellectual and ratiocinative explanation of things. Nevertheless, there were systems like the Pythagorean, Stoic, and Epicurean, which were dynamic not only for thought but for conduct of life and developed a discipline, an effort at inner perfection of the being; this reached a higher spiritual plane of knowledge in later Christian or Neopagan thought-structures where East and West met together. But later on the intellectualization became complete and the connection of philosophy with life and its energies or spirit and its dynamism was either cut or confined to the little that the metaphysical idea can impress on life and action by an abstract and secondary influence. Religion has supported itself in the West not by philosophy but by a credal theology; sometimes a spiritual philosophy emerges by sheer force of individual genius, but it has not been as in the East a necessary adjunct to every considerable line of spiritual experience and endeavour. It is true that a philosophic development of spiritual thought is not entirely indispensable; for the truths of spirit can be reached more directly and completely by intuition and by a concrete inner contact. It must also be said that the critical control of the intellect over spiritual experience can be hampering and unreliable, for it is an inferior light turned upon a field of higher illumination; the true controlling power is an inner discrimination, a psychic sense and tact, a superior intervention of guidance from above or an innate and luminous inner guidance. But still this line of development too is necessary, because there must be a bridge between the spirit and the intellectual reason: the light of a spiritual or at least a spiritualized intelligence is necessary for the fullness of our total inner evolution, and without it, if another deeper guidance is lacking, the inner movement may be erratic and undisciplined, turbid and mixed with unspiritual elements or one-sided or incomplete in its catholicity. For the transformation of the Ignorance into the integral Knowledge the growth in us of a spiritual intelligence ready to receive a higher light and canalize it for all the parts of our nature is an intermediate necessity of greater importance.

[1] E.g. the six classical systems of Hindu philosophy.
[2] E.g. the Yoga philosophy of Patanjali.

But none of these three lines of approach can by themselves entirely fulfil the greater and ulterior intention of Nature; they cannot create in mental man the spiritual being, unless and until they open the door to spiritual experience. It is only by an inner realization of what these approaches are seeking after, by an overwhelming experience or by many experiences building up an inner change, by a transmutation of the consciousness, by a liberation of the spirit from its present veil of mind, life, and body that there can emerge the spiritual being. That is the final line of the soul's progress towards which the others are pointing and, when it is ready to disengage itself from the preliminary approaches, then the real work has begun and the turning-point of the change is no longer distant....

The question inevitably comes to the mind of a Westerner whether or not the foregoing descriptions, contrasts, and criticisms are justified and what is their precise origin and basis. There are major difficulties here, but the value to be derived from setting the account straight, as it were, may outweigh the difficulties and the probably to-be-challenged interpretations expressed.

What, then, is the basis and validity of Sri Aurobindo's sharp contrast of East and West, his setting of one over against the other rather constantly, and his consistent and comprehensive criticisms of the West from the Indian perspective and from the point of view of the integral or total truth which he is seeking? Sri Aurobindo himself admits the significance of what I have previously called the psychological factors which make it difficult for a representative of one tradition adequately to appreciate, or even to understand, the ideas and ideals, the intuitions and insights, of another tradition.[1] It is submitted here that, in spite of Sri Aurobindo's intimate relationship with and knowledge of the West, he is still looking for the light with Indian or Eastern eyes. To use an expression employed by Dr S. Radhakrishnan in another connection, we are all likely to consider the defects of another culture as central to that culture, whereas we consider the defects of our own culture as merely peripheral. Sri Aurobindo seems to follow this pattern too often. The Westerner does not look at Western thought and culture as does Sri Aurobindo—and as do most

[1] See his *The Significance of Indian Art*, Chapter I; see also note, p. 98 below.

Asians. Sri Aurobindo constantly criticizes the Western interpretations of Eastern thought on the ground that they are guilty of easy over-generalization or over-simplification of description and definition in terms of extremes and non-typical points of view or attitudes or points of view which he considers aberrations of the Indian tradition. If there is any unsound note in Sri Aurobindo's treatment of the East-West problem, it is in this respect, namely, that he over-simplifies the West, identifies it with points of view which are not universal, points of view which many in the West would reject, points of view which also, as a matter of fact, the 'Great Tradition' of Western thought has denied.

The West—a vast over-simplification in itself: 'the West'— is not materialistic, is not a slave to science, is not devoted to the limitation that all reality consists of the physical, the vital, and the mental—every one of the very many idealists in the entire Western tradition and in what has been called the 'Great Tradition' would deny these allegations and interpretations. The West's goal is the truth, and to a great part of the West's tradition that truth, that goal, is spiritual as is India's. Nor has the West limited itself to truth of life without regard for 'truth of spirit'. There are many similar misunderstandings which unjustifiably serve to isolate the West from the East. Perhaps there is a difference of emphasis, a difference of preoccupation to a certain extent with differing approaches to life and reality, with different values, but, just as Sri Aurobindo rejects interpretations of India and Indian culture in terms of certain specific, though emphasized, characteristics, so the West should not be interpreted in a similar fashion. Nor is it quite sound to judge the significance of another's point of view strictly from one's own point of view—as, for example, Sri Aurobindo does in evaluating Western religion. Sri Aurobindo puts this extremely important point in a very telling manner by saying that ideas are to be accepted and judged by their applicability in 'opening the door to spiritual experience', and that it is 'an inner realization of what these approaches are seeking after, a liberation of the spirit from its present veil of mind, life and body', which is to be the basis of judgment.[1]

[1] *The Renaissance in India*, pp. 77–8.

This is assuming the sole validity of this point of view and judging other ideas and even ideals strictly in the light of this, his own or his own tradition's particular interpretation. To a Westerner this is an approach, a method, a basis of interpretation which is open to question, and which is no better in this respect than his own provincial and question-begging tendency to reject the East on a similar basis.

Furthermore, to emphasize a point already made in this connection, it would seem that Sri Aurobindo may be encouraging misunderstanding of the West by ignoring the presence there of tendencies of which he approves but which may seem to be less prominent, less emphasized, in the West than in India—the very procedure which he rejects in the West's interpretation of India in terms of some but not all basic points of view. It will be recalled that he rejects the Western interpretations of India in terms strictly of its metaphysical, other-worldly, and ascetic attitudes, although these emphases are undoubtedly a major part of the Indian thought-tradition.[1] So, in the West, for all its use of reason and intellect, for all its recognition of science, for all its interest in social welfare and in worldly improvement, for all its interest in Nature, for all its interest in the individual—it is not justifiable to identify the West with these points of view, because there are also strong elements of religion, spirituality, idealism, social harmony, opposition to individualistic concern and selfishness, interest in man and in the soul and spirit of man,[2] as well as in Nature, a deep concern about the inner spirit of man as well as outer man and outer Nature,[3] and, much more often than realized, a recognition of intuition and an insistence on the limits of reason and science.[4] The West, too, as well as India, sees 'the infinite behind all things finite and it adjudges the values of the finite by higher infinite values of which they are the

[1] *The Renaissance in India*, pp. 21–3.

[2] This is certainly true in Judaism and Christianity, which have been very significant—though greatly ignored—influences in and upon Western thought and culture.

[3] The West is often thought of as a combination of Christianity (and idealism) and science, not one of these alone.

[4] Kant—the only one prominently noticed in India—and many other idealists in the West have called attention to the limits of reason and science.

imperfect translation and towards which, to a truer expression
of them, they are always trying to arrive'.[1] The West also 'sees
a greater reality than the apparent not only behind man and
the world, but within man and the world, and this soul, self,
divine thing in man it holds to be that in him which is of the
highest importance. . . .'[2] It is not sound to say that for the
Westerner religion smacks too much of things external such
as creeds, rights, external piety. Religion in both East and
West consists essentially of 'the attempt to know and live in
the highest self'.[3] The West, too, holds to the spiritual view
that 'mind, life, body are man's means and not his aims. . . .'[4]

Sri Aurobindo often expresses forthright appreciation of
specific points of view which are common in the West, such as
science, reason, progressiveness, the humanitarian attitude,
and social service—but with all of these, as well as in the
metaphysical points of view which he ascribes to the West, he
always finds that the purpose or goal is worldly and materialistic. This is not the interpretation with which higher-minded
Westerners, corresponding to the higher-minded thinkers of
India, and higher-souled thinkers of both, would describe the
ultimate purpose of life and thought. The spiritual goal is to a
very great extent the predominant—or at least an important—
goal of the Western thought-tradition, certainly of the Great
Tradition of Western culture. Without much doubt, the Indian
perspective has emphasized more strongly the infinite, the
ultimate, the absolute spirituality of man and the world, but
not exclusively, as Sri Aurobindo himself insists.[5] It is
unquestionably true that the general tenor of much of Indian
thought often goes beyond the reaches of Western thought—
especially the more naturalistic or materialistic aspect—but
this does not imply lack of ultimate perspective, lack of
spiritual concern, or lack of spiritual aspiration as the dominating motive and goal of thought (and life) in the West.

Be all this as it may, what has been said certainly does not
belittle the tremendous achievement of Sri Aurobindo as a
result of his thinking in terms of the East in relation to the
West. He himself says that the comparative approach is of

[1] *The Renaissance in India*, p. 70.   [2] *Ibid.*, p. 70.
[3] *Ibid.*, p. 80.   [4] *Ibid.*, p. 69.   [5] *Ibid.*, pp. 6–7.

vital importance in helping one understand his own culture and tradition. As he says, 'There is . . . still a utility in fathoming the depths and causes of the divergence.' And, '. . . by the appreciation excited by an opposing view it' (a tradition) 'will be better able to understand itself. . . .'[1] The comparative approach to the ultimate truth leads Sri Aurobindo to interpret and explain for all—Easterners and Westerners—the rich, full, comprehensive, and real content, substance, and meaning of Indian philosophy in a way which makes it infinitely more open to appreciation and understanding by the West and also infinitely more capable of accounting for and including the great variety and range of life, experience, and reality, than earlier, restricted, almost emancipated interpretations have been. This is one facet of the greatness of Sri Aurobindo in the East-West situation. In this achievement he has not only brought Eastern and Western cultures and thought-traditions closer in appreciation and understanding but has also suggested, in his final achievement of the integral philosophy, a world philosophy which does justice to both East and West and also provides at least one formulation of the goal of modern man, a philosophy for humanity as a whole, devoid of the antagonizing, narrowing provincialisms of East and West.

In this elaboration of basic Indian thought in its fullness he may or may not have been directly or indirectly conscious of East and West—he may have derived none of his ideas from the West—but he has shown the world that Indian philosophy *in its fullness*, without its extremes and aberrations and distortions, is able to meet not only the problems of man and his destiny in terms of the ultimate spiritual Absolute but also the problems of man's life and experiences in the here and now in a way which avoids the extremes of East ('denial', 'asceticism') *and* West ('materialism' and 'intellectualism'). He also provides an answer to the exaggerated distortions and misinterpretations of the rich Indian heritage which have made it, in the eyes of many in East and West, able to meet the needs of the man of the spirit but not of man in the world. Sri Aurobindo's integral philosophy, being as he contends only the

[1] *The Significance of Indian Art*, p. 12; see also passages referred to in note 2, p. 89, and note 2, p. 90, above.

explanation of traditional Vedānta, provides for the world an all-comprehensive perspective in which both East and West can feel at home and which can meet the aspirations of all men.

Here, now, in his own words, to illustrate the in-fact synthesis of East and West and to provide a basis for decision on our question, are statements of the essential principles, properly interpreted, of the wisdom of the Indian philosophical tradition—after the quoting of which some possibly significant pertinent observations will be suggested.

Spirit without mind, spirit without body is not the type of man, therefore a human spirituality must not belittle the mind, life or body or hold them of small account: it will rather hold them of high account, of immense importance, precisely because they are the conditions and instruments of the life of the spirit in man. The ancient Indian culture attached quite as much value to the soundness, growth and strength of the mind, life and body as the old Hellenic or the modern scientific thought, although for a different end and a greater motive. Therefore to everything that serves and belongs to the healthy fullness of these things, it gave free play, to the activity of the reason, to science and philosophy, to the satisfaction of the aesthetic being and to all the many arts great or small, to the health and strength of the body, to the physical and economical well-being, ease, opulence of the race. . . . Spirituality is not necessarily exclusive; it can be and in its fullness must be all-inclusive.[1]

Therefore the time grows ripe and the tendency of the world moves towards a new and comprehensive affirmation in thought and in inner and outer experience and to its corollary, a new and rich self-fulfilment in an integral human existence for the individual and for the race.[2]

We perceive that in the Indian ascetic ideal the great Vedāntic formula, 'One without a second', has not been read sufficiently in the light of that other formula equally imperative, 'All this is the Brahman'. The passionate aspiration of man upward to the Divine has not been sufficiently related to the descending movement of the Divine leaning downward to embrace eternally Its manifestation. Its meaning in Matter has not been so well understood as Its truth in the Spirit. . . . As we have seen how greatly Materialism has served the ends of the Divine, so we must acknowledge the still

---

[1] *The Renaissance in India*, pp. 68–9.   [2] *The Life Divine*, p. 11.

greater service rendered by Asceticism to Life. We shall preserve the truths of material Science and its real utilities in the final harmony, even if many or even if all of its existing forms have to be broken or left aside. An even greater scruple of right preservation must guide us in our dealing with the legacy, however actually diminished or depreciated, of the Aryan past.[1]

. . . spirituality itself does not flourish on earth in the void, even as our mountain-tops do not rise like those of an enchantment of dream out of the clouds without a base. When we look at the past of India, what strikes us next is her stupendous vitality, her inexhaustible power of life and joy of life, her almost unimaginably prolific creativeness. For three thousand years at least—it is indeed much longer—she has been creating abundantly and incessantly, lavishly, with an inexhaustible many-sidedness, republics and kingdoms and empires, philosophies and cosmogonies and sciences and creeds and arts and poems and all kinds of monuments, palaces and temples and public works, communities and societies and religious orders, laws and codes and rituals, physical sciences, psychic sciences, systems of Yoga, systems of politics and adminis-tration, arts spiritual, arts worldly, trades, industries, fine crafts—the list is endless. . . . Everywhere, as on her soil, so in her works there is the teeming of a superabundant energy of life. . . . She lavishes her riches because she must, as the Infinite fills every inch of space with the stirring of life and energy because it is the Infinite.[2]

Such then is the view of the universe which arises out of the integral Vedāntic affirmation. An infinite, indivisible existence all-blissful in its pure self-consciousness moves out of its funda-mental purity into the varied play of Force that is consciousness, into the movement of Prakṛti which is the play of Māyā. The delight of its existence is at first self-gathered, absorbed, sub-conscious in the basis of the physical universe; then emergent in a great mass of neutral movement which is not yet what we call sensation; then further emergent with the growth of mind and ego in the triple vibration of pain, pleasure and indifference originating from the limitation of the force of consciousness in the form and from its exposure to shocks of the universal Force which it finds alien to it and out of harmony with its own measure and standard; finally, the conscious emergence of the full Saccidānanda in its creations by universality, by equality, by self-possession and conquest of Nature. This is the course and movement of the world.

---

[1] Aurobindo, *The Life Divine*, pp. 24–5.
[2] *The Renaissance in India*, pp. 11–13.

If it then be asked why the One Existence should take delight in such a movement, the answer lies in the fact that all possibilities are inherent in Its infinity and that the delight of existence—in its mutable becoming, not in its immutable being, lies precisely in the variable realization of its possibilities. . . . In this creation the real Saccidānanda has to emerge.[1]

Thus by the very nature of the world-play as it has been realized by Saccidānanda in the vastness of his existence extended as Space and Time, we have to conceive first of an involution and a self-absorption of conscious being into the density and infinite divisibility of substance, for otherwise there can be no finite variation; next, an emergence of the self-imprisoned force into formal being, living being, thinking being; and finally a release of the formed thinking being into the free realization of itself as the One and the Infinite at play in the world and by the release its recovery of the boundless existence-consciousness-bliss that even now it is secretly, really and eternally. This triple movement is the whole key of the world-enigma.

It is so that the ancient and eternal truth of Vedānta receives into itself and illumines, justifies and shows us all the meaning of the modern and phenomenal truth of evolution in the universe. . . . To this mutual self-discovery and self-illumination by the fusion of the old Eastern and the new Western knowledge the thought of the world is already turning.[2]

Therefore we arrive at this truth of Matter that there is a conceptive self-extension of being which works itself out in the universe as substance or object of consciousness and which cosmic Mind and Life in their creative action represent through atomic division and aggregation as the thing we call Matter. But this Matter, like Mind and Life, is still Being or Brahman in its self-creative action. It is a form of the force of conscious Being, a form given by Mind and realized by Life. . . . Matter is Saccidānanda represented to His own mental experience as a formal basis of objective knowledge, action and delight of existence.[3]

A purely impersonal existence and consciousness is true and possible, but also an entirely personal consciousness and existence; the Impersonal Divine, Nirguṇa Brahman, and the Personal Divine, Saguna Brahman, are here equal and coexistent aspects of the Eternal. Impersonality can manifest with person subordinated to it as a mode of expression; but, equally, Person can be the reality with

[1] Aurobindo, *The Life Divine*, pp. 102–3.   [2] *Ibid.*, pp. 106–7.
[3] *Ibid.*, p. 220.

impersonality as a mode of its nature: both aspects of manifestation face each other in the infinite variety of conscious Existence. . . .[1]

The first aspect of cosmic existence is an Infinite which is to our perception an indeterminate, if not indeterminable. In this Infinite the universe itself, whether in its aspect of Energy or its aspect of structure, appears as an indeterminate determination, a 'boundless finite', paradoxical but necessary expressions which would seem to indicate that we are face to face with a suprarational mystery as the base of things; in that universe arise—from where?—a vast number and variety of general and particular determinates which do not appear to be warranted by anything perceptible in the nature of the Infinite, but seem to be imposed—or, it may be, self-imposed—upon it. We give to the Energy which produces them the name of Nature, but the word conveys no meaning unless it is that the nature of things is what it is by virtue of a Force which arranges them according to an inherent Truth in them; but the nature of that Truth itself, the reason why these determinates are what they are is nowhere visible. It has been possible indeed for human Science to detect the process or many processes of material things, but this knowledge does not throw any light on the major question; we do not know even the rationale of the original cosmic processes, for the results do not present themselves as their necessary but only their pragmatic and actual consequence. In the end we do not know how these determinates came into or out of the original Indeterminate or Indeterminable on which they stand forth as on a blank and flat background in the riddle of their ordered occurrence. At the origin of things we are faced with an Infinite containing a mass of unexplained finites, an Indivisible full of endless divisions, an Immutable teeming with mutations and differentiae. A cosmic paradox is the beginning of all things, a paradox without any key to its significance.

It is possible indeed to question the need of positing an Infinite which contains our formed universe, although this conception is imperatively demanded by our mind as a necessary basis to its conceptions,—for it is unable to fix or assign a limit whether in Space or Time or essential existence beyond which there is nothing or before or after which there is nothing,—although too the alternative is a Void or Nihil which can be only an abyss of the Infinite into which we refuse to look; an infinite mystic zero of Non-Existence would replace an infinite x as a necessary postulate, a basis for our seeing of all that is to us existence. . . .[2]

---

[1] Aurobindo, *The Life Divine*, p. 258.　　　　[2] *Ibid.*, pp. 270–1.

It might be said again that, even so, in Saccidānanda itself at least, above all worlds of manifestation, there could be nothing but the self-awareness of pure existence and consciousness and a pure delight of existence. Or, indeed, this triune being itself might well be only a trinity of original spiritual self-determinations of the Infinite; these too, like all determinations, would cease to exist in the ineffable Absolute. But our position is that these must be inherent truths of the supreme being; their utmost reality must be pre-existent in the Absolute even if they are ineffably other there than what they are in the spiritual mind's highest possible experience. The Absolute is not a mystery of infinite blankness nor a supreme sum of negations; nothing can manifest that is not justified by some self-power of the original and omnipresent Reality.[1]

It may be noted, however, that nowhere in the Upaniṣads is it actually laid down that the threefold status is a condition of illusion or the creation of an unreality; it is constantly affirmed that all this that is,—this universe we are now supposing to have been constructed by Māyā,—is the Brahman, the Reality. The Brahman becomes all these beings; all beings must be seen in the Self, the Reality, and the Reality must be seen in them, the Reality must be seen as being actually all these beings; for not only the Self is Brahman, but all is the Self, all this that is is the Brahman, the Reality. That emphatic asseveration leaves no room for an illusory Māyā. . . .[2]

At the basis of the refusal to recognize the universe as real is the concept or experience of the Reality as immutable, featureless, non-active and realized through a consciousness that has itself fallen into a status of silence and is immobile . . . there is no reason why we should not conceive of the Reality as at once static and dynamic. It is perfectly rational to suppose that the eternal status of being of the Reality contains in it an eternal force of being, and this dynamis must necessarily carry in itself a power of action and movement, a kinesis; both status of being and movement of being can be real. . . .[3]

The one thing that can be described as an unreal reality is our individual sense of separativeness and the conception of the finite as a self-existent object in the Infinite. . . .[4]

In ancient Indian spiritual thought there was a clearer perception of the difficulty; the practice of truth, virtue, right will and right doing was regarded as a necessity of the approach to spiritual

[1] Aurobindo, *The Life Divine*, p. 291. [2] *Ibid.*, p. 405.
[3] *Ibid.*, pp. 410–11. [4] *Ibid.*, p. 417.

realization, but in the realization itself the being arises to the greater consciousness of the Infinite and Eternal and shakes away from itself the burden of sin and virtue, for that belongs to the relativity and the Ignorance. Behind this larger truer perception lay the intuition that a relative good is a training imposed by World-Nature upon us so that we may pass through it towards the true Good which is absolute. These problems are of the mind and the ignorant life, they do not accompany us beyond mind; as there is a cessation of the duality of truth and error in an infinite Truth-Consciousness, so there is a liberation from the duality of good and evil in an infinite Good, there is transcendence. . . .[1]

The absolutist view of reality, consciousness and knowledge is founded on one side of the earliest Vedāntic thought, but it is not the whole of that thinking. In the Upaniṣads, in the inspired scripture of the most ancient Vedānta, we find the affirmation of the Absolute, the experience-concept of the utter and ineffable Transcendence; but we find also, not in contradiction to it but as its corollary, an affirmation of the cosmic Divinity, an experience-concept of the cosmic Self and the becoming of Brahman in the universe. Equally, we find the affirmation of the Divine Reality in the individual: this too is an experience-concept; it is seized upon not as an appearance, but as an actual becoming. In place of a sole supreme exclusive affirmation negating all else than the transcendent Absolute we find a comprehensive affirmation carried to its farthest conclusion: this concept of Reality and of Knowledge enveloping in one view the cosmic and the Absolute coincides fundamentally with our own; for it implies that the Ignorance too is a half-veiled part of the Knowledge and world-knowledge a part of self-knowledge. The Isha Upanishad insists on the unity and reality of all the manifestations of the Absolute. . . .[2]

For we have in this unfolding of knowledge the two terms of the One and the Many, as we have the two terms of the finite and the infinite, of that which becomes and of that which does not become but for ever is, of that which takes form and of that which does not take form, of Spirit and Matter, of the supreme Superconscient and the nethermost Inconscience; in this dualism, and to get away from it, it is open to us to define Knowledge as the possession of one term and the possession of the other as Ignorance. The ultimate of our life would then be a drawing away from the lower reality of the Becoming to the greater reality of the Being, a leap from the Ignorance to the Knowledge and a rejection of the Ignorance, a

<hr>

[1] Aurobindo, *The Life Divine*, p. 557.   [2] *Ibid.*, p. 567.

departure from the many into the One, from the finite into the infinite, from form into the formless, from the life of the material universe into the Spirit, from the hold of the inconscient upon us into the superconscient Existence. In this solution there is supposed to be a fixed opposition, an ultimate irreconcilability in each case between the two terms of our being. . . .

Our conception of the Knowledge and the Ignorance rejects this negation and the oppositions on which it is founded: it points to a larger if more difficult issue of reconciliation. For we see that these apparently opposite terms of One and Many, Form and the Formless, Finite and Infinite, are not so much opposites as complements of each other; not alternating values of the Brahman which in its creation perpetually loses oneness to find itself in multiplicity and, unable to discover itself in multiplicity, loses it again to recover oneness, but double and concurrent values which explain each other; not hopelessly incompatible alternatives, but two faces of the one Reality which can lead us to it by our realization of both together and not only by testing each separately—even though such separate testing may be a legitimate or even an inevitable step or part of the process of knowledge. . . .[1]

A spiritual evolution, an unfolding here of the Being within from birth to birth, of which man becomes the central instrument and human life at its highest offers the critical turning-point, is the link needed for the reconciliation of life and spirit; for it allows us to take into account the total nature of man and to recognize the legitimate place of his triple attraction, to earth, to heaven and to the supreme Reality. But a complete solution of its oppositions can be arrived at only on this basis that the lower consciousness of mind, life and body cannot arrive at its full meaning until it is taken up, restated, transformed by the light and power and joy of the higher spiritual consciousness, while the higher too does not stand in its full right relation to the lower by mere rejection, but by this assumption and domination, this taking up of its unfulfilled values, this restatement and transformation—a spiritualizing and supramentalizing of the mental, vital and physical nature. . . .

Mind and life themselves cannot grow into their fullness except by the opening up of the larger and greater consciousness to which mind only approaches. Such a larger and greater consciousness is the spiritual, for the spiritual consciousness is not only higher than the rest but more embracing. Universal as well as transcendent, it can take up mind and life into its light and give them the true and

---

[1] Aurobindo, *The Life Divine*, pp. 570–1.

utmost realization of all for which they are seeking: for it has a greater instrumentality of knowledge, a fountain of deeper power and will, an unlimited reach and intensity of love and joy and beauty. These are the things for which our mind, life and body are seeking, knowledge, power and joy, and to reject that by which all these arrive at their utmost plenitude is to shut them out from their own highest consummation. An opposite exaggeration demanding only some colourless purity of spiritual existence nullifies the creative action of the spirit and excludes from us all that the Divine manifests in its being: it leaves room only for an evolution without sense or fulfilment—for a cutting off of all that has been evolved is the sole culmination; it turns the process of our being into the meaningless curve of a plunge into Ignorance and return out of it or erects a wheel of cosmic Becoming with only an escape-issue. . . . A large relation of unity, an integration, restores the balance, illumines the whole truth of being and links together the steps of Nature.

In this integration the supracosmic Reality stands as the supreme Truth of being; to realize it is the highest reach of our consciousness. But it is this highest Reality which is also the cosmic being, the cosmic consciousness, the cosmic will and life: it has put these things forth, not outside itself but in its own being, not as an opposite principle but as its own self-unfolding and self-expression. Cosmic being is not a meaningless freak or fantasy or a chance error; there is a divine significance and truth in it: the manifold self-expression of the spirit is its high sense, the Divine Itself is the key of its enigma. A perfect self-expression of the spirit is the object of our terrestrial existence. This cannot be achieved if we have not grown conscious of the supreme Reality; for it is only by the touch of the Absolute that we can arrive at our own absolute. But neither can it be done to the exclusion of the cosmic Reality: we must become universal. . . .

It is true that the soul can ascend into worlds of a greater consciousness beyond the earth, but it is also true that the power of these worlds, the power of a greater consciousness has to develop itself here; the embodiment of the soul is the means for that embodiment. . . .

A complete involution of all that the Spirit is and its evolutionary self-unfolding are the double term of our material existence. . . . It is a perfected and divinized life for which the earth-nature is seeking, and this seeking is a sign of the Divine Will in Nature.[1]

[1] Aurobindo, *The Life Divine*, pp. 603–7.

This, then, is the true wisdom of the Indian mind. It is truly comprehensive. It includes the insights of the East and the insights of the West. It combines their respective unique emphases. It provides, from the point of view of idealism and the significance of spirituality, what might be the inevitable synthesis of what is called the wisdom of the East and the knowledge of the West.

Sri Aurobindo has thus arrived at a comprehensive and, to all intents and purposes, all-inclusive view of the universe and life, providing a world philosophy which in effect brings together the East and the West. The question of the basis upon which this philosophy is founded and its source or sources inevitably arises. There are three possibilities that come to mind. First, this may be, as Sri Aurobindo feels, the true conception of Indian traditional thought, properly and fully explained and interpreted, but a Westerner cannot help wondering if all the West-like ideas and all the arguments he uses (e.g. in treating the problem of evil) are fully and exclusively drawn from the Indian scene. Second, this philosophy may be the result of Sri Aurobindo's own experience, derived mystically rather than merely by bringing out the truth embodied in traditional Indian wisdom. Or, third, it may be, though not consciously so, the inevitable synthesis of the thought of the East and the thought of the West as a result of his intimate knowledge of and experience in both traditions. (It is most difficult to avoid this interpretation, that the West has been significant in his thinking, although, *as far as I know*, he never once admits such influence.) The investigating mind inevitably asks which of these is the true source of Sri Aurobindo's complete philosophy. As already suggested, it may be next to impossible even for Sri Aurobindo himself to identify any one source to the elimination of others. It is very probably the result of an extremely complex mind ready to bring to bear all of its many and profound experiences. The language of the quotations just cited sometimes seems purely Indian, sometimes significantly Western. To the superficially minded Westerner it is quite remarkable, and surprising, to find that such a comprehensive, worldly as well as other-worldly, personal as well as impersonal, rational as well as intuitive, pluralistic as well as monistic, human as well as superhuman, philosophy is the true essence of Indian traditional thought. It is to Sri Aurobindo's everlasting credit that he has overcome the error of such limited thinking by pointing out the remarkable richness of the Indian tradition.

As said, the investigating and inquiring mind inevitably asks for the source, but, as a matter of fact, is it necessary to answer this question, is it possible, is it important? The suggestion is offered that, regardless of source, Sri Aurobindo's philosophy provides the two great needs of the time, namely, a virtual synthesis of East and West looking toward a philosophy acceptable to all mankind and, second, a rich, full interpretation of Indian thought, correcting abuses and aberrations, thus providing a point of view which will not only prepare spiritual-minded India for the maintenance of its deep spirituality but also prepare the new and modern India for a healthy and vigorous—but not exaggerated—interest and activity in the contemporary world.

While these seem to be the outstanding results of Sri Aurobindo's integral philosophy, as far as East and West are concerned, it seems to this writer that there are two other results or by-products which, from a slightly different point of view, are just as important, possibly more so.

The first of these is one which Sri Aurobindo himself might reject, namely, that through his East-West considerations and through his inclusion in a properly interpreted Indian point of view of many of the major and generally considered unique Western attitudes he has thereby indicated that the East and the West do not stand at opposite poles of the philosophical spectrum, that they are not substantial opposites, that, in a word, they have very much in common. It is important to note this, because such agreement in so many fundamentals—and the noting of that agreement—would seem to be the most fruitful basis of an approach to improved mutual understanding between the two great philosophical traditions.

The second by-product, and one which Sri Aurobindo would probably accept because he has made the point many times in his writings, is that, as just indicated, East and West—or

India and the West—do have very much in common in terms of fundamental convictions, but the great wisdom of India and of Sri Aurobindo lies in the view, barely touched upon in the foregoing, that both in the details of many of its particular doctrines and in its overall point of view the West does not go far enough and that, therefore, it is essential to go beyond the more-or-less typical Western points of view—in practically all areas of philosophy—in order to reach a comprehensive and therefore adequate philosophy. It is contended all along by Sri Aurobindo, in what I have called his synthesis of East and West, that typical Western points of view have a place in his total or integral philosophy. The fallacy of the West lies, as said above, in the exclusiveness of its ideas and in their limited applicability and validity.

Sri Aurobindo does not reject the West's interest in the physical, the vital, the mental, but it is necessary to go beyond these to the spiritual in order to provide an adequate explanation of the world we know. He does not reject the West's interest in and use of the intellect, reason, logic, and science, but he does insist that these cannot reach integral knowledge or the truth; it being necessary to supplement them by intuition, insight, direct experience. He does not reject the religious ideas of the West, even the West's interest in a personal deity, but points out simply that these do not represent the last step in the search for or nature of spirituality and spiritual perfection. He does not reject the ethical, the aesthetic, and other spiritual values of life, with which the West is so seriously concerned, but, again, simply points out that they are not representatives of real spirituality. And so on through practically all of the major ideas which he has considered in his work: we must for the truth go beyond matter, life, and mind (the intellectual, mental),[1] beyond Nature and the terrestrial,[2] beyond mind to supermind,[3] beyond mind to soul,[4] beyond mind by *yoga* to the deeper recesses of the subliminal mind,[5] beyond God to Supermind,[6] beyond the individual to the One and the whole,[7] beyond the differentiated many to the

---

[1] E.g. Aurobindo, *The Life Divine*, p. 130.   [2] *Ibid.*, pp. 601, 604.
[3] *Ibid.*, pp. 114, 151.   [4] *Ibid.*, p. 157.   [5] *Ibid.*, p. 280.
[6] *Ibid.*, pp. 123, 139.   [7] See above, note 6, p. 85.

undifferentiated One,[1] beyond man and humanity to Divinity,[2] beyond reason, intellect, science, and ordinary logic, to intuition,[3] beyond metaphysics to integral being,[4] etc.

In other words, it may be that the greatest single contribution of Sri Aurobindo—and it seems that this is to be found in much of Indian traditional philosophy, especially in the Upaniṣads and Indian philosophy derived therefrom—is the need to advance beyond even the highest reaches of traditional Western philosophy so as to attain a higher and more comprehensive, truer view which will not only include the partial points of view of the West but also bring to light the highest truth, the highest reality, spiritual perfection. In this sense, the West is not wrong but is merely inadequate in its search for truth. But it is mandatory to reach higher and deeper. This inadequacy and limitation the West must recognize—at least as worthy of or requiring most serious consideration. The necessity to go beyond the limits of the restricted Western points of view does not set East and West over against each other, does not constitute a rejection of the West, but provides a means both for a synthesis of East and West and also for a better mutual understanding between them. This is most effectively brought out by Sri Aurobindo because by 'going beyond' (my phrase) he does not reject either but includes both in his total vision, which is the essence of all true philosophy.

[1] Aurobindo, *The Life Divine*, Book II, Part I, Chapter I.
[2] *Ibid.*, pp. 601, 929, 938; see also *Evolution*, p. 36.
[3] See above, note 6, p. 89. [4] *Ibid.*, p. 59.

6

K. C. VARADACHARI

Sri Aurobindo and the Future of Philosophical Studies

AMONG the many important discoveries of the twentieth century the discovery of Sri Aurobindo must be reckoned as one. The developments in the fields of science and political theory had their impacts on cultural valuations. The seesaw of interests and the dialectics of thought had their importance realized in the diverse ways the cultural process had moved. It is indeed a very significant fact that during these five decades, the world has tended to come together and its parts have begun to realize that though each area has its distinctive treasures of thought and culture to preserve and offer to the whole, the total picture of the world culture is bound to sacrifice some of the 'essentials' so called of each. It is, however, not easy to estimate the extent of sacrifices. A world government or an agency that will look after the whole area of human civilization is already in embryo. All these have not been achieved in a day. Two wars have certainly aided this movement towards world government. It must be remembered that the work of promoting, or more fundamentally, of germinating these creative thoughts has been through the most spiritual beings. Significantly the work was undertaken in the last quarter of the last century and we owe a deep debt of gratitude to all those who brought the world's ends together, who worked for the present experimentation in common government, common welfare without considerations of race or colour, ideology or forms of government. Swami Vivekananda brought America and India together and some of the finest minds of America had impressed India with a love for human dignity, and years that have rolled by have only enhanced the reputation of America, because it has been dynamically experimenting with common solutions in the idea of One World.

We have, however, passed these many years by way of preparation. The dignity of man has been recognized but man himself has been at pains to discover his real universal nature. Humanity has itself to undergo a lot of change; it has to pass beyond the fragmentary ways of thinking, and piecemeal planning; it has to adapt itself to universal needs and not merely collective security (as the latter involves some of the most ugly features of the maxim: 'all ways are good so long as we win or hold what we have'). The world requires of man quite a different kind of yoga or method of realizing the goal of man. The goal of man cannot be man himself, for this self-concern for mankind, however laudable, finally makes man a stagnant being caring only for his physical existence. Man is not a value intrinsic; what is intrinsically valuable is surely something more than man. Whenever a living being rests on its own achievement and begins to contemplate on its own beauty or narcisstically adores itself, that living being cannot evolve, and must in due course become static and arrested and live a life of gradual degeneration. Mankind in several parts had gone through this experience whenever it arrived at this conclusion, consciously or unconsciously. One of the important ideas thrown up during the last century was the idea of evolution and many have been the writers who have discussed it threadbare as a scheme of philosophy or as a theory of science. India too had not remained unaffected by this doctrine. The idea that man is not the goal of man is an ancient one. Men-like-gods has been a common conception. Man must surpass his mere humanity and rise to divinity. The concept itself of a higher evolution or future for man has been the implicit faith of all spiritual striving, and that entailed the discrimination of the nature of man and his body and the nature of individual life and spirit or self. Sri Aurobindo had the fortune of being alive to this basic stimulus of the evolution theory to the modern world. Though it had a restricted scientific application in the biological theories, following Herbert Spencer and Henri Bergson he saw that it was a vital force in the evolution of the human consciousness itself and would set free the forces of humanity to new and fuller endeavours for the reconstruction of a new One World.

Man must be surpassed or transcended, not of course in the sense assumed by Nietzsche by denying humanity or by enslaving it, but by getting rid of his ignorance that in a myriad ways distorts the unity, pulverizes it and makes it impossible for it to have a grasp of the reality.

Intellectual thought has, despite its most brilliant exponents, failed to generate that dynamic element that makes for higher evolution. Evolution itself has been expounded by means of the dialectical process by rationalistic idealism, and, by a strange irony, it has been expounded by even inverting that philosophical position. Intellect reveals more paradoxes that arrest evolution rather than stimulate it. The escape into irrationalism or other scientific substitutes for it has not been successful. Intellect becomes a mere tool and no more. Its high prestige has suffered grievously. It is impossible to think that we can have philosophies of the intellect at all in the future. Though it is the finest tool or instrument or organon of knowledge that man has devised and perfected in a sense that even the earliest of the geniuses could never have envisaged, it has become just a human instrument, useful for man as he is and wishes to be—it cannot lead man to higher perceptions or help crossing his ignorance.

Sri Aurobindo sees that the present age requires a new organon, a need felt also by the Russian Ouspensky. It is not for me here to enter into a comparative appraisal of the merits of the tertium organum of the latter writer. The ways of intellect had led to a lot of scholastic word-chopping and humanity has not moved forward. Intellectual activity, instead of being moulded in the patterns of growth, has become a mere tool of stabilizing and preserving old patterns of thought and action; in other words, it has become incapable of inspiring one to move up to the higher levels of thought-existence so clearly declared by the master-seers of humanity at the dawn of human history. The mystical writings or revelational scriptures all bear witness to a power of intellectual activity that urged man to grow beyond his intellect itself. This transcending function of intellect seems to have lost force during the centuries that followed and mankind has been left with an intellect that is incapable of performing this high evolutionary function. Thus we have the growth of several divergent schools of intellectual thought so called, ranging from rank scepticism and materialism to idealistic absolutism, static and impotent. There are many things that had made the renunciation of intellect in favour of some kind of irrationalism very unsavoury—especially the history of irrationalism in the fields of political theories had been bitter. Suspicion of any kind of anti-intellectualism is justified. But it is precisely here that mankind has to be wary and vigilant. Any irrationalism that abridges the liberty of the individual must be false and condemnable, but such non-intellectualism as enhances the liberty of the individual by dispensing the perception of higher values must be considered different. It would not be irrational, nor regressive, but super-rational and progressive. Indian thought had from the beginning sought to arrive at a vision of reality that discloses the higher values of life such as can transform and integrate our actual living.

Sri Aurobindo in showing the limits of intellect did not merely rest content with widening the operations of the intellect by applying it to wider fields and areas of human understanding and work, but showed also that such 'transcendental' applications, if we may so speak of these wider applications, entailed the very modification of the principles of intellectual activity. Not merely does the instrument of human understanding, intellect or reason, undergo change in this process of self-adaptation to cosmic needs, it also reveals its incapacity to change or adapt beyond a particular limit. A new faculty in man has to be drawn out, latent as it is in him, the true spiritual force or psychic truth in him, and that would be able to do the work of a cosmic existence and a new world would be opened to the vision of man. Such a faculty or power is not only a psychological possibility but also an evolutionary principle emerging in man at the present time. This evolutionary force is the supermind or gnostic mind; its operations far exceed the operations of the human intellect, both in respect of the finite world and the infinite spirit.

No longer is man satisfied with an intellectual apprehension or systematization of reality which he grasps by sections and fragments and unifies in terms of his own laws of systematization, such as consistency or coherency, which indeed are incapable of achieving their own ideal. Man lives in a world of increasing complexity in social and international and inter-racial relationships as well as inter-ideological perceptions. To plead for the *status quo* or to seek a divorce between different areas of human life cannot carry him far. The fundamental need today is that of integrating the different segments of human life, and the ultimate integrating principle is that higher power of consciousness which Sri Aurobindo has called the supermind. Sri Aurobindo has clearly seen that the operations of the supermind are necessary and inevitable, sooner or later. Global thinking demands universal perceptions rather than collective thinking, which is all that the human mind has been able to improvise at the present time. The notion of the general will in politics during the past two centuries has this forestalling effect of the real universal will, though the Absolute of the Hegelians as the rational is a pseudo-universal, which has failed of its purpose.

The intuition of philosophers has its own history, even as the intellect has. The higher consciousness alone synthetically presents the truth of Reality which somehow comes to man severed as intuition and intellection, as apprehension and coherence. The operation of the higher mind is something known to all those who have closely studied the facts of perception and reasoning. We shall not enter into a survey of the history of philosophy to show how analytical thinking prone to atomistic intellectuality makes it impossible to arrive at the original synthesis presented to the higher consciousness of man. The unity of the inward psychological life, thanks to ignorance or attachment to particularities and fragments of experience or concentration on them, gets divided and hence arises the difficulty of restoring the original oneness or synthesis.

Though mankind in the course of its cultural history became

aware of several levels of mind beyond the intellect, such as
inspiration, overmental consciousness, intuition, and so on, it
was rather a difficult thing for them to present a comprehensive
account of Reality. There is one exception however. Indian
thought had reckoned as the most important *pramāṇa* or
source of right knowledge in respect of transcendental facts,
Śabda or Śruti. The whole of the Vedas was considered to be
the direct perception of Reality, not by sense nor by reason or
intellect, nor even by the analogizing mind of the poet. It is
something that is granted by the divine vision or *divya-jñāna*
or *ātma darśana*. Its knowledge about Reality is intimate and
is available in Yoga and is achieved by *yajña* (self-offering)
and *yāga* (self-sacrifice)—all understood in the psychological
sense (*adhyātma*). Veda is a *pramāṇa*, and it is only when man
becomes possessed of this seer-vision (*ṛṣi-jñāna*), that he begins
to perceive Reality wholly and as indivisible and transcendental
(*nirguṇa*), and as supreme value (that which grants value to
everything, being the ground of all). Sri Aurobindo thus found
that this achievement of the Veda-pramāṇa in one's psychological consciousness is the most urgent need, for therein lies a
key to the new philosophical understanding of Reality. But
when he himself undertook this task of applying this supramental understanding or Vedic understanding to the Vedas
themselves, he found that it was the first step rather than the
final step in knowledge or integral knowledge. He, therefore,
declared that the Veda opens a way to the still higher levels
and *pramāṇas* (instruments of knowledge). The understanding
of the Veda-pramāṇa unfortunately became so thoroughly
scholastic and intellectual during the past thousand and odd
years that it no longer was considered to be an organon of
knowledge like the intellect or mind but a book and a scripture,
to be understood as best as one may. This seems to have been
much more serious in the case of other sacred revelational
literatures also. The spiritual instrument of transcendental
Reality was not used at all; instead the intellect was made to
interpret and exegetize them. The result was scholasticism, and
divergences in interpretations, clever, contradictory and
confusing. Systems (*darśanas*) began to spring up instead of a
darśana, the integral vision. Schisms developed within them.

Heretical systems, first differing from certain accepted kinds of interpretation, later abandoned dependence on the original revelational scriptures, feeling that intellect can explain adequately the Reality. A careful look at the *darśanas* or schools of thought will present certain circumscribing limits fixed for the understanding, and the total apprehension was surrendered even as an ideal. Some like Buddhism and Jainism and the other *darśanas* gave up the attempt to see the whole steadily and as one. Sri Aurobindo seeks in his *magnum opus* to undo precisely this disintegrative process of the *dārśanikas*, though his presentation was addressed to all philosophical and other enterprises of the schools Eastern and Western. Underlying his great and original exposition through his *pramāṇa* (*divyānubhava*) so nearly resembling the Veda-pramāṇa, and supplementing and correcting it, is this discernment of the defects of an intellectualizing of scholasticism, which even the modern mind has not escaped from. We are yet governed by the logic of the finitizing mind, its dichotomies and dialectical procedures.

If Sri Aurobindo had not throughout his work proceeded to expound his vision of the one integral Reality through the supermind, it might have become utterly alien to the human mind of the present age. One suspects that the perception would be as radically distinct even as Śaṅkara had stated about his two worlds, the *pāramārthika* and *vyavahārika*, the ultimate and the conventional. But the integral conception of Sri Aurobindo bridges the gulf and shows that in the vast perception of the supermind, the appearance gains rather than loses the Real, and the Real permeates the appearance; the supermind transfigures the mental world and rids it of the ignorance and mortality. The logic of the supermind is the 'logic of the Infinite', it is usually said. That at many times in history men thought of the logic of the Infinite is true. But the definitions of the nature of the Infinite and the lack of perception that it is not merely a limiting concept of the intellect prevented a more definite formulation of the logic and law of the Infinite Being. Ideational mathematics had somehow developed on abstract lines. It must be said that after the complete overthrow of the abstract ideas from the field of philosophy, thanks to

British empiricists, it was found that they can have play only in mathematics. Modern mathematical and symbolic logicians have unfortunately not learnt the lesson of history. The Infinite is not only a category of mathematics but is, as Being, a category of integral philosophy, recognized by the integral *pramāṇa* or consciousness, as experience.

A full and fair presentation of this application of the integral consciousness to the several problems of philosophy has been done by distinguished exponents of Sri Aurobindonian thought, such as Dr S. K. Maitra and Dr Haridas Chaudhuri, in recent years.

Thus the future of philosophical studies should be considered to be bright. The inanities of the past twenty years would be things of the past. Aware that there is a new method of approaching the problems of philosophy and life, and indeed a true creative method is inevitable if human intellect itself should cease to despair of its own future, man may boldly go forward towards an international discovery of this new principle in himself. We know that though all men are rational, it is hardly this reason that we draw out in the affairs of the world. Democracy in its true sense should attempt to draw out this inward principle of man in all affairs social, political and spiritual, so that the universality affirmed of reason might be operating at all times and continuously. This, however, is not being done, or else it is seen that this reason is circumscribed and limited to welfare socialisms and politics which more often than not divide nations and people. The creative obligation is forgotten and man tends to wither for lack of incentives to inward peace and spiritual progress.

Supramental Yoga would entail the constant attempt to apply the logic of the supermind or the infinite. In all affairs there is need for drawing out this inward psychic principle, for the very fulfilment of man entails this self-transcendence.

Sri Aurobindo has with a penetrating insight surveyed the fields of sociology and political theory for the reformulation of the *dharma* of the modern age in terms of eternal values. Individual psychology has itself to undergo modifications; and the regressive interpretations of the human in terms of the rabbit and the rat and other species or in terms of the abnormal have to be checked and revalued. A large 'transvaluation of values' not in terms of Nietzschean ideology but in terms of the supermind has to take place and the theory of 'beyond good and evil' has to be reformulated in terms of the Real Good. But all these do not involve the liquidation of the human and his world and values but 'open' up the 'closed' societal conditions and individual consciousness.

In religious consciousness and the methods of attainment of the supramental experience again one has to pass beyond the purely aesthetical conception and limitation of religious experience and arrive at the integral method of total approach. Thus to the psychology of religious experience and the science of yoga Sri Aurobindo has brought the approach of the integral mind.

Daring and original as these contributions have been, it must be clear that the philosophical method of the integral consciousness or supermind is not capable of being appreciated at once. The integral approach releases a new creative movement that 'breaks' through the shell of 'closed' finite mental intellections as well as abstract intellectual constructs, even as the *élan vital* of Bergson is said to do. But with a difference; the integral approach seeks to comprehend both being and becoming, eternity and time, status and dynamis, in its sweeping vision. The Infinite opens up its unlimited horizons to the supermind and man realizes his real being and existence in terms of it.

Thus it can be seen that Sri Aurobindo reveals a new and dynamic possibility for the philosophical enterprise in the years to come, different from any past renaissance or mystical resurgence or intellectual revival, based upon sceptical modes of thought and contradictions between theory and practice.

From an unbiased and open-minded study of Sri Aurobindonian literature, it would be plain that Sri Aurobindo has opened a new chapter in philosophic thinking—a chapter of all-embracing integration of the fundamental categories of existence and values of life. In the years to come he would more and more be recognized as the most dynamic thinker of the twentieth century.

7

ERNEST WOOD

The Concept of Integral Unity

It is well known that men are never satisfied with their human situation. Man, it has been said, will never be happy until he is God and knows himself as such. There must be no more worlds to conquer before he can contemplate a future eternity of happiness. It seems, therefore, that there is something wrong with himself rather than with either chaos or cosmos. On this ground some of the ancient thinkers of India developed a triple classification of the causes of human trouble, which may be expressed in modern terms as troubles arising from the material world, troubles arising from others, and troubles arising from oneself. This practical issue culminated in the Yoga and Vedānta schools, which announced that man acts wrongly, feels wrongly and thinks wrongly, when he has not understood himself. The Yoga school gives five troubles thus arising: ignorance, egotism, emotional attachments and repulsions, and material possessiveness, which have to be first weakened by good conduct towards the world and oneself (*yama* and *niyama*)[1] and finally removed by deep meditation. The Vedānta schools proceeded on the basis of the question: 'Do you want heaven or do you want God?' The last line of Emerson's well known poem 'Brahma' puts the Vedāntic advice in a nutshell with the words: 'Seek Me and turn your back on heaven.' Heaven, it is to be noted, involves the five sources of trouble (*kleśas*) including possessiveness, liking and egotism; in that state man has what he likes and does what he likes. The three

[1] Patanjali, *Yoga Sutras*, II, pp. 30–45.

fundamental verbs of human language, *to be, to do* and *to have*, corresponding to our being, doing and having—the mental, the emotional and the material—sum up the heaven situation pretty well. These verbs are also connected with the three great laws of life and the world—unity (or entity), harmony and variety. Man wants to have all these. He wants to be an entity among entities, a conscious entity among material entities. 'It is quite clear in the world', he says to himself, 'that variety is subordinate to unity, since it is all one universe, and not a speck of dust can get away by itself, separate from the rest.' The human body, he also sees, now exemplifies these three principles—the limbs and organs the variety, the fact that they work to sustain one another the harmony, and the deeper cause for them to do so (that impulse of the conscious-ness which we call the instinct of self-preservation—'the first law of nature') the unity. It is good science as well as good philosophy to recognize the supremacy of unity in the world and in the human being; indeed, in the latter, when the conscious impulse is not there, the harmony goes and even the varieties disintegrate.

When, then, the classical Vedāntic philosophers set themselves to interpret the relation of man to God, they followed the same three lines, according to their preferences. We find Śaṅkara holding the position that the unity in man is absolutely the same nature as the unity of God, so that the two are indis-tinguishable, since it excludes variety. Ramanuja, however, found man's ultimate goal in harmony with God, and Madhva found it in his difference but eternal presence. So were set up these three distinct schools of thought, which have fought one another verbally through the centuries.

Modern Vedāntists often carry on this contest, but Sri Aurobindo has been conspicuous by his insistence that the three are not inconsistent and can be combined in one integral conception.

It appears that man's error has been not so much in his seeing of variety and harmony as in his failure to see the unity, and the fact of his divine discontent as the indication of the supremacy of unity over the other two. To realize this one must perceive what was pointed out by a less known thinker,

H. P. Blavatsky,[1] about eighty years ago, that unity has nothing to do with number—not even the number one—but is more in the nature of a power, indeed a supreme power in man and in the world. Number one does not differ in nature from number two or any other number. Five, for example, is *a five*—five trees constitute a five of trees—and is thus a one, and one is two from the standpoint of a half or a four from the standpoint of a quarter. So unity is *not to be contrasted* with variety, but is something that permeates it and does not exclude it. It is, in fact, a totally different conception, not based on any sensuous perception as to what things *are*.

Thus God is not one among many, differing from the others in being all-powerful, but is inherently different and totally unrelated, as unaffected by them as space is unaffected by the objects which in popular speech we say are 'in it'.

Metaphysically, if we then call the Unity the Absolute or the Unlimited, we are bound to admit the paradox that the unlimited can at the same time be the limited, for if one denies its capacity for being limited one denies the unlimitedness. When the philosopher refers to it as 'not this', one remembers that 'this' includes the 'not', and one is at the same time faced with 'not not' and a whole Chinese nest of paradoxes.

This does not mean that man cannot know the Unity, the Self, or the God. He does know it, but he cannot *compare* it with various or particular objects or their qualities and actions. He knows it because it is with him, and is indeed himself. He has to look at it with a looking which is not that of a subject perceiving an object, but one in which subject and object are a pair of varieties existing in harmony with each other. But he has to beware of making this pair into a new combined object, and the Self into a new subject. There is no such relation, nor anything which we can call relation, in terms of either presence or absence.

I have not attempted in these few remarks to present the reasons and arguments given by Sri Aurobindo in his voluminous works, but merely to indicate the importance of his integral 'truth-vision' in reference to the conflict of opinions

[1] H. P. Blavatsky, *The Secret Doctrine*, Vol. I (London: The Theosophical Publishing House, 1952), p. 152.

among the followers of the schools of the classical thinkers on this subject. But I do wish to offer my respectful tribute to him for his assiduous labours to prevent us, the moderns, from falling into the error of accepting 'simple solutions' of the age-old problems and paradoxes which beset the path of the Vedāntic thinker, and no doubt ultimately provoke his awakening and illumination.

8

RAYMOND F. PIPER

Cosmic Integration

THE INCLUSIVE PROCESS OF CUMULATIVE TRANSFIGURATION OF THINGS, PERSONS, AND SOCIETIES IN SPIRITUAL EVOLUTION

This action of elevation and expansion . . . includes a taking up of that which is lower into the higher values: the divine or spiritual life will not only assume into itself the mental, vital, physical life transformed and spiritualized, but it will give them a much wider and fuller play than was open to them so long as they were living on their own level. . . . They can and do become much richer, greater, more powerful and more perfect: in their divine change they break into possibilities which in their unspiritualized condition could not be practicable or imaginable.[1]

IN the three-stage transmutation of the dialectical method of the eminent German philosopher, G. W. F. Hegel, there is an illuminating similarity to the integral transformation of Sri Aurobindo. In both thinkers the process is precisely integral in the basic sense of lifting up and linking components of one stage into a whole which is higher and richer in spiritual values, and which contains a more solid harmony.

Hegel's striking technical name for this transformation is *aufheben* (to lift up; past participle, *aufgehoben*). J. G. Hibben declares, 'The verb *aufheben* possesses the three-fold meaning in Hegel: to destroy, to re-create in a new form, and at the same time to elevate'. For example, a lumberman cuts down a tree and throws away the branches; the sawmiller saws it into various boards; the cabinet-maker constructs out of them a

---

[1] Aurobindo, *The Life Divine*, pp. 648–9.

piece of furniture to contribute to the comfort and harmony of a beautiful living room. Thus Frank Thilly points out, 'What is implicit in the lower form becomes explicit or is made manifest in the higher. Every stage in the process contains all the preceding stages and foreshadows all future ones.'

In establishing his theory, Hegel illuminated many phases of history by showing how antithetical ideas or movements became differentiated, correlated, and transmuted into higher truths. Thus in early Greek philosophy Parmenides said that being is permanent; Heraclitus, that it is in constant change; the Atomists asserted that being is neither but both: atoms abide while their relations change.

Both Hegel and Sri Aurobindo apply the principle of evolutionary integration to all existence. Hegel excels in the logical compactness and tightness of his system, and in the abundance of his historical illustrations. Sri Aurobindo shines and excels in presenting four monumental achievements: (a) 'The sevenfold chord of being',[1] which includes the descent or involution from supermind to matter and the reverse of synthetic evolution from matter to supermind. (b) Cosmic integration, which displays, with unparalleled richness and grandeur, the phases and ideals of evolving spiritual or divine life. The two preceding achievements, set forth in The Life Divine, represent perhaps the most profound, comprehensive, and creative metaphysics in human history. (c) 'Synthetic yoga', with its wealth of psychological and mystical wisdom and techniques for realizing spiritual evolution. (d) The cosmic epic poem called Savitri: A Legend and a Symbol, in 23,813 lines of exquisite English blank verse, probably the greatest epic in any language.

This little essay is concerned with fact (b). The stages of waking, elevation, and transmutation pass from the atom to life, to mind, and finally to spirit. The first step is the elevation of physical atoms or the unconscious energy of matter. This happens when the life-force organizes atoms into the cells, functions, and sensitive characteristics of living organisms. Vital organisms are lifted and intensified by the emergence in them of mind, which is marked by perceptual and intellectual

[1] Aurobindo, The Life Divine, p. 243.

capacities, individual subject-object consciousness, and purposive action. Thus, 'mind takes up the lower grades and gives to their action and reaction intelligent values'.[1] Spirit imparts to mind vast powers for growth in consciousness and divine living which mind by itself could not attain.

Thus at every stage the lower factors are *aufgehoben* or lifted up into a new whole which integrates everything valuable which has gone before into a more worthful and powerful plane of consciousness. This process is called 'ascent and integration',[2] 'synthetic evolution', or often transmutation. Each advance deserves the wonderful name of transfiguration—mud becomes roses; roses become aesthetic perception and delight; aesthetic perception and reflection become spiritual intuition, cosmic truth—the fullness and bliss of gnostic being.

Let us examine how the senses may be intensified and expanded on the astral plane of being as reported in Chapter 43 of *Autobiography of a Yogi*, by Paramhansa Yogananda. His deceased master, Sri Yukteswar, is resurrected before his astonished eyes and tells how he had been sent by God as a saviour to the 'illumined astral planet' called Hiranyaloka. The astral beings there have more senses than we do, especially a third eye and 'the all-inclusive intuitional sense'. All their senses manifest an increased range, refinement, and capacity of response to 'subtle vibrations' of many kinds, especially of light and colour and 'the ethereal music of the spheres'. Because these beings may change themselves or the astral cosmos as they wish, within the laws of astral being, they may enjoy, by the thousand, whatever fragrant flowers, fruits of indescribable flavours, 'luminous raylike vegetables', variegated costumes, jewels, or palaces they may wish. They communicate by telepathy and television, travel through space freely by levitation, develop rich and extensive friendships, and enjoy the 'infinitely beautiful, clean, pure, and orderly astral world'.

The fruitful, unwitting use of the principle of integral transformation in a wide variety of institutions and situations confirms its validity and value. Thus the venerable Chinese practice of compromise illustrates the process. I was in Shanghai once when sugar dealers and customs officers had to determine

---

[1] Aurobindo, *The Life Divine*, p. 636.   [2] *Ibid*., p. 626.

the rate of import duty. The dealers confessed that they might accept one cent, while the officers insisted that they must have at least ten cents (my figures may be incorrect). After three days of festivities and discussion, mostly irrelevant, they shortly decided on five cents and everybody went home happy.

The method of creative conference employed by Bahais, Quakers, certain business firms, and other groups has the purpose of discovering, purifying, enlarging, and combining the suggestions of individuals until a satisfactory solution may be reached which no individual could have attained by himself.

T. V. Smith is noted for his elaboration, in political philosophy, of the idea that the indispensable essence and means of successful democratic government is the compromise and balance of the conflicting interests of diverse parties into a workable common plan which is acceptable to the majority and experimentally observed by all.

Transfiguring integration is illustrated also in the principle of reconciliation set forth in the letters of St Paul: each hostile or contending party is persuaded to accept the spirit of love as proposed by a mediating friend, and often this goodwill will grow until an adjustment or integration is realized in which past grudges are forgotten and all persons involved become far finer, happier, and more winsome personalities.

This principle of spiritual integration will apply more and more to the growing interrelations among the world's religions. These religions will both learn from each other and at the same time encourage each faith to cultivate the special religious values that distinguish them in the hope that others may eventually benefit. As Professor Hocking has said, we do not want any religion to disappear without bequeathing to the rest of us whatever values it has verified.

Sri Aurobindo, in his extensive writings on social philosophy, applies the principle of transfiguration to social interrelations for the purpose of attaining the important desideratum of 'a new world, a change in the total life of humanity, . . . by the evolution of the Truth-consciousness, . . . consolidating a common life'.[1] 'Unity, mutuality, and harmony must be the inescapable law of a common or collective gnostic life.'[2]

---

[1] Aurobindo, *The Life Divine*, p. 914.   [2] *Ibid.*, p. 916.

'A perfected community can exist only by the perfection of its individuals . . . and the discovery by all of their spiritual unity.'[1]

The comprehensive goal of spiritual or gnostic life is described in the incomparable last two chapters of *The Life Divine*. The plan of this chapter does not include a description of that life. Here is a condensed statement of its chief aspects: 'There is an exaltation, exultation, excitement, a highest intensity of the joy of the heart. . . . In the highest ascents of spiritual bliss . . . there is an illimitable intensity of participation in an eternal ecstasy which is founded on the eternal Existence and therefore on a beatific tranquillity of eternal peace.'[2]

The ideal of balance and harmony in spiritual integration is so difficult to realize that history exhibits many failures. For example, Nietzsche proposed the fertile idea of a transvaluation of all values (*Umwertung aller Werte*) which was to create new values and a new civilization of the superman, but he destroyed the symmetry and usefulness of his system by exaggerating egoistic power at the cost of goodwill. Sri Aurobindo explains how the Hindu ideal of self-realization through the four stages of life failed because it persisted in assigning an excessive weight to the principle of renunciation.

Let us now seek a more definite conception of the grandeur of spiritual integration by the study of a particular field of values; namely, the expansion of aesthetic values of beauty. First, we need to view it among its associates in an inclusive table of seventeen human values in which every value should have a fitting place. The following table expresses a three-dimensional theory of value:

A. The horizontal dimension: the kinds, range, or quantity of values:

1. Utilitarian or material values: health, wealth, work.
2. Social values: love, justice or social security, co-operation (skill in social adjustments).
3. Cultural values: wisdom, beauty, recreation, goodness, hardihood (capacity to deal with suffering or evil).

[1] Aurobindo, *The Life Divine*, p. 931. [2] *Ibid.*, p. 879.

4. Philosophic or total values:
Personal existence: life and self-consciousness.
Integration or unity of self or personality, aided by: self-realization through education.
Holiness, wholeness, or religious values of all kinds.
Freedom and self-reliance, where freedom means all the skills presupposed above, for the mastery of the conditions necessary for realizing one's legitimate wishes in this kind of world.
Adventure: the joys from realizing and expanding the preceding values and discovering new ones.

B. The vertical dimension: quality or degree in each kind of value. Each type has many levels and ramifications of realization from rudimentary beginning of appreciation to comprehensive grasp and synthetic bliss. For example, there exist many degrees of sensitivity and capacity in the enjoyment of symphonic music.

C. The spherical dimension or spiritual integration: the realization of possible values in a balanced proportion through a long well-ordered unfoldment in time. The interpretation of every kind of value as a form or aspect of love offers one way of unifying them.

Spiritual evolution is postulated as eternal since we cannot picture perfection as a fixed terminal state or condition of spirit. Perfection rather is a direction or process of endless expansions, rhythms of consciousness, and combinations of values. Sri Aurobindo likes to call the supreme cosmic Being Saccidānanda: existence-consciousness-bliss. Bliss encompasses three factors: love, beauty, and joy. Joy is the climactic good of reality but it is an effulgence that interpenetrates all other aspects of the divine life. Note the important fact that beauty is an integral attribute of the supermind.

Let us now stretch our thought and imagination to the utmost to envisage some of the possible developments of beauty. This inclusive name embraces all the aesthetic delights realized in the vast ranges of nature and in the endless artistic creations of spiritual beings. In *The Journal of Aesthetics and*

Art Criticism for September 1957, Thomas Munro classifies more than 400 arts and types of art. Each of these arts has its own kind of vast potentialities for expansion and enjoyment. Let us confine our attention to one of the 400, painting, the art that exploits light and colour in expressive forms. In 1949 the Museum of Art in Providence, Rhode Island, exhibited samples of twenty-nine isms or styles of recent painting. All of these styles invite exploration, and after rejecting all that is bad in the history of painting, there remain multitudes of creations that will add to our aesthetic enjoyment, not to mention the thousands that are being added daily to earth's treasurehouse of beauty.

But in painting we have only begun to set forth the possibilities of light and colour. Released from static canvas, luminous colour may be aesthetically developed in many other ways, some of which, as Sri Aurobindo would say, are now 'impracticable and unimaginable'. Some of these future wonders are suggested by the marvellous colour effects realized in more or less abstract motion pictures like *Fantasia*, in lumia (the art of mobile colour as developed by the genius of Thomas Wilfred), in fireworks or in fountains of water. Even the beginnings of lumia are so magnificent that it is difficult to imagine how in the future it will be developed to beautify our homes, temples, and public buildings, by the play of appropriate living light and colour.

I cannot resist some speculations about new arts of luminous colour which may be developed on a plane like Hiraṇyaloka. If astral people, for instance, have twice as many colours as we enjoy, with expanded vision to receive them, the possibilities of new combinations and of aesthetic enjoyment are infinitely multiplied. These creative beings might invent controls for producing colour symphonies that would resemble a sustained, ordered, magnified aurora borealis. From radiant disks and planes suspended in the sky, from flashing fountains in variegated lakes and seas, and from other unforeseeable constructions, such beings could produce colour symphonies of indescribable grandeur, accompanied by vast mystical music and breezes of gently rhythmic fragrances, produced by vast perfumery organs or gardens of multifarious flowers.

Such remote speculations force upon us by contrast the urgency of using the vast knowledge and skills we now possess for the increase of human happiness on earth. In every realm of value there are prophets and masters who know the secrets for bringing to mankind vast expansions of their special kinds of good, if only the masses would listen. Because of the perennial difficulties of awakening lower minds to the treasures of the spiritual life, masters and *avatārs* will always be needed and summoned to descend in order, skilfully and gently, to release those who dwell in the great ignorance, and to lead them up the stairway of spiritual evolution. 'This taking up of the lower parts of life reveals itself as a turning downward of the master eye of the secret evolving spirit or of the universal Being in the individual from the height to which he has reached on all that now lies below him.'[1]

Thus finally we come to perhaps the most distinctive characteristic of Sri Aurobindo's conception of spiritual integration: the powerful, redemptive retroaction of every advance in insight, illumination, or love. We read that 'that downward eye of knowledge and will with a view to an all-round heightening, deepening and subtler, finer and richer intensification is the secret Spirit's way from the beginning'.[2]

A few examples follow of the retroactive, permeating effect of a new insight or emotion. Thus a young man who has fallen in love awakens to many new values in his daily work, observations, and social relations. In *Pilgrim's Progress*, when the pilgrim discovered the Christ consciousness, the whole universe was transmuted for him into beauty and joy. During an art exhibition in 1921 of 4,000 works of the 'independent artists' in Paris, I encountered a painting called *The Infinite* which suddenly brought forth in me an aesthetic conversion in which I discovered the beauty, power, and wonder of colour. For the first time in my life I saw, in a kind of expansive explosion, the enchantments, the adventures, and the possibilities of coloured patterns. This one fresh insight radically changed my whole successive life. It inspired extensive new researches in the fine arts, new university courses, books, and travel. It transformed my home life: progressively improved interior

[1] Aurobindo, *The Life Divine*, p. 636.   [2] *Ibid.*, p. 637.

decorations from basement to attic, and stimulated the development of landscaping and flower growing outside the house. The most important consequence has been the establishment of scores of delightful new friendships around the world. In short, a fundamental principle in Sri Aurobindo's philosophy is that any advance in value appreciation reacts to lift all of one's lower or earlier life into richer perspectives and harmony.

We end by three more statements by Sri Aurobindo himself, selected from hundreds: 'An integral spiritual consciousness . . . links the highest to the lowest through all the mediating terms and achieves an indivisible whole.'[1] 'The lower consciousness of mind, life and body cannot arrive at its full meaning until it is taken up, restated, transformed by the light and power and joy of the higher spiritual consciousness.'[2] 'An integral consciousness will become the basis of an entire harmonization of life through the total transformation, unification, integration of the being and the nature.'[3]

---

[1] Aurobindo, *The Life Divine*, p. 566.
[2] *Ibid.*, p. 604. [3] *Ibid.*, p. 646.

9

R. S. SRIVASTAVA

The Integralist Theory of Evolution

IN the renaissance of Indian Philosophy, Sri Aurobindo may be regarded as the most revolutionary and creative thinker. Evolution is the pivot on which his whole philosophy rotates. He synthesizes the truths of both the Eastern and the Western theories of evolution. The Western theories are existential, intellectual and cosmic in outlook, but they lack the requisite spiritual standpoint. The West require conversion from their excessive realistic approach to the idealistic and spiritual one. The Indian views are thoroughly spiritual. But their main defect is that they have an individualistic outlook and they are static in character. The Indian theories of evolution concentrate upon the evolution of the individual—in all his stages, purpose, self-realization and attainment of salvation. They neglect the cosmic aspect of evolution, but they must break the bonds of narrow individualistic outlook and acquire a dynamic and cosmic character.

Sri Aurobindo is a synthetic thinker in the sense that for him the truth of evolution lies in the assimilation of the Indian and Western theories in a spiritual, integral, cosmic and dynamic philosophy of evolution. Evolution is the process of the revelation of the Spirit. The Supreme Spirit (Saccidānanda) creates the universe and manifests itself in higher, spiritual and divine principles. The unfoldment of consciousness in matter is the ceaseless process of evolution. The Divine involves itself in ignorance and inconscience. It apparently negates itself in matter or non-being and gradually manifests its spiritual and divine character. The full emergence of Saccidānanda in the cosmos brings about the life divine on earth.

SPIRITUAL VIEW OF EVOLUTION

Sri Aurobindo's philosophy of evolution is thoroughly spiritual. Spirit is the source of creation and evolution and also the final end of realization. The materialistic, vitalistic and idealistic theories cannot adequately explain the truth of evolution. The materialistic theories are self-contradictory, for an unconscious principle cannot evolve life and consciousness from it. In a purely materialistic philosophy, there is an unconscious movement of development, and we cannot talk of any direction or goal. The biological theories of evolution, propounded by Darwin, Spencer, Lamarck and others, believed in the progressive adjustment of the individual to his environment, leading ultimately to the annulment of all conflict between the two, as the goal of evolution. But the human individual must not accept his environment as something fixed and immutable. The vitalistic theories fail to explain evolution, because in the ordinary version of vitalism, such as that of Bergson, there is only a ceaseless process without a goal. Bergson speaks of an unchecked and unimpeded flow which is not a movement towards any goal. Evolution, for him, is not a process of ascent and steady manifestation of the higher spiritual and divine principle. It is an aimless flow without direction, with up and down, blind movements leading to blind alleys. Bergson tried to give us deliverance from the mechanical theory of evolution, but in rejecting all teleology he has himself fallen into the same dreaded mechanistic theory. If creative movement is not a movement towards anything, if it does not know what it is to create and if it is not guided by any purpose, how, we ask, can it be called 'creative'? Bergson's sourceless and aimless evolution is a temporal mechanism in place of the spatial mechanism of the biologist. Bergson calls his view of evolution 'creative', but unless evolution has a goal it can in no way be called 'creative'. The idealistic theories of evolution which believe reason to be the ultimate principle give also an entirely unsatisfactory account of evolution. If reason be the highest principle, then assuredly there can be no evolution beyond it. Having reached the stage of reason, evolution must cease forever. We should bid farewell to all cosmic evolution. The destiny of man is also very dismal on such a theory. He remains a finite, limited, ephemeral, and ignorant being forever. A higher destiny of man is only possible in a philosophy which admits higher grades of consciousness that are incomprehensible to human reason.

Sri Aurobindo envisages a thoroughly spiritual view of evolution. It is an evolution of consciousness in matter until the former becomes explicit, open, revealed and perceptible. As spirit is involved in matter, its manifestation in grades of consciousness is the 'truth' of evolution. Sri Aurobindo says: 'A spiritual evolution, an evolution of Consciousness in Matter as a constant developing self-formation until the form can reveal the indwelling spirit, is then the key-note, the central significant motive of this terrestrial existence. This significance is concealed at the outset by the involution of the Spirit, the Divine Reality, in a dense material Inconscience, a veil of Inconscience; a veil of insensibility of Matter hides the Universal Consciousness-Force which works within it, so that the Energy, which is the first form the Force of creation assumes in the physical universe, appears to be itself inconscient and yet does the work of a vast occult Intelligence.'[1]

INVOLUTION AND EVOLUTION

Evolution is the reverse of the process of involution. Evolution of higher principles from the lower ones is possible only when the former are already involved implicitly in the matter. Life emerges from matter, only because it is already involved in the latter. The emergence of mind from physical and vital realities is possible because it lies embedded in them. There is no magical emergence of the non-existent realities. All the higher spiritual and divine grades of principles remain implicitly embedded in the lower reality. 'For there seems to be no reason', says Sri Aurobindo, 'why life should evolve out of material elements or Mind out of living form, unless we accept the Vedāntic solution that Life is already involved in Matter and Mind in Life, Life a form of veiled consciousness—and

[1] Aurobindo, *The Life Divine*, Book II, Part II, pp. 734–5.

then there seems to be little objection to a further step in the series and the admission that mental consciousness may itself be only a form and a veil of higher states which are beyond Mind.'[1] Involution of Saccidānanda precedes Its manifestation. The act of involution is graded descent from Saccidānanda to supermind, overmind, intuition, illumined mind, higher mind, mind, soul, life and finally to matter. As Sri Aurobindo remarks: 'Evolution is an inverse action of the involution, what is an ultimate and last derivation in the involution is the first to appear in the evolution, what was original and primal in the involution is in the evolution the last and supreme emergence.'[2]

The immanent dynamic movement of the Supreme Spirit (Saccidānanda) takes place because of the involution–evolution process in diverse and multiple forms. Though the Absolute is transcendent even to its manifestations, and is not limited by its expression, it remains immanent in the cosmos. Involution–evolution is the mode in which the power of the Absolute becomes active, i.e. expresses itself. The Absolute is absolute because it is not bound by its self-expression and it remains the Absolute both in and beyond its self-expression.

TRIPLE PROCESS OF EVOLUTION

Evolution has a triple character, viz. *widening*, *heightening*, and *integration*. The lower principles become wide, open, receptive, sublime, refined and adaptive when it has to ascend to a higher state. For instance, matter must undergo a process of complication, self-differentiation, subtle and intricate organization in order that the higher principle, life, may evolve in it. If matter remains a simple, hard, and therefore an unadjustable stuff, life can never evolve in it. The process of widening of a principle means its increasing organization, expression and differentiation so that it may be capable of evolution of higher principles from it and within it as a base. If there is life in an animal, it is only because its body has become sufficiently organized, subtle and complex. If mind inhabits a man, it is because his body has a higher degree of

---

[1] Aurobindo, *The Life Divine*, Book I, p. 5.
[2] *Ibid.*, Book II, Part II, pp. 759–60.

complexity than plants and stones and has the capacity and organization for the reception of the mental consciousness.

Secondly, evolution is a process of heightening of the force of consciousness to higher and higher grades. Matter evolves into life, mind and other grades of consciousness until the consciousness-force (*cit-śakti*) becomes explicit and fully manifest. Sri Aurobindo states with characteristic lucidity thus: 'All evolution is in essence a heightening of the force of consciousness in the manifest being, so that it may be raised into the greater intensity of what is still unmanifest, from matter into life, from life into mind, from the mind into the spirit.'[1]

Integration of the new higher principle with the lower principles is the essential feature of evolution. Evolution is not confined to the manifestation of higher principles in abstraction from the lower evolved beings; it establishes a larger field of life in which the power of the new principle may have sufficient play and room for its emergence. Evolution is a triple and indivisible process of heightening, widening and integration of the lower principles.

INTEGRAL EVOLUTION

Sri Aurobindo takes an 'integral' view of evolution. Evolution is not a process of the addition of higher principles to the realities that are pre-existent in relation thereto. When a higher principle emerges, the lower realities get transformed. With emergence of life, matter does not cease to evolve. Both matter and life are together transformed, when the higher principle of mind emerges in a being possessed of these realities. Matter becomes more sensitive and life more powerful in the human beings. Similarly, when the supermind emerges, the entire cosmos of matter, life and mind is vitally transformed. Samuel Alexander commits a blunder when he conceives the emergence of higher beings which have no capacity to transform the lower realities. The lower principles are not affected and benefited in the least by the emergence of the higher principles. When the higher principle emerges, the lower

---

[1] Aurobindo, *The Life Divine*, Book II, Part II, p. 634.

principle ceases to evolve. It is forever dominated by the higher principle. In opposition to Samuel Alexander, Sri Aurobindo conceives an integral ascent of all the lower principles. The principles have infinite capacity to develop and become a mould and form fit for the truer manifestation of the Divine. Even the entire cosmos undergoes a gradual process of radical transformation. Sri Aurobindo very strongly refutes the mistaken view that in evolutionary development the new principles emerge only on the condition that the lower principles be condemned to remain forever in their lower state of existence.

It is also quite wrong to hold that the realization of higher principles or grades of consciousness is possible only when there is an absolute dissociation of the lower principles. Similarly it is also erroneous to suppose that man only advances when he dissociates himself from the baser principles of body, life and mind. The Advaita-Vedantins commit this error. They believe that the soul can only realize the Divine when it is absolutely dissociated from the lower principles. The ordinary view that the lower principles remain always lower and are to be dropped in the spiritual ascent of man is absolutely wrong. If body, life and mind are simply rejected and not taken up and transformed, then there can be no evolution in the stricter sense of the term. For Sri Aurobindo, when man is supramentalized, his body, life and mind are also transformed supremely. As Sri Aurobindo strongly asserts: 'The divine or spiritual life will not only assume into itself the mental, vital, physical life transformed and spiritualized, but it will give them a much wider and fuller play than was open to them so long as they were living upon their own level. Our mental, physical, vital existence need not be destroyed by our self-exceeding nor are they lessened and impaired by being spiritualized, they can and do become much richer, greater, more powerful and more perfect: in their divine change they break into possibilities which in their unspiritualized condition could not be practicable or imaginable.'[1]

The lower principles are lower creations of Saccidānanda in which the superconscient existence, consciousness-force, bliss and supermind secretly lie concealed. It is the constant

[1] Aurobindo, *The Life Divine*, Book II, Part II, pp. 648–9.

sādhanā, or yoga of nature itself, to manifest the superconscient powers in the evolving matter, life, soul and mind.

Nature labours to ascend with all its principles. But the process of transformation is a slow process and the complete transformation and perfect integration is not possible until the supramental gnosis emerges in material nature. It is by the continuous working of the supermind in the principles of inconscience and ignorance that there can be total conversion of the realities of the universe.

It is the supreme supramental gnosis which thoroughly divinizes the principles and effects their inherent integration with one another. As the three constituent principles of Saccidānanda, viz. existence, consciousness-force and bliss, are one in being and yet serve as differentiated powers and have an absolute integration, so also matter, life and mind, which are nothing else than the Spirit at different levels, are integrated by the action of the supermind. The indwelling divine principles then become explicit in these lower principles. Matter reveals the existence, life manifests the consciousness-force, the soul realizes the bliss and mind expresses the supermind. But such a radical conversion is possible only when the supermind descends into the lower nature. In his inspiring way, Sri Aurobindo says: 'If there is to be an entire transformation, it can only be by the full emergence of the law of the spirit, its power of supermind or gnosis must have entered into matter and it must evolve in matter. It must change the mental into the supramental being, make the inconscient in us conscious, spiritualize our material substance, erect its law or gnostic consciousness in our whole evolutionary being and nature.'[1]

The supermind uncovers the veil of ignorance and inconscience and envisages the integral transformation of man. *Salvation* of the individual means the realization of the highest consciousness, blessedness, omnipotence and perfection. It is a state of being transformed into gnostic being or superman. It is a divine birth. To become a gnostic being is to have omniscience, omnipotence, blessedness and immortality. It is to realize the supermind or God, where mind recovers its divine light, the soul realizes its divine self in the all-blissful *ānanda,* life regains

[1] Aurobindo, *The Life Divine,* Book II, Part II, p. 629.

its divine power in the omnipotent conscious-force, and body reveals its divine existence.

COSMIC YOGA

The integral divinization of man into the gnostic being is possible only when the cosmos manifests and reveals the Spirit. Both the individual and the cosmos evolve simultaneously. As the individual realizes spiritual and divine existence, the world is also gradually transformed into an unveiled manifestation of the Divine. There is integral evolution of man and nature. A divine being cannot emerge in an undivine universe. Nature seeks to manifest the Divine in the individual, and the individual being so divinely transformed, remains ever engaged in the act of the divinization of nature. The supramental consciousness of the gnostic being is one and continuous with the earth-consciousness. He transforms material nature into the divine nature by his conscious-force. 'A complete and radical change can only be brought about by bringing persistently the spiritual light and intimate experience of the spiritual truth, power, bliss into the recalcitrant elements until they too recognize that their own way of fulfilment lies there, that they are themselves a diminished power of the spirit and can recover by this new way of being their own truth and integral nature.'[1] But such a divine transformation of the cosmos is only possible by the supramental conscious-force. The lower principles can only partially transform and imperfectly integrate the cosmic principles. It is the gnostic beings that supramentalize the inconscient earth. The ascent of the human consciousness to the supramental consciousness has the cosmic purpose of supramentalization of the very earth-consciousness. It may be considered as a vast yoga of nature. But cosmic yoga is possible only through the supramental beings. Individual yoga, therefore, is only a prelude to cosmic yoga or the union and oneness of Nature with God. Unless God and Nature unite in the supramental gnosis, the synthesis of yoga cannot be considered complete.

The gnostic individual will gradually transform nature into

[1] Aurobindo, *The Life Divine*, Book II, Part II, pp. 831–2.

the superconscient supernature. The divine consciousness will, through the medium of superman, descend on earth and will manifest its consciousness-force in nature. Sri Aurobindo very beautifully expresses it in the following stanzas of *Savitri*:

> When superman is born as Nature's King
> His presence shall transfigure Matter's work.
> He shall light up Truth's fire in Nature's night,
> He shall lay upon the earth Truth's greater law;
> Man too shall turn towards the Spirit's call.[1]

EVOLUTION IN KNOWLEDGE

Supramental evolution is evolution through knowledge. *Evolution in knowledge is a process of the pure manifestation of the Spirit in myriad illumined expressions of consciousness-force and bliss.* It is a process of the glorious revelation of the Divine in newer and infinite diverse vistas. As Sri Aurobindo remarks: 'The evolution in the Knowledge would be a more beautiful and glorious manifestation with more vistas ever unfolding themselves and more intensive in all ways than any evolution could be in the Ignorance. The delight of the Spirit is ever new, the forms of beauty it takes innumerable, its godhead ever young and the taste of delight, *rasa*, of the Infinite eternal and inexhaustible.'[2]

The consummation of the evolution in knowledge is the realization of the triune aspect of Saccidānanda. The integral supramental consciousness, in the process of evolution, merges in the unitarian consciousness of Saccidānanda. The highest summit of supramental consciousness is Saccidānanda and, therefore, the descent of Saccidānanda will be the consummation of the spiritual and supramental evolution of nature. As Sri Aurobindo observes: 'At the higher end of the evolution the ascending ranges and summits of supermind would begin to rise towards some supreme manifestation of the pure spiritual existence, consciousness and delight of being of Saccidānanda.'[3]

In conclusion, we may reaffirm our faith that Sri Aurobindo's

---

[1] *Savitri*, Book XI, Canto I (Pondicherry: Sri Aurobindo Ashram, 1950), p. 331.   [2] Aurobindo, *The Life Divine*, Book II, Part II, p. 861.
[3] *Ibid.*, p. 861.

philosophy of evolution has certain tendencies which dominantly influence the growth of modern Eastern and Western philosophies. *Firstly*, the conception of cosmic salvation (*sarva-mukti*) appeals to all shades of mind in the world of today. We are all thinking in terms of world-economy, world government, world-peace and world-soul. Sri Aurobindo envisages the salvation of the entire humanity. *Secondly*, salvation means the rebirth of an individual into the Divine Life. It is to become God incarnate with transformed body, life and mind. He discards the view that in salvation the soul enters into a calm, serene and unchangeable consciousness of the Divine, whereas mind, life and body perish in nature. *Thirdly*, the destiny of man, as Sri Aurobindo conceives it, is to become superman. It is to attain divine transformation of his entire embodied existence. It is to achieve an unveiled manifestation of the Divine in human society.

N. A. NIKAM

The Problem of Creation:
Concepts of Māyā and Līlā

IT is the merit of Sri Aurobindo's philosophy to treat the problem of 'creation' as a problem of the *nature* of existence. Why is there 'creation'? is a question which is a question about: *what* is the nature of reality, of existence?

BEING, FREEDOM, DELIGHT

The Upaniṣads state the problem of existence, of being, thus: being is freedom: 'to be' is 'to be free'. The Upaniṣads distinguish, however, between two senses of freedom: (*a*) 'to be' is 'to be free', i.e. to be free from fear; (*b*) 'to be' is 'to be free', i.e. to be free because of the discovery of the delight of existence (*ānanda*). But there is a gap between the two; for one may be free from fear and yet not have discovered 'the delight of existence' (*ānanda*). This distinction may be indicated by citing the following passage from the Fourth Brāhmaṇa of the *Brihad-Āraṇyaka Upaniṣad*: the passage speaks of the creation of the manifold world from the Unitary Soul:

1. In the beginning, this world was Soul (*Ātman*) alone, in the form of a Person. Looking around, he saw nothing else than himself. He said, first: 'I am . . .'

2. He was afraid. Therefore, one who is alone is afraid. This one then thought to himself: 'Since there is nothing else than myself, of what am I afraid?' *Thereupon, verily, his fear departed*, for of what should he have been afraid? Assuredly it is from a second that fear arises.

3. *Verily he had no delight*. Therefore one alone has no delight. He desired a second . . . (The italics are mine.)

COMMENT

Removal of fear is a necessary condition for the discovery of the delight of existence. The awareness that there is no 'other'—no 'second'—is an awareness of absoluteness: of absoluteness of conscious existence. 'Absoluteness of conscious existence is', Sri Aurobindo says, 'illimitable bliss of conscious existence; the two are only different phrases for the same thing. All illimitableness, all infinite, all absoluteness is pure delight.'[1]

What is 'absoluteness of conscious existence'? In absolute existence 'there can be no nothingness, no night of inconscience, no deficiency'. Yet, the Upaniṣad says, there was no delight; for, 'one who is alone has no delight'. Therefore, as the Upaniṣad says, 'He desired a second'. This means that while removal of fear is a 'necessary' condition it is not a 'sufficient' condition for the discovery of the delight of existence. To affirm absoluteness of one's existence is only a phase of the discovery of the delight of existence. To 'loose forth' this delight in the discovery of one's self in a 'second' is a self-delight which is not content to possess merely its absoluteness of self-being. If this movement of loosing forth in the discovery of one's self in others were not possible, it would be a limitation of absoluteness of self-being. Therefore, 'The self-delight of Brahman', as Sri Aurobindo says, 'is not limited, however, by the still and motionless possession of its absolute self-being'.[2]

The passage cited from the Upaniṣad distinguishes between two senses of the 'second'. It is from a 'second' that fear arises. Therefore, absoluteness of existence is the 'conquest' or removal of the 'second' from whom fear arises. This is a movement within the nature of absoluteness of existence, necessary for the affirmation of the absoluteness. There is another sense of a 'second' which is the source of the delight of existence; for absoluteness of conscious existence is another movement which is a 'loosing forth' in the discovery of one's self in a 'second'. This movement is also a necessary part of the affirmation of the absoluteness of conscious being. The nature of reality is an interplay of movement between these two apparently opposed and antinomial movements.

[1] Aurobindo, *The Life Divine*, p. 86.   [2] *Ibid.*, p. 87.

The Upaniṣad says, 'He *desired* a second'. Now, desire is 'want'; it is a 'deficiency' as we know it in our experience. But we must distinguish between the desire which is 'want' and 'deficiency' and, as such, arises from limitation and finitude, and the 'desire' which arises out of the fullness of being. Desire in the first sense is something which issues forth in an activity whose end is economic satisfaction. This raises no problems. It is 'desire' arising in the absolute consciousness of existence which raises the problem: Why should Brahman, perfect, absolute, and 'desiring nothing', yet 'desire for a second'? The answer must be discoverable in the nature of the 'absoluteness' of conscious being; for its nature is such that it is free; and *it is so free that it is not bound either by desire, or even by desirelessness.*

Furthermore, the nature of the 'absoluteness' of conscious existence is a 'creative' or self-expressive activity or force, which has the centre of its being in self-delight, and it enjoys issuing forth, in endless forms, the fundamental fact of its existence. Delight and freedom are the two 'attributes' of its self-expression. If this is the case, then 'creation' is not an 'illusion'. It is not the transformation into actuality of what is merely 'potential'. Creation is not an 'accident'; it is not even purposive' in the usual sense of the term. '*Why* should Brahman, perfect, absolute, infinite, needing nothing, desiring nothing at all, throw out force of consciousness to create in itself these worlds of forms?' This question cannot be answered if the 'why' seeks to discover a 'purpose' in or behind creation.[1]

In Sri Aurobindo's treatment of the problem there are two points to be noted: (*a*) Why the Infinite becomes the finite is a wrong question because we do not understand the true meaning of the word 'Infinite'. The Infinite is that in which 'all possibilities are inherent in its Infinity', as Sri Aurobindo says, and so, the 'delight' of its existence 'lies precisely in the variable realization of its possibilities'. The 'possibilities' are not there in the Infinite as unrealized potentialities, but are there in their eternal realization: 'Form in itself, world in itself, are eternal..., they have an eternal recurrence if not an eternal persistence, an eternal immutability in sum and foundation along with an

---

[1] Aurobindo, *The Life Divine*, p. 86–7.

eternal mutability in aspect and apparition.'[1] Secondly: (b) The variable realization of its possibilities is a movement in which the Infinite 'looses itself', as Sri Aurobindo says, by 'concealment' in that which seems to be its own *opposite*; so, in another sense, 'creation' is a process of evolution in which the absoluteness of conscious existence, or Saccidānanda, has to 'emerge'. All creation or Becoming is nothing but this self-manifestation.[2]

MĀYĀ

According to Sri Aurobindo there are two ways in which we can regard world-existence: (a) 'in relation to pure, infinite, indivisible, immutable existence'; (b) 'in its relation to the self-delight of eternally existent being'. In its first relation, Sri Aurobindo admits that we are entitled to regard world-existence and to describe and realize it as *Māyā* in the *original* sense of this term, as that which *limits*, *measures* and *gives form to the formless*. The original sense of Māyā in the Vedānta seems to correspond to the Pythagorean philosophy of Form, and the opposition between the Limit and the Unlimited. 'The Unlimited is that which is potentially capable of Form; it is that which receives and becomes Form. Both the Unlimited and the Limit or Form, are areas of change. Form is the Actuality of the Unlimited; it is ever-changing. The Unlimited is the ever-lasting possibility of a change which is never constant. . . . Form is the condition of change, of multiplicity; everything takes on Form in proportion, i.e. in Number and Measure.'[3]

Later in the development of the Vedānta the term māyā acquired, as Sri Aurobindo indicates, 'a pejorative sense of cunning, fraud or illusion'.[4] It is in this sense that the term is used in the schools of the later Vedānta. The world is *māyā* because it is not the essential truth of infinite existence, but rather a creation of self-conscious being: a phenomenal truth of its free multiplicity and infinite mutability, and not truth

---

[1] Aurobindo, *The Life Divine*, p. 95. [2] *Ibid.*, p. 103.

[3] N. A. Nikam, article on 'Pythagoras' (Amalner, India: *The Philosophical Quarterly*, January 1958). [4] Aurobindo, *The Life Divine*, p. 95.

of its fundamental and immutable unity. The world is not the essential truth but a phenomenal truth in the sense that what 'appears' or is manifested, is capable of manifestation, capable of non-manifestation, or capable of other-manifestation.

LĪLĀ

In relation to *Saccidānanda*, or the self-delight of the eternally self-existing being, the world, according to Sri Aurobindo, is not *māyā* but *līlā:* i.e. a play, and joy of play, wherever this is found: 'the child's joy, the poet's joy, the actor's joy, the mechanician's joy . . .'; the cause and purpose of play is: 'being ever busy with its own innumerable self-representations. . . . Himself the play, Himself the player, Himself the playground.'[1]

There is behind all our experiences one reality, one indivisible conscious being, supporting our experiences by its inalienable delight. The delight of being is, or ought to be, therefore, our real response in all situations. The experience of pain, pleasure, and indifference, is only a superficial arrangement effected by the limited part of our selves, caused by what is uppermost in our waking consciousness.[2] There is the *ānandamaya* behind the *manomaya*, as the Upaniṣad states it: a vast bliss behind our mental being.

Sri Aurobindo indicates that this conception of reality as the self-delight of being has practical consequences; and this is the most attractive and liberating part of his teaching. There is a 'discovery' which we have yet to make, the discovery of the self-delight of being. When the discovery of self-delight of being is really made—this is possible for everyone—then we have mastered the great art of living. The *habitual* way of our life is to feel pain when things go wrong, and to feel pleasure, when they go according to our wishes. But, 'there is no real obligation on us to return to a particular contact a particular response of pleasure, pain or neutral reaction, there is only an *obligation of habit*'.[3] (The italics are mine.)

If we discover the real nature of our self as the self-delight of being, then we could alter the habitual mode of our living. 'It is equally within our competence to return quite the opposite

---

[1] Aurobindo, *The Life Divine*, p. 96.   [2] *Ibid.*, p. 98.   [3] *Ibid.*, p. 98.

response, pleasure where we used to feel pain, pain where we used to have pleasure'[1]—*Sama duḥkha sukham,* as the *Gītā* says, a perfect gladness, or a perfect indifference in all situations of pain or pleasure.

The human individual has this destiny before him: 'to become the master of his own responses to the world's contacts. . . .'[2] How this may be possible is the practical teaching of the 'integral' yoga of Sri Aurobindo.

[1] Aurobindo, *The Life Divine,* p. 98. [2] *Ibid.,* p. 99.

RUTH REYNA

Integralism: A Philosophie Perennis

THE insistent demand of reason for essential and permanent verities in a world characterized by change and inconstancy, has been the force precipitating man's quest for a universal view, a search for a perspective that will not only embrace all the aspects of human experience, but at the same time will relate human values and ideals to the ultimate ground of the universe.

As a result of this seeking there have emerged sharp contradictions of philosophical systems, effecting a fragmentation of philosophy into totally diverse sections and preventing the examination of philosophical problems from a truly universal point of view. Were we to review the evolution of doctrines from the primitive ages of India down to the present time and take cognizance of the progress achieved by contemporary scientific philosophy, we could do no less than infer the indefinite progress of philosophical thought. There are those who have allowed themselves to be enamoured of this ideal dream. Auguste Compte's 'law of the three stages', Herbert Spencer's evolutionism, Hegel's indefinite becoming of the spirit, the Marxian historical materialism and the like, sweep philosophy along in an ever cresting tide toward an ideal perfection, dependent upon a pertinent time and upon an interminable course of evolution, a perfection whose finality is inaccessible to the clairvoyant genius of man.

There have been attempts to mediate between those systems that hold philosophy to be variable and relative and those which claim to have discovered a criterion of certainty, an attempt, that is, to point the way to a coherent and ultimately satisfactory view of the world that allows for the integration of the material and spiritual values of life. So it is formulated by Sidgwick, who lays down as 'the final and most important task of philosophy, the problem of connecting fact and ideal in some rational and satisfactory manner'.[1] Philosophy thus becomes the struggle for a *Weltanschauung* in which the experiences of mankind can be brought into a common pool of human knowledge; and this is altogether possible, for side by side with the changes that belong to the condition of man's finitude, there is a fragment of unchangeable truth underlying his most patent systems and haunting the human mind in its most incurious investigations.

Secretly operative within the variations of historic systems there lies a *philosophie perennis*, which embodies those universal truths to which no one people or era can make an exclusive claim—a clear atmosphere of truth circumscribing the centuries, its subtle presence somehow sensed in spite of illusion and mist. The truth Pythagoras sought, and Plato, and Aristotle, is the same that Augustine and Aquinas pursued. So far as it is developed in history, truth is the daughter of time; so far as it contains within itself a content independent of time and therefore of history, it is the daughter of eternity.[2]

It is this conflict—the attempts of man to convert his obscure physical mentality into supramental illumination, to recognize and to possess a self-existent and permanent truth in the face of transitory persuasions—to seek an infinite freedom in a world governed by mechanical inevitabilities, and to realize immortal life in a body subjected to death and decay, that makes the search for a world philosophy not only one of curious theoretical speculation, but of the greatest practical urgency. The fuller idea of life demands of man that he find an integral living based upon a permanent truth, a way that will provide him the joy of the creative fulfilment inherent in his nature, yet resting upon an unchanging premise of truth—the

---

[1] Sidgwick, *Philosophy, Its Scope and Relations* (London: The Macmillan Co., 1902), p. 30.
[2] Willman, *Geschichte des Idealismus*, II (Braunschweig: Friedrich Vieweg und Sohn, 1907), p. 472 ff.

way of creative living in conscious union with the one universal creative principle.

This, then, is the basic problem of a *philosophie perennis*—it must satisfy man as to the fundamental truth of existence, and at the same time offer a motility for his self-expression that will enable him to conform to the creative purposes of life. It must provide for the agreement of unchangeable truths with the intellectual life while retaining that fluidity indispensable to spiritual unfoldment.

The philosophical position of Sri Aurobindo comes auspiciously close to meeting the requirements for a universal point of view. By a unique spiritual perception he has conceived the universe through a fresh vision of reality, and has comprehended into one concordant whole a total response to our human situation, thereby presenting an intellectually acceptable integration of the material and spiritual values of life while at the same time making possible the retention of man's loyalties in the plurality of human cultures.

Since the individual as functional uniqueness, in the view of Aurobindo, is none other than ultimate reality in differential mode, the highest goal of human life cannot consist of self-annihilation into a static and absolute truth. The path of fulfilment lies rather, as Integralism points out, in the active self-identification with the creative purposes of life, that is, with the ultimate integrating principle of the universe—the principle of infinite creativity.

What differentiates integral idealism with its principle of unending creativity, from the eternal variabilities and the indefinite evolutionism of certain western philosophies, is its confinement of variability within a field of manifestation typal in nature. In this integralism posits a seeming logical impossibility—that of including both immutability and mobility as coattributes of the one Reality. But in spite of this logical contradiction it is quite possible to reconcile the idea of fixed and definite goals with a progressive self-manifestation of the Spirit in time and in infinitely variant conditions embracing all the diverse forms of human experience. In the meaning of integralism, the ultimate nature of the Real is a composite of the Spirit existing simultaneously in different poises; that is to say, there are different orders of self-fulfilment of the Supreme Spirit: as supra-cosmic Transcendence and absolute freedom beyond the sphere of relativity; as infinite Consciousness creatively sustaining the sphere of relativity; and as the multiplicity of unique individuals functioning as channels of self-expression of the universal reality.

The supreme spirit as the cosmic creative principle sustains various planes of existence and consciousness as diversified modes of its self-fulfilment. While the visible material world is the sphere of evolutionary growth, the invisible planes of pure mind, supermind, etc., are typal or non-evolutionary in character, with fixed forms, modes of existence and patterns of perfection. These are 'fields of manifestation of fixed types, and whatever takes place in them is in the nature of increasing self-expression within the limits of these types'.[1]

The material world is that in which matter functions as the basic and dominant principle; and while the other planes are typal in nature, the material world is essentially evolutionary, for teaches Aurobindo, 'An involution of the Divine Existence, the spiritual Reality, in the apparent inconscience of Matter is the starting-point of the evolution'.[2] Matter, therefore, being the lower form of manifestation of the Spirit in the element of *sat* (existence) must implicitly contain within itself such other powers of the Spirit as life and mind and all the others. It is because these principles are from the beginning present and secretly operative in matter that it can be said that 'matter then contains the promise and potency of all terrestrial life, not as an absolutely non-spiritual blind entity, but as an apparently unconscious mode of operation of the super-conscient creative energy of the Spirit'.[3]

Matter is, without doubt, the starting point of the divine manifestation in the terrestrial plane. 'My supreme Nature has become the living being and the world is upheld by it . . . all beings have this for their source of birth.'[4] Thus we come to the understanding that the creative will of the divine Śakti,

---

[1] Haridas Chaudhuri, *The Philosophy of Integralism* (Pondicherry: Sri Aurobindo Ashram Press, 1954), p. 215.

[2] Aurobindo, *The Life Divine*, p. 814

[3] Haridas Chaudhuri, *op. cit.*, p. 157.   [4] *Gītā*, VII, pp. 5, 6.

functioning through the medium of matter endowed as it is with all of the principles of the Spirit, brings forth into articulate expression on ascending planes of consciousness, forms more and more adapted to its own completer expression. This integral emergence is the goal of evolving Nature.

Consciousness in life, responding to the pressures from above of vital, mental, and supramental planes of existence, throws off the primal inconscience of material nescience, and in evolutionary phases strives for emergence into true Reality, an eternal existence (*sat*), consciousness (*cit*), and delight of existence (*ānanda*). In man, the enlivening consciousness appears as mind, more clearly aware of itself and things, but still fragmentary and limited, yet possessing an irrepressible urge from within, and vividly aware of an ennobling force from above. It is the co-operation of this '*upward-tending force from below*' and the '*upward-drawing force from above*'[1] that compels man to ascend on the path of spiritual progress, and through which his first conceptive potentiality and the promise of integral emergence is revealed.

The philosophy of integralism points up the responsibility of the individual to follow his inward urge of aspiration, to strive toward an ever higher consciousness; for it is only through growth of the individual that the cosmic Spirit can organize the collective being and make itself expressive. It is only through the individual that nature is raised from the inconscience to the superconscience and exalted to meet the transcendent. 'I have arisen from earth to the mid-world, I have arisen from the mid-world to heaven, from the level of the firmament of heaven I have gone to the Sun-world, the Light.'[2]

It is the first duty of man, using the material instruments at hand, to evolve into ever higher consciousness and finally to exceed himself. He must gather his fragmentary being into a complete being, his partial consciousness into an integral consciousness; he must master his own environment and apply it to world-union and world-harmony; he must discover his

---

[1] Haridas Chaudhuri, *op. cit.*, p. 231.

[2] Yajur Veda, 17.67. These correspond with what Sri Aurobindo has called the planes of matter, life, pure mind, and supermind.

individuality and then extend it into a greater cosmic self in the universal harmony of the spiritual delight of existence. 'To exceed ego and be our own true self, to be aware of our real being, to possess it, to possess a real delight of being, is therefore the ultimate meaning of our life here; it is the concealed sense of our terrestrial existence.'[1]

Sri Aurobindo's theory of evolution as the Spirit's progressive self-manifestation in infinitely variable conditions, offers a rational and integral expression of immediate contact with the Real by embodying a reconciliation of the reality of the world-process with the eternal perfection of the Spirit. In this light, the philosophy of integralism is seen as an art of life fashioned from the continuity of the creative process which integrates man with mankind, quickening each individual to a genuinely creative self-reliance while deepening and enhancing his communion with the universe. Its purpose is to show that the integral experience of the Spirit imparts meaning and significance to the whole universe, offering a new vision in terms of world and human development while revealing and securing the intimate correlation between universality and individuality.

In an enlarged meaning of life, integralism has widened human spiritual horizons beyond all parochial and sectarian restrictions; it implies a new vision of man in his organic and spiritual unity, and envisages what man may yet attain when enjoined by an unyielding inner necessity, to press forward to the aspiration that is most exalted in him.

[1] Aurobindo, *The Life Divine*, pp. 817–8.

12

J. N. MOHANTY

Integralism and Modern
Philosophical Anthropology

THE purpose of this discussion will be to help an assessment of
the concept of man in Sri Aurobindo's philosophy in the light
of what is getting known, on the European continent, as
'philosophical anthropology'. Our procedure will be to start
with laying down the main lines of research brought together
under the title 'Philosophical Anthropology' and then to
follow it up with a statement of Sri Aurobindo's concept of
man, assessing its value and relevance for the contemporary
discussion of this theme.[1]

I

The term 'Philosophical Anthropology' was introduced in our
time, and the task of the discipline outlined, by Max Scheler
in his *Die Stellung des Menschen im Kosmos* (1928). But Scheler
had already formulated the main ideas in an essay 'Zur Idee
des Menschen' as early as 1914. The central problem with
which Scheler's philosophy is concerned is: What is man? And,
what is his status in relation to Being? This problem is handled
by Scheler in many of its aspects. The specific nature of human
feelings is discussed in *Wesen und Formen der Sympathie*: the
relation of man to history is discussed in the essay 'Mensch
und Geschichte'; the possibility of human development is

---

[1] Compare, for this entire theme, the author's *Modern Philosophical
Anthropology and the Concept of Man in Sri Aurobindo's Philosophy* (Bombay:
Sri Aurobindo Circle Annual, 1956).

the theme of a lecture, 'Der Mensch im Weltalter des Ausgleichs'.[1]

Two passages from Scheler may be quoted to outline the major themes:

Philosophical anthropology is a fundamental science of the essence and essential structure of man; of his relation to the realms of Nature (the inorganic, plants and animals), as well as to the basis of all things; of his metaphysical origin as well as of his physical, psychical and spiritual beginning in the world; of the forces and powers that move him and which he sets in motion, of the basic directions and laws of his biological, psychical, cultural-historical and social development, of their essential possibilities as much as of their actualities.[2]

It is the task of a philosophical anthropology to show exactly how, from the basic structure of human being, all the specific monopolies, creations and activities of man follow: language, conscience, crafts, weapons, ideas of justice and injustice, state, leadership, the representative functions of the arts, mythology, religion, science, historicality, and sociality.[3]

It will readily be appreciated by those acquainted with the contents of Sri Aurobindo's works, that his philosophy has to make a substantial contribution to these themes.

Philosophical anthropology on the European continent has: (1) tried to isolate the distinctive nature and status of man, as compared with the other realms of being, living and non-living. In doing this, philosophical anthropology has (2) freed itself from a narrow 'naturalistic-scientific' approach. It has rightly seen that neither physics nor chemistry, neither biology nor physiology, nor even psychology can adequately study the nature of man, although the data of each of these sciences are not without any relevance. A truer indication of man's essential nature is in language, mythology and poetry, art and religion, science considered as man's achievement, and history, that is to say, through what is vaguely called 'culture'. Hence the intimate connection between philosophical anthropology and

___

[1] These essays are included in the volume *Philosophische Weltanschauung* (München, 1954).   [2] *Ibid.*, p. 62.

[3] Max Scheler, *Die Stellung des Menschen im Kosmos* (München, 1947), p. 80.

what is called cultural anthropology in the United States.[1]
Further, insight is provided by analysis of the basic feeling-
tones of human existence: hope and despair, love and hatred,
trust and anxiety; hence, the inevitable alliance between
philosophical anthropology and 'existence'-philosophy. As
much attention is to be paid to a static-morphological study as
to a historical study, for man's understanding of himself has
unfolded itself in history and an important part of a study of
man is the study of man's growing understanding of himself.
Such understanding of himself constitutes an essential feature
of man's nature. (3) With this comprehensive programme
before it, it is but natural that modern philosophical anthropology cannot rest satisfied with any one-sided formulation of
human nature but struggles *towards an integral philosophy of
man*. The spirit of it is best expressed again by Max Scheler:

> Through his process of becoming, man has proved himself to be a
> being of enormous *plasticity*. It is therefore of the greatest danger
> for any philosophical opinion to formulate the Idea of Man too
> *narrowly*, to derive it from any one naturalistic or only historical
> form. . . . The idea of 'animal rationale' in the classical sense was
> much too narrow; the 'homo faber' of the positivists, the 'dionysian
> Man' of Nietzsche, Man as 'the disease of life' of the new panromantic
> teachings, the 'Superman', the 'homo sapiens' of Linné, the 'l'homme
> machine' of Lemettries, the merely 'Power'—the merely 'libido'—
> the merely 'economic'—man of Machiavelli, Freud and Marx, the
> fallen creature Adam—*all* these representations are much too
> narrow, since they are required to comprehend the *whole* man.
> Further, they all are at the same time Ideas of *Things*. Man, how-
> ever, is not a thing—he is a *direction of movement of the universe
> itself*. . . .[2] (The italics are mine.)

II

Sri Aurobindo has given us such an integral philosophy of man.
The cardinal principle of this philosophy is the principle that
man is what he can be; that human existence is full of possi-

[1] Compare H. Wein, 'Trends in Philosophical Anthropology and Cultural
Anthropology in Postwar Germany' (*Philosophy of Science*, Vol. 24, No. 1,
January 1957), pp. 46–56.
[2] *Philosophische Weltanschauung* (München, 1954), p. 96.

bilities; that man as such has an unavoidable tendency towards self-exceeding. 'It is in his human nature, in all human nature, to exceed itself by conscious evolution, to climb beyond what he is.'[1] This coincides with the findings of such researchers as Martin Heidegger: what distinguishes human existence from other lower modes of being is that whereas in those modes of being actuality dominates over possibility, human existence consists in its possibilities. Heidegger, however, is concerned with what may be called 'horizontal' possibility: the possibility of oscillating on the genuine dimension of existing. Sri Aurobindo supplements this phenomenological with a genetic-evolutionary standpoint. Man has not only the possibility of leading a more inwardized, more self-conscious (i.e. the 'existentialistic') life as contrasted with the externalized life of the sensational man; he has also the possibility of growing beyond himself as the spearhead of the cosmic evolutionary process.

This integral philosophy of man has two major aspects: morphological and genetic-evolutionary. The former reveals a horizontal cross-section of human existence, brings to light the sedimented structures within it, the immense complexity of man's nature; but it has also to show the endless existential possibilities according as man lets any one of the principles dominate the rest. The latter, i.e. the genetic-evolutionary aspect locates man in the cosmic evolutionary process and thereby determines his status and destiny. These two aspects are not unconnected, for which one reason amongst others is that the morphological complexity of human existence is but a consequence of the precise place man occupies in the cosmic-evolutionary process. Before we enter into short sketches of these major aspects, we may mention that the evolutionary aspect again shall include within it a subordinate theme: the evolution of man himself, as contrasted with cosmic evolution!

III

Looking for the complexity of human existence, one has learnt in our times to go beyond the simple rationalism of the past

[1] Aurobindo, *The Life Divine*, p. 638, also cp. p. 750.

centuries. Christianity had already challenged the Greek rationalism and had set up against the latter the extremely difficult notion of 'sin', of the powerful irrationalism before which reason is helpless and to get rid of which one has to take the help of 'faith' and 'grace'. In recent times, Marxism and psycho-analysis have, in different ways, undermined the eighteenth-century rationalism by exhibiting the irrational forces, economic and vital, that dominate man's rational activities. The concept of 'sin' continues to influence even these anti-religious modes of thought. The overall picture that today is in our mind is that of the dark irrational dominating reason—'moral sin', 'class interest', 'will to power', 'libido' are only different aspects of this infra-rational part of our nature.

In fact, 'infra-rational' is too vague a designation of this part of our being. Lowest are *the physical and vital* strata; for the body is there with a physical existence, just as there is also 'a vitality working in this bodily form and structure as in the plant or lower animal'. Yet, of both these strata of our existence, we are aware only of a little.[1] The true subconscious lies above these basic strata: 'it is *the Inconscient* vibrating on the borders of consciousness sending up its motions to be changed into conscious stuff, swallowing into its depths impressions of past experience as seeds of unconscious habit and returning them constantly but often chaotically to the surface consciousness.'[2] (The italics are mine.) This is what has been recognized in modern psycho-analysis, the '*ālaya-vijñāna*' of the Vijñānavādin Buddhists. It is this subconscious which is the 'dream-builder'.

But the word 'subconscious' may be used in a wider sense, in which case the subconscious cannot be taken to be identical with the infra-rational, but the infra-rational would only be the lower part of the subconscious. For, the subconscious would also include the subliminal. The subliminal is not like the unconscious a storehouse of irrational impulses, but has its own powers and modes of action that surpass the capacities of the waking consciousness. Such phenomena as clairvoyance, telepathy, thought-reading are only manifestations of this

---

[1] Aurobindo, *The Life Divine*, p. 498.   [2] *Ibid.*, pp. 499, 654.

subliminal part of our being.[1] Besides, it is the subliminal which can directly enter into other people's consciousness and accounts for many supernormal experiences. The subliminal is responsible for much of the best in art and literature, and it is false to trace all human culture to the infra-rational, the unconscious alone, as psycho-analysis has tried to do.

Besides the subconscious and the subliminal parts of our being, there is the higher, the superconscient. Whereas modern psychology has got hold of the first and, at its best (as with Jung), has got glimpses of the second, we are to turn to the yogic psychology and also to the spiritual psychologies of all countries to get to know about the last, i.e. the superconscient.

Sri Aurobindo has given us a rich phenomenology of these three spheres of our being, especially of the subliminal and the superconscient. Each of these spheres has its own inner stratification, and, of course, points of contact between them are not lacking. There is no rigid pigeon-holing, but there are left possibilities of movement from the one into the other.[2]

It is interesting to see how the status and function of reason is delimited upon this canvas. Lying midway between two spheres, the infra-rational and the supra-rational (including the subliminal and the superconscient), reason is no original law-giver, no autonomous faculty, not its own master (except, perhaps, in a limited region of purely formal thinking). Reason is a mediator 'between the subconscient All that we come from in our evolution upwards and the superconscient All towards which we are impelled by that evolution'.[3] In the subconscient, consciousness is involved in action; in the superconscient, action is transformed into knowledge. Standing in between them, reason fulfils an evolutionary role: it releases consciousness as it were from its 'imprisonment in the act' and prepares it 'to resume its essential primacy'.[4] While this is the evolutionary function of reason, in its multifarious activities reason is not under any one master. Now she obeys the lower vital, now the higher vital, now the subconscious, now the subliminal and at rare moments also the superconscient. In ordinary life, reason justifies one's physical-vital tendencies, economic class-

---

[1] Aurobindo, *The Life Divine*, p. 479.   [2] *Ibid.*, p. 480 f.
[3] *Ibid.*, p. 62.   [4] *Ibid.*, p. 63.

interests, traditional beliefs, etc. To turn reason from its servitude to the lower strata of our being and to make it a luminous medium for the truths of the higher regions is the task before every individual.

IV

The above sketch of a phenomenology of human nature is connected, in Sri Aurobindo's philosophy, with an evolutionary account of the origin and destiny of man. Sri Aurobindo, as is well known, advocates a kind of evolutionary philosophy in which there is a series of successive emergents, the whole process of emergence following upon a prior process of involution. These emergents have been: matter, life, animal consciousness and human self-consciousness. This process of emergence is characterized by three features: first, as the lower stratum advances sufficiently in complexity and configuration, a higher form emerges. Secondly, this higher—inert matter, life or consciousness as the case may be—when it appears does not reject the lower but takes it up as it were (compare Hegel's *aufheben*) and transforms it radically; thus life transforms matter in the sense that a living organism though material yet exhibits properties not to be found in inert matter! While the old and the lower is thus taken up and transformed, the new and the higher seeks to expand its own domain and to prepare itself for the emergent next-to-appear!

Man, standing as he does at the apex of the evolutionary process, includes in himself all the lower principles, not as such but as transformed and integrated under the dominant principle of his being: mental consciousness. He is a material body and also a living organism; but he is primarily a self-conscious mental being. Not only are the lower principles integrated in his being under the dominant principle of mental awareness; but even the higher principles, higher forms of awareness, are involved in him, even if under the limitations permitted by mental awareness. Hence the immense complexity of his nature, as well as the way the various aspects of his being cluster around man's self-consciousness.

In the preceding paragraph, we have spoken of integration

under a dominant principle. It should immediately be added, if we are to be true to the facts, that this integration, so far as man's present stage of self-awareness is concerned, is too imperfect. The elements of that complex nature which is man's do jar and conflict; hence, the conflicts within the individual and also in human history. The growth of man's self-awareness is a growing process of integration, rather—what amounts to the same—a search for a mode of self-awareness which would prove more effective in harmonizing the lower and the higher! It is Sri Aurobindo's singular vision that this mode of self-awareness is beyond the separative mental consciousness and nearer that divine self-consciousness—towards which man is growing—for which unity and plurality do not jar.

The evolutionary philosophy, while it provides, as we have seen, the rationale of the peculiar complexity as well as the plasticity of human nature, also affords us with the fundamental *existential responsibility* that is man's and from which should follow all his religious, ethical and social 'ought-to-do's' and 'ought-to-be's'.

The evolutionary philosophy teaches that the appearance of man signifies a 'crucial step, a decisive change in the cause and process of the evolution; it is not merely a continuation of the old lines'.[1] 'In him . . . the substitution of a conscious for a subconscious evolution has become conceivable and practicable. . . . In the previous stages of the evolution Nature's first care and effort had to be directed towards a change in the physical organization, for only so could there be a change of consciousness. . . . But in man a reversal is possible, indeed inevitable; for it is through his consciousness, through its transmutation . . . that the evolution can and must be effected.'[2]

It is possible now, and indeed it is his spiritual responsibility, that man should consciously co-operate with the cosmic process. The *urge* is towards a higher (in the sense of being more integrated, harmonious, all-comprehensive and based not on separation but on identity) mode of consciousness. The *task* is to prepare the ground for the emergence of such a mode of consciousness, morality, individual and social, religion, personal and institutional, art and literature, science and technology,

[1] Aurobindo, *The Life Divine*, p. 750.   [2] *Ibid.*, p. 751.

education and social ordering—all these activities of man may be understood and evaluated in the light of this most funda-mental responsibility that is placed on man by virtue of his unique position in the evolutionary process. Man, to recall Scheler's words (quoted above), is 'a direction of movement of the universe itself'; he is not only a direction, but *the* dominant direction.

V

While the preceding section lays down the basis of Sri Aurobindo's philosophy, to this must be added an account of *the spiritual evolution of man himself*. For this one has to turn, to start with, to the chapter entitled, 'The Evolution of the Spiritual Man' in *The Life Divine*; but to be able to appreciate the comprehensiveness of Sri Aurobindo's approach, one must inevitably take into consideration *The Human Cycle*.

Since the evolutionary process is everywhere aiming at a comprehensive change, and not merely at emergence of some-thing new, the evolution of the spiritual man is bound to be a slow and laborious process. For, it is not enough if the spiritual being alone is developed; it is also required that the outer crusts of our being also shall be developed and transformed. The evolution of man therefore has a twofold aspect; an evolution of our outward nature and an evolution of our inner being. In the case of man, the former means primarily the development of our mind 'to its greatest possible range, height, subtlety; for only so can be prepared the unveiling of an entirely intuitive intelligence'.[1]

There is an original 'amalgam of religion, occultism and mystic experience',[2] which characterizes the early human mind. This belongs to what is called in *The Human Cycle* the symbolic age. There is however a growing 'tendency towards intellectuali-zation', along with which the occult element diminishes; and there arises 'a movement to cut out everything but creed, institution, formal practice and ethics'. This characterizes the typal age of *The Human Cycle*. Soon all spiritual content vanishes, leaving behind nothing but conventions. It seems as

---

[1] Aurobindo, *The Life Divine*, p. 763.   [2] *Ibid.*, p. 771.

if the spiritual evolution of man would be totally frustrated. But Nature has her own way of working. The age of convention helps the dawning of a new era of individualism and rationalism. The individual revolts against conventions and takes to reason as his guiding principle—science and socialism are the twin outcome of this era. Curiously enough, as *The Human Cycle* vividly portrays, in the hands of both the individual is swallowed up, and reason proves a poor guiding principle. After attaining to a high watermark of development, rationalism has yielded room to a new search for the soul, a deeper subjectivism which according to Sri Aurobindo would provide the basis for the future of mankind.

It is clear that here again the emphasis is on integration. The future of mankind lies in more and more of integration of the different principles constituting his complex nature.

Intellectualization of the earlier spiritual cultures was not a falling away, a retrogression; it was the beginning of a new line of development, an attempt towards the perfecting of a new faculty, i.e. intellect. What the primitive man had vaguely sensed through intuition was later sought to be apprehended through a perfected reason. The consequence was beneficial to both. For we cannot say that the vague intuitions of the primitive man were perfect; all that was only a beginning. Ages of human experiments through which human mind has been perfecting itself are making possible a richer intuitive grasp of the truth of things and therefore a more integrated form of awareness.

We have considered Sri Aurobindo's philosophy of man in three of its aspects: (1) in the morphological analysis of human nature, (2) in relation to the cosmic evolutionary process, and finally (3) in relation to the story of the spiritual evolution of man himself. Bearing in mind Scheler's demand for an integral philosophy of man, we may look up to Sri Aurobindo's works for a satisfying answer.

PART TWO

EPISTEMOLOGY AND PSYCHOLOGY

13

NINIAN SMART

Integral Knowledge and the Four Theories
of Existence

THE massive yet intricate beauty of *The Life Divine* can
conceal from us how a paragraph, a sentence even, may contain
within itself a vast range of thought. It is part of the genius
of the work that its doctrines are exhibited not in a dry, and
therefore unilluminating, sequence, but in the manner of a
painting: each new brush-stroke gives novel significance to the
others, and the features emerge not by being mechanically
filled in, but by a kind of patterned growth. It is therefore
hard to deal briefly even with what at first seems a small
fragment. For instance, one reads that 'the hard logical and
intellectual notion of truth as a single idea which all must
accept, one idea or system of ideas defeating all other ideas or
systems, . . . is an illegitimate transference from the limited
truth of the physical field to the much more complex and
plastic field of life and mind and spirit';[1] yet one can hardly
discuss this vital point without adverting to the whole edifice
of Sri Aurobindo's thought. But perhaps it is not entirely
nugatory to link this sentence specifically to his classification
of different kinds of metaphysical or religious theories.[2]

But first, a general word about schemes of classification. It
is evident that any metaphysical view must give some account
of its possible competitors. For instance, some views (ones
which are indirectly criticized in the above quotation and
which I shall refer to as 'exclusivist', since they hold that one

[1] Aurobindo, *The Life Divine*, p. 788.
[2] *Ibid.*, the classification is elaborated in Part II, Chapter XVII, p. 609.

picture or other of spiritual truth is exclusively correct) have a simple account of their rivals: that they are just wrong. Opposed to this way of treating possible opponents is the synthetic approach, whereby other doctrines are absorbed, not rejected.[1] The Judaic religions, for instance, tend to be exclusivist, Hinduism synthetic. And in particular, Sri Aurobindo's integralism is a majestic attempt at synthesis. But perhaps, though the contrast here depicted is just, it should not be drawn too sharply; for it often comes about that a religion, in so far as it is at all missionary and inasmuch as it encounters other faiths that cannot just be dismissed as demonic,[2] must provide some convincing interpretation of the spiritual experience and dynamism of others. This usually involves a description of other faiths, not quite in their own terms, but in terms of one's own.[3] A similar remark may apply to Sri Aurobindo's classification of the theories of existence. To this we now turn.

The four theories are respectively: the supracosmic; the cosmic and terrestrial; the supraterrestrial; and the integral or synthetic or composite. The first of these holds that the supreme Reality is alone entirely real; while the second takes cosmic and terrestrial reality (or becoming) as alone real. The third recognizes both the reality of the world and that of something higher—characteristically, we have here belief in human immortality and a view of life as a temporary sojourn in which ethical and spiritual development constitutes the path to ultimate salvation. Finally, there are views built up out of two or more of these, and in particular there is the integral theory of Sri Aurobindo himself. The most typical instance of supracosmicism is the *Advaita Vedānta*; on the other hand the cosmic view is more characteristically found in Western tradition. This is not to say that there are no instances of the former

---

[1] Absorbed, or sublated; see Appendix A, *A Glossary of Sanskrit Terms in the Life Divine* (Pondicherry, 1952).

[2] Consider, e.g. the view of Roman and Greek gods in early Christianity.

[3] Cp., for a similar point, Austin Farrer in his article on 'Examination of Theological Belief' in *Faith and Logic*, ed. Basil Mitchell (London: Allen & Unwin Ltd., 1957), p. 13, where he distinguishes between those things *off* which we read religious truths and those *into* which we read them; a like remark applies to the histories and doctrines of religions.

theory in the West, for there are systems of idealistic metaphysics such as that of Bradley, which in some respects bear
a remarkable formal resemblance to Śaṅkara's—though in view
of the directly *spiritual* reference of *Advaita*, a nearer parallel
would be found in some of the writings of Eckhart.[1] On the
other hand, though naturalistic views have, in consonance with
the rise of science and the decline of Christendom, become
widespread in the West, there are instances of them in the
East, e.g. the *Cārvāka* metaphysics.

Sri Aurobindo criticizes these two theories as being incomplete. In regard to cosmicism: it denies the simple affirmation
that there is a 'beyond'.[2] It ignores the teaching of spiritual
experience and so will not ultimately satisfy human nature. On
the other hand, supracosmicism normally issues in the feeling
that the world is illusory, a dream, a mirage; and, even where
it does not, it yet assigns no ultimate significance to the individual being. And thus it negates something which cannot be
dismissed 'as a device for a minor operation, the coiling and
uncoiling of an insignificant spiral amid the vast circlings of
the Eternal's becoming in the universe'.[3]

But when we turn to supraterrestrialism, we might think at
first glance that it is a kind of synthesis, for it affirms the
reality of both the Transcendent and the material cosmos.
Thus, it has been remarked by William Temple that Christianity
is the most materialistic of the world's religions. This is partly
because theistic faiths do not normally stress the illusoriness
of the cosmos (for the dualism implicit in theism—the dualism
between Creator and creature, Object of worship and wor-
shipper—must affirm the reality of each term in the relation
and must also see the world as purposive and hence becoming
in its own right subsistent); and partly because in particular
the Christian doctrine of the Incarnation contains the idea that
God Himself sanctifies material existence. It may be noted in

[1] See Rudolf Otto's classic, *Mysticism East and West* (London: Macmillan
& Co. Ltd., 1932). Eckhart's description of the world, on one occasion, as
'a mere nothing' is reminiscent of what Sri Aurobindo calls a sense of 'the
vanity of cosmic existence' (*The Life Divine*, p. 436).

[2] Cp. *The Life Divine*, p. 18.

[3] *Ibid.*, p. 459: the reference is to the *Vedānta* of the *Upaniṣads*, where,
says Sri Aurobindo, the becoming of *Brahman* is accepted as a reality.

passing that the prevalent materialism in some Western societies is perhaps a reflection of this feature of Christianity: theism without the *Theos* leaves matter; whereas the equation does not quite hold in India: remove the personal God and you may be left with the Absolute. There are two directions in which one may desert an Īśvara.[1]

Why then is supraterrestrialism not a synthesis in Sri Aurobindo's sense? It must be borne in mind that on his view there are three elements which must be preserved, and held together, in any picture of reality which paints it in its full richness: first, the reality of the cosmos; second, the reality of that which transcends it; and third, the reality of the individual being. Now certainly—at least superficially—theistic religion preserves these three elements. But if we consider Sri Aurobindo's main criticisms of supraterrestrialism, we gain a clue towards understanding the matter. For he remarks that its defect lies in the way it treats man's existence in the present world; for although the view contains the truth that there is a higher realm of being (often described as a heaven or paradise), the picture of man as in a fallen or unsatisfactory state in this world, such that his ultimate salvation lies in another realm, neglects the truth that the worlds of higher consciousness are not the only possible habitation for a perfected soul.[2] This life also is part of the Spirit's self-expression. Hence, supraterrestrialism falls into an error similar to that of supracosmicism —it represents an improper notion of the status of the cosmos and of human existence.

One or two subsidiary questions arise out of the above scheme of classification of views. A notoriously difficult metaphysical system to dovetail into any general account of religions is that of Buddhism and in particular the *Theravāda*. For it cannot be said that according to the latter there is a unitary absolute; hence, it is hard to count it as supracosmic. Moreover, the impermanence of all entities in the cosmos is not full-blown unreality. On the other hand, the *Theravāda* is not, in the sense

[1] Aurobindo, *The Life Divine*, p. 621: 'The higher self-knowledge begins therefore as soon as man has got beyond his preoccupation with the relation of Nature and God to his superficial being, his most apparent self.'
[2] *Ibid.*, p. 472.

in which the Judaic group of faiths is, supraterrestrial, in that it is agnostic about individual immortality,[1] and there is no God to provide a heaven for His creatures. But neither is it simple cosmicism, for there is an unborn, an uncompounded: there is *nirvāṇa*. Perhaps it is best to see the *Theravāda* as combining elements of the cosmic and supracosmic views. For, like supracosmicism, its supreme goal is a kind of self-annihilation; but like cosmicism, it does not preach a substantive Reality beyond the cosmos.

This points to a formal or logical feature of composite and synthetic theories. For the two simpler views, cosmicism and supracosmicism, are overtly exclusivist: not merely is it said that the cosmos or the Absolute is reality, but that it is the *only* reality. Materialism, for instance, rejects what is yielded in spiritual experience. It is absurd to suppose that a synthetic view can absorb *all* the features of that which it synthesizes; for clearly the synthesis itself cannot reject spiritual intuition, even though it may delight in the clearing away of cobwebs induced by such a rejection.[2] What it admires is the positive elements, or at least some of these; what it denies is the rejections. But how is one to hit upon the right method of synthesizing? Sri Aurobindo's procedure here is of the greatest moment—for, as glimmers forth from his reflections upon the fundamental theories, he is illumined by experience in selecting the main facts to be accounted for. And the dark flaw in cosmicism, for example, is that it is blind to, and denies, a living facet of experience, just as supracosmicism rejects the witness of the individual being. Similarly, but for different reasons, supraterrestrialism—at least as it is found in the West—is exclusivist; and we have in Sri Aurobindo's strictures a reflection of the long tradition of Hinduism: that no one theory can declare others to be utterly false. Yet the real defect in supraterrestrialism, on his view, is again that it neglects the possible opening up of a wider experience, as implied in the notion of a higher existence, in this visible world that we know

[1] *Majjhima-Nikaya*, Vol. I, p. 483 ff., etc.

[2] Aurobindo, *The Life Divine*, p. 13: 'Rather we shall observe with respect and wonder the work that Atheism has done for the Divine and admire the services that Agnosticism has rendered in preparing the illimitable increase of knowledge.'

so well. It wrongly creates a great gulf between the cosmos and the higher realm, to the detriment ultimately of the former and the distortion, in some degree, of the latter.

So much then, all too briefly, for the reasons why the synthesis has to embrace the insights of the three fundamental world-views. It is now perhaps worth reflecting on some points about the synthetic method. I have remarked above that Sri Aurobindo looks to experience and intuition[1] for the basic facts of existence which need to be woven together into an integral theory. And indeed it may be said that it is different varieties of experience which yield the three fundamental views. Now this points towards an important aspect of the present predicament. In the West, with the permeation of society by science and naturalism and the decay, in some regions, of traditional religion, there exist two main ways in which spiritual truth can be defended. The first is by philosophical metaphysics and the second is by appeal to experience and intuition. Yet, as Sri Aurobindo remarks, 'the concepts of metaphysical knowledge do not in themselves fully satisfy the demand of our integral being. . . . Our nature sees things through two eyes always, for it views them doubly as idea and as fact and therefore every concept is incomplete for us and to a part of our nature almost unreal. . . .'[2] But worse; it is doubtful whether much trust can be placed in philosophical metaphysics of the old sort—for the play of logic upon concepts such as *causality*, to generate conclusions about a First Cause, and so on, is by no means evidently legitimate. It may be true that those who have intimations of the spiritual find their beliefs encouraged by the natural metaphysical feeling that the existence of the cosmos cries for an explanation. Yet it can hardly be thought that there is a method of *a priori* reasoning which can by itself yield sure truths about reality.[3] Hence, belief must defend itself by reference to experience, and this is where there arises a painful paradox for exclusivism. To claim there is one revelation, and to back the claim by appeal

---

[1] For the use of this term see *The Life Divine*, footnote p. 63.

[2] Aurobindo, *The Life Divine*, p. 59.

[3] *Ibid.*, p. 64: 'Intuition brings to man those brilliant messages from the Unknown which are the beginning of his higher knowledge. Reason only comes in afterwards to see what profit it can have of the shining harvest.'

to humanity's deeper intuitions, is seemingly, in the light of the facts, a contradiction. For the facts tell us unmistakably that the spiritual adventure of men, whether at a superficial or profound level, is not constricted to one culture or family of cultures. Such an illusion has been generated by ignorance of others, but neither the Holy Roman Empire nor *Jambudvīpa* was the full circle of humanity, nor was the outsider justly named *barbarous* or *mleccha*. A deeper acquaintance with alien cultures must lead one to recognize their spiritual as well as their other glories. Hence an appeal to experience, though it may be harmonized with the view that one's own *Weltans-chauung* gives the fullest picture, or the quintessential picture, cannot be consonant with extreme exclusivism.

It therefore seems inevitable at the present juncture for religions to take the path towards synthesis. Hinduism, it may be replied, does not need to do this, since it has already done it. Yet there are points where traditional Hindu theories need supplementation perhaps; and indeed it is Sri Aurobindo's genius that he has provided a framework of thought which, while it grows out of such ancient concepts as *Brahman, puruṣa, prakṛti, prāṇa*, etc., yet does not have merely a static view of things, but absorbs the sense, gained from both science and history, of the unfolding of man's spirit. The importance of this lies not just in its presentation of matter and life as evolving, but in its evolutionary description of religion and metaphysics. Fogazzaro, in his moving novel *Il Santo*, made the point that a new set of teachings, a new spiritual movement, needs not merely ideas to express it, but a saint to give it power and legitimacy. Even those who do not adhere to Sri Aurobindo's teachings must surely ask—though without the irony of the original:

> *kavīyamānah ka iha pra vocad?*
> *devaṁ manah kuto adhi prajātam?*[1]

('Who has here, like a poet-seer, given this teaching?
Where has this divine mind sprung from?')

And to ask the question is already to grant the need for some synthesis or reinterpretation of belief.

[1] *Rg-Veda*, I.164.18.

14

H. P. SULLIVAN

The Integration of Knowledge

'KNOWLEDGE', as this word is commonly understood and used in Western philosophy, refers to those thought-constructs of the rational mind which arise in the intellective process of unifying, interpreting and verifying sensory data. To some philosophers knowledge must possess a testable logical certainty as articulated statements. To yet others any external validation or test of logical certainty applied to knowledge is irrelevant, contradictory and in the last analysis impossible, since basically all knowledge is of a 'subjective' nature, derived from an irreversible causal activity within the brain.

Apart from this sort of difference of definition and others perhaps somewhat more basic (such as whether or not knowledge is an activity or relationship between subject and object or whether it is already self-contained in the mind), contemporary Western epistemological theory and speculation is with few exceptions preoccupied with 'objective' knowledge, knowledge of the external world of objects. It is indeed rare that one finds serious discussion of the possibility or actuality of suprasensory cognition such as intuitive or non-rational knowledge, experience of spiritual truth and 'pure consciousness' or supraconscious awareness. More often than not, such modes of knowing and the knowledge derived are characterized as 'unscientific', 'fantasy', or at the best 'faith' or 'belief' as opposed to testable or tested 'knowledge'. True knowledge of ultimate Reality, in so far as most professional philosophy (apart from surviving Hegelian elements and occasional 'right-wing' existentialists like Marcel and Jaspers) is concerned, is highly suspect and is usually relegated to the realm of pious opinion and even superstition of the religionist and theologian.

The traditions of Eastern philosophy and metaphysics to the present day stand in sharp contrast to Western traditions in their final elevation of the intuitive and suprarational or spiritual over the rational intellect as the means of valid knowledge. Rather than being the most reliable and infallible means of knowledge (as it is in the West) the rational intellect is the most uncertain means, just because the primary sensory data upon which it must rely come from a world of impermanence, change and illusion, and are filtered through a not altogether reliable sense-mind. In the last analysis, it is from the non-rational, the highest intuition, the 'spiritual experience', that the truest knowledge of Reality comes.

In the metaphysical system of Sri Aurobindo, we find the consummation of this approach to knowledge. What is unique in his treatment of the epistemological problem is the attempt to reconcile the rational-theoretical standpoint of Western metaphysics with the suprarational-practical understanding of Eastern (and primarily Indian) traditions in a grand synthesis. In doing so he avoids two extremes: the denial of spirit by the West and the annihilation of intellect by the East. Each knowledge, the spiritual and the rational, is necessary to the other if there is to be achieved an integral knowledge, a wholistic understanding of Reality, both empirical and absolute; one is incomplete without the other. Sri Aurobindo recognizes that there are levels of knowledge with corresponding levels of consciousness and ways of knowing. His goal is to arrive at an integration of knowledge through an integration of the various levels of consciousness.

Sri Aurobindo distinguishes four main ways of knowing Reality: knowledge by identity; knowledge by direct contact; knowledge by separation from the object of observation; and knowledge gained through a completely separate and indirect contact with the object. On the cognitive mode employed will, of course, depend the level and type of Reality known. Knowledge is, in other words, teleological; it is selective of its own content and determined by its own interests and motivation. Thus it is that most of the time we operate in terms of a separative cognition of subject and object (rather than a knowledge by identity) and gain only a knowledge of separate existence. Whereas in self-awareness we directly experience ourselves—that is, part of the subjective consciousness can remain detached from the flow of thought and sensation and observe and even control this flow while another part of consciousness enters into and becomes completely identified with the internal states—in our knowledge of things and events outside us, we distinguish ourselves from that which is not-self. We function as knowing subjects separate from an objective reality external to consciousness. As Aurobindo points out: 'We do not identify ourselves with external objects, not even with other men though they are beings of our own nature; we cannot enter into their existence as if it were our own, we cannot know them and their movements with the directness, immediateness, intimacy with which we know—even though incompletely—ourselves and our movements.'[1]

Our knowledge of others, however, most often lacks not only identity, but direct contact as well. There is no real participation of one being in another being; no true meeting of one consciousness with another. Our awareness of most of the external world is confined to generalized sensory impressions which lack any real directness or intimacy. If, however, we were to remain at the level of mere sensible impressions of our external world, we would not be able to function effectively in that world. At this point reason operates upon the chaotic mass of sense data to achieve some sort of structured order whereby we are able to relate our existence to other existents. This action of the human reason is what Aurobindo characterizes as 'mixed' or 'dependent'.[2] It is confined to sensible experience, regards only phenomena and is concerned only with appearances.

There is, however, another action of the mind which may be termed 'pure'. This occurs when the mind starts with appearances but instead of stopping there, it goes beyond them and strives for general principles and concepts which will give a wholistic meaning to the appearances. This 'pure' action of the mind is eminently necessary since our field of sensible experience is so restricted and the knowledge derived there-

[1] Aurobindo, *The Life Divine*, p. 472.　　　　[2] *Ibid.*, p. 59 f.

from so limited and fractionated. It is of the very nature of the pure reason to exceed the mass of sensible phenomena in the quest for those unifying principles which offer the greatest possible truth of things.

This, then, is the movement of the mind from purely physical knowledge to metaphysical knowledge. But something more is demanded by our integral being, a knowledge greater than mere intellectual truth or a mental conception concerning the nature of ultimate Reality; for no concept of metaphysical knowledge—no matter how 'polished'—is really in itself complete. We see existence through two eyes, the eye of sensory experience and the eye of pure reason, and thus it is seen doubly as fact and as idea. As a consequence, metaphysical concepts do not provide truly integral knowledge, for they have a 'split' existence. The truths which constitute the innermost reality of our existence are derived neither from observations of the senses nor from the constructions of the pure reason; they are truths of the supraphysical which can be had only through suprarational and super-psychological experience. 'The central aim of Knowledge', says Aurobindo, 'is the recovery of the Self, of our true self-existence. . . .'[1] To know the truth of our own being—to detect and set right its disorders, confusions, and its false identifications with aspects of its surface nature such as mind, body, emotions, desires, etc.—is the goal of all knowledge. This is the task of self-knowledge, self-identity, integrity, or what Jaspers calls 'authentic selfhood'. Only in knowing ourselves do we truly know the self in others and the Reality in Nature and History and that which is the All behind all Reality. By discovering the truth of our own being we overcome the barrier between our individuality and the universe and achieve a 'correspondence' of truth and an identity between our particularity and the totality of existence. Only then do we universalize our conscious existence and know all Being through identity with our own being. Realizing in ourselves the 'I am He' of the Vedānta, we cannot but realize in looking upon all around us the identical knowledge on its other side, 'Thou art That'.

[1] Aurobindo, *The Synthesis of Yoga* (Pondicherry: Sri Aurobindo Ashram, 1955), p. 382.

For Aurobindo, therefore, the 'true truth of things' as distinguished from the 'practical truth of relation' is knowledge by identity—that which is known apart from the media of sense or ratiocination. It is knowledge of ourselves derived solely from psychological experience, but psychological experience on a certain level and of an exact kind. For in a sense all our experience is psychological experience. But the psychological experience in question, too, like the cognitions of the reason, is of a mixed and a pure nature. When we seek to become aware of the external world in any of its features or dimensions, we employ the five senses to collect the data which we refer to our 'sixth sense', or what the ancient Indian philosophers called *manas*, the sense-mind. This is the mixed nature of psychological experience; the sense-mind is wholly dependent upon the senses. However, when it seeks to become aware of itself—the subject—then its nature is pure, for its perception of itself is one by identity. That is to say, we are capable of an immediate experience of ourselves; we are aware directly of our thoughts and emotions, of our existence. This, then, is the autonomous nature or functioning of psychological experience which produces knowledge by identity and is that very knowledge. Moreover, this knowledge by identity is the only means to the 'true truth of things'; the knowledge derived from sensible experience is but the 'practical truth of things'.

It is Aurobindo's contention that the real nature of all cognitive experience is knowledge by identity, but because of the exclusive demands of the ego, we have separated ourselves from that which we now know as 'external reality', creating distinctions of 'subject' and 'object' and necessitating thereby the development of processes and organs whereby we can achieve contact with and knowledge of that which by force of the ego we have excluded from the consciousness of our being.[1]

[1] Gabriel Marcel propounds a similar view of what he terms 'knowledge by participation'. In knowledge of oneself, which is the only real knowledge, since it is knowledge of the knower, Descartes' *cogito* formulation is of no help since it is not related to the whole self of will, body, feelings, consciousness, but only to the ego as an organ of cognition. Descartes was concerned with a thinking subject standing over against a world of objects and not with the whole Self as contained in Being-Itself. As Marcel says, 'knowledge is contingent on a participation in being for which no epistemology can account because it continually presupposes it' (*The Philosophy of Existence*, p. 8).

In order to regain knowledge by identity, we must regain knowledge of our true self. For only when we know the self of our own being can we know the Self in all being *by identity*. That which is the ultimate reality of the individual is the ultimate reality of all existence. At the base of all true knowledge of existence is a consciousness of identity and by identity; a full awareness of all as oneself and oneself in all. This consciousness lies behind all mental awareness but is not subject to the distinctions of temporal modes of separate knowledge, for it possesses an integral knowledge of self-existence in time and in all modes of past, present and future at once and totally. To enter into this supramental consciousness, to know all being as one's own being and all selves as one's own self, is the goal, the perfection and the integration of all knowledge.

To become aware of this consciousness and to enter into it, we must withdraw from our usual mental activity of fragmented and separative knowing and from the abstractions and rigid constructions of our ego-controlled rational intellect. For if we are confined to mind and its temporarily determined perceptions and constructions, we can never achieve a knowledge which is more than that of our immediate time-space relationships. In other words, we can never know reality which is other than spatial or temporal.[1] We must instead radically 'open' ourselves to that consciousness which stands behind our ordinary mental-knowing and conscious self-experience. We must see ourselves as more than a particular mind-body complex and go beyond our separative individuality and self-limiting ego construction to the realization of an existence behind and beyond the phenomenal flow of differentiated

---

[1] As Pascal pointed out, man cannot hope to comprehend his own nature by means of the sort of knowledge whereby as a subject he apprehends the external world of 'things'. 'The nature of our existence hides from us the knowledge of our first beginnings which are born of the Nothing; and the littleness of our being conceals from us the sight of the Infinite. Our intellect holds the same position in the world of thought as our body occupies in the expanse of nature. . . . This is our true state; this is what makes us incapable of certain knowledge and of absolute ignorance. When we think to attach ourselves to any point and fasten to it, it wavers and leaves us; and if we follow it, it eludes our grasp, slips past us and vanishes forever' (*Pensées*, Modern Library Edition, No. 72).

self-experience, of a timelessness of an eternal present beyond all temporal distinctions.

In short we must have an experience of that ultimate Reality which is the ground and essence of all existence, empirical and absolute. Such an experience is not a fantasy. On the contrary, it is possible for man to enter into the consciousness of the Absolute since it is that very consciousness which is involved in and is the essence of his own consciousness and of his very existence. Thus, the experience of absolute Consciousness, of the individual self as one with the universal and ultimate Self, is the highest knowledge; it is the culmination of knowledge by identity. Human consciousness, therefore, contains within itself the consciousness of the Absolute as a light whereby all things are made known. As St Thomas Aquinas declared, *'praeexistunt in nobis quaedam scientiarum semina'*[1] ('We possess within ourselves the germ of all knowledge').

The problem of the integration of knowledge thus demands an exploration of all possible levels of consciousness, including that of spiritual experience; for the supraphysical is as real as the physical and in order to have complete knowledge of Reality, it is essential that we know all realms of existence.

Such knowledge, however, is often branded as occultism. Nonetheless it is part of human experience, and the secret inner workings of mind, life and matter can and must be known. The spiritual domain is occult only in the sense that it transcends normal experience, but just because it does, it is possible to discover here the inner nature of consciousness and being and by the discovery of the inner laws of psychical and spiritual nature to transform human existence. In a similar sense science is occultism in that it seeks to discover and to bring into effect the laws of physical nature. It discovers the hidden knowledge of nature and uses that knowledge to control the operations of natural energies. In its own way it has evolved as a vast system of physical magic, utilizing the secret powers and processes of nature.

Supraphysical knowledge is necessary for the completion of

---

[1] *Contra Gentiles*, IV, 2, ad *Rursus considerandum est*, quoted in Etienne Gilson, *The Christian Philosophy of St Thomas Aquinas*, p. 215.

physical knowledge; for in themselves, materialistic doctrines of knowledge are inadequate.[1] This is not to say, however, that such doctrines are unnecessary. On the contrary, it would be

[1] At this point Aurobindo has a strong Western ally in the person of Karl Jaspers (vide Von der Wahrheit, Munich, 1947, and Der Philosophische Glaube, Basel, 1948, translated by R. Manheim and published in English under the title: The Perennial Scope of Philosophy, London, 1950).

Jaspers distinguishes between 'understanding' (Verstand), whereby we are able to deal with the objective world and obtain phenomenal knowledge, and 'reason' (Vernunft), which is involved in 'transcending thinking'. Vernunft penetrates beyond finitude, seeks the Transcendent which is behind concepts, and goes beyond both the surface knowledge of things which science provides and the common-sense conventional meanings which we attach to our everyday empirical existence. By virtue of Vernunft we are able to transcend immanence (Dasein) and attain true Selfhood (Existenz).

Both Aurobindo and Jaspers agree that agnosticism and nihilism play a necessary transitional role in the quest after ultimate truths in that they reveal the precariousness of any attempt to construct a total interpretation of Reality within the confines of objective knowledge. Also, they both agree that science cannot provide a comprehensive and unified view of existence, since the existing individual is always more than the sum total of what can be known about him objectively. Even if it were possible to construct a single, consistent system from the totality of our phenomenal knowledge derived from the natural and human sciences, the complex of meaning which is man could still not be fully contained in that system. Cognition of the phenomenal, objective world can never grasp that ultimate primal ground (Ursprung, Brahman) of our existence. The sciences—even the human or social sciences such as psychology and sociology—do not grasp the essential nature, the selfhood of man qua personal existence, but rather they characterize aspects of him in terms of psychological, sociological and biological forces. But the self is more than any force or the totality of forces. Conceptual knowledge may throw some light on man's essential existence (what Jaspers calls Existenzerhellung—'lighting up existence'), but it can never directly illumine his self.

Aurobindo, however, goes beyond Jaspers by extending the possible boundaries of knowledge to include ultimate Reality. Jaspers seems to deny the possibility of man ever really having any direct and immediate consciousness and thus knowledge of what he calls the Transcendence—ultimate Reality; we must instead rely on symbolic revelations ('ciphers') (vide D. E. Roberts, Existentialism and Religious Belief, New York, 1957, pp. 257–68). Being itself forever transcends us; there is ever a hiatus between human consciousness and the Ultimate. Aurobindo would agree with Jaspers's insistence that no predicates derived from ordinary knowledge and experience are applicable to Being-Itself. For as the ancients declared, all that can be said of Brahman is 'neti, neti!'—'not this, not this!' But, on the other hand, men can and do have an experience of ultimate Reality and are compelled to express that experience in word and deed even though the expression is always inadequate to the original experience. There is a verifiable conscious experience of the Many in the One and the One becoming the Many, of the absolute unity of all modes of reality contained in Being-Itself.

difficult to assess fully the indispensable role played by rationalistic materialism in leading man to true knowledge. By its insistence upon a chastened and disciplined intellect in dealing with natural phenomena it has saved us from much superstition and irrational dogma which in the past often impeded the advance of knowledge. As Aurobindo declares: 'It is necessary, therefore, that advancing Knowledge should base herself on a clear, pure and disciplined intellect. . . . It may even be said that the supraphysical can only be really mastered in its fullness—to its heights we can always reach— when we keep our feet firmly on the physical.'[1]

Granting the relative value and truth of the materialistic critique of knowledge, we must yet not lose sight of the fact that behind physical nature is a supraphysical force. Matter is not the sole or fundamental reality; it is but the structure of a primal energy, of conscious force. The exclusively materialistic interpretation of existence reveals a one-sided preoccupation with one aspect of total reality, just as does an exclusive concentration upon either life or mind regarded as the sole and fundamental reality. Spirit, the Self in all things, is the fundamental reality of existence. But even asserting that fact, we must not be exclusively preoccupied with spirit if we are to achieve a truly integrated knowledge of all existence.

Integral knowledge is not an intellectual knowledge which can be learned; it is knowledge which must be experienced and 'realized'. In the last analysis the highest integration of knowledge can come only through an evolution of consciousness which will transform our total being—mind, body and spirit. To use Aurobindo's own words:

. . . it will mean the knowledge of the Absolute as the origin of all things; the knowledge of the Self, the Spirit, the Being and of the cosmos as the Self's becoming, the becoming of the Being, a manifestation of the Spirit; the knowledge of the world as one with us in the consciousness of our true self, thus cancelling our division from it by the separative idea and life of ego; the knowledge of our psychic entity and its immortal persistence in Time beyond death and earth-existence; the knowledge of our greater and inner existence behind the surface; the knowledge of our mind, life and body in its

[1] Aurobindo, *The Life Divine*, pp. 12–13.

true relation to the self within and the superconscient spiritual and supramental being above them; the knowledge, finally, of the true harmony and true use of our thought, will and action and a change of all our nature into a conscious expression of the truth of the Spirit, the Self, the Divinity, the integral spiritual Reality.[1]

[1] Aurobindo, *The Life Divine*, p. 584.

15

INDRA SEN

The Indian Approach to Psychology

IN order to be able to understand the distinctive Indian approach to psychology and evaluate its insights and judgments, it is necessary that we must not allow ourselves to be limited by any of the particular conceptions and definitions of psychology evolved in recent years and current now. All great cultures of world history present distinctive patterns, and their motivations in the pursuit of life and knowledge have been peculiar to them. The scientific age, whose child modern psychology is, has been essentially built upon a concept of nature, a method of analysis and experimentation and a separation of the empirical from the Real. Indian culture, on the other hand, founded itself on the idea of the unity of all existence, and all disciplines of knowledge were to it different approaches to and expressions of the same ultimate Reality. Here the empirical was an intimate part of the Real, the theoretical, the seeking for knowledge as such, essentially bound up with the practical, the seeking for growth in consciousness, and psychology, in particular, was closely connected with ethics and metaphysics. Evidently, if we wish to understand Indian psychology, we cannot afford to take the approach of any such concept of psychology, which excludes by assumption any part of the data, methods or judgments of Indian psychology. We must, therefore, take psychology in the broadest, widest and a plastic sense as a discipline of life and knowledge concerned with human personality and its consciousness. This is, however, altogether provisional and experimental, intended to facilitate the best perception and appreciation of things psychological in Indian culture, life and knowledge.

The Indian Approach to Psychology

There is no doubt that psychology has been a great and persistent interest in India. Its expression has been the characteristic Indian seeking of *Ātmānam Viddhi* (Know Thyself). This seeking has been perhaps the strongest and the most popular in all Indian culture and it differentiated itself out in innumerable forms resulting in a large number of *sādhanās* or *yogas*. These *sādhanās* or *yogas* are often present as an integral part of almost all philosophies as well as religions, and also as independent disciplines of knowledge. These are essentially psychological in their standpoint, method, scope and important judgments, since the human consciousness is their essential concern. They study the human consciousness in its present form as also its possibilities of growth and perfection. In doing so introspection is the essential and the most important method and the human experience in the widest and the highest ranges is the scope. And the judgments they arrive at all concern human personality, at its average level as well as the highest level. Thus psychology has been a traditional interest in India and introspection is almost a national habit. However, its form has been distinctive and it needs to be properly formulated so that it may be correctly understood and appreciated.

Not only has psychology been a great interest, it even determined the standpoint for philosophy and religion in India. Philosophy and religion here have conceded that truths, in order to be real, must admit of being experienced. Thus, they submit to the test of psychological experience as the last proof of validity. Psychology, therefore, enters intimately into the structure and thought of philosophy as well as religion. The advantage of it to them has been very great. They have remained close to life. They have really guided life and have been themselves moulded and modified by it. But that shows that the standpoint of psychology, that of conscious experience, was widely determining for Indian life and culture.

It is evident that 'Know Thyself' has been the basic urge for psychology in India and that the different systems of *sādhanā* and *yoga* are the Indian counterpart of Western psychology. Now, what has been their characteristic approach?

The approach of Indian psychology, covering under the

term all the systems of *sādhanā* or *yoga* existing either as independent formulations and treatments of psychological issues or as integral parts of philosophy and religion, shows a certain community of outlook and we will have to define it carefully. Western psychology is a natural science. It deals with the phenomena of mind and behaviour. The psychologist treats them as objects, impersonal events and as they are. In Indian psychology, the psychological interest seems to take the form: 'What I am at present, what I can become in future, and how can that be achieved?' This seems to be the essential attitude of the yogic systems and the same they tend to evoke in the mind of a student. In this attitude the theoretical and the practical motives of life are combined. However, both of them are to be disinterested. The practical is not utilitarian. It is that of seeking growth of life and consciousness for its own sake. The same is true of Indian philosophy too. There knowledge of existence as such is not entirely satisfying. That is to enable and facilitate the growth of personal life to the status of Reality. The knowledge of Reality is not divorced from the will to be real as Reality is. This personal will to grow is considered necessary on another ground also. Sri Aurobindo argues with evident cogency that 'the capacity to know should be equal to the object to be known'. Ultimate Reality, which is infinite, requires other cognitive functions to those adapted to the perception of the finite objects. These must be developed as a part of the philosophical seeking to know ultimate Reality. Otherwise this seeking itself cannot succeed. On this account, some Western thinkers continue to hold that Indian philosophy is not philosophy. It is religion. We have here, in fact, two standpoints as to the relation of the theoretical and the practical. The aforesaid argument applies to our knowledge of personality too. So far as the normal functions of the waking consciousness are concerned our normal introspection is adequate. But if we wish to have a direct access to the subconscious or the superconscious, then certain distinct developments of introspection are needed.

In a sense and degree this emphasis of Indian philosophy and psychology on the growth and perfection of the knower is admitted by Western science. The scientist has to be trained to observe. He must learn to be dispassionate and impartial. Bacon had wanted the scientific investigator to free his mind from a number of deep-seated prejudices. However, the Indian demand is much greater and if that is incorporated into psychology, psychology will become a system of yoga and a student of psychology an aspiring practitioner of yoga.

Indian psychology is, therefore, deliberately not a natural science concerned with the 'is' of mental life. It is also not a normative science concerned with the 'ought', the ideal alone. It is, we might say, a science of the 'becoming' of conscious life, that of growth from the actual to the possible. This characterization gives us the first determinant of the Indian approach to psychology.

The second factor in the approach may be described as the insistence on taking conscious life as a whole and refusing to be limited to the empirical function of the waking consciousness alone. The empirical and the real are a single unity to the Indian standpoint. It, therefore, does not divide and separate the two. In fact, it rightly seeks the true explanations of the empirical issues in the Real. However, the Real is for psychology as even for philosophy not a speculative reference, but a fact to be experienced. Thus, the soul in psychology is no mere metaphysical assumption or affirmation. It is the self-existent consciousness, as distinct from the environment-dependent consciousness of mind, which can, through proper training and discipline, be experienced, as we do our normal mental processes.

In the West, Jung is the one psychologist who has had the urge and the impulse to inquire into the nature of personality to its very roots. And this he has carried out by means of the various pathways of dreams, cultural history, mythology and analysis. By all these he finds himself impelled to posit a 'centre' in personality, which he endows with the capacity of integrating all the experiences of life. This 'centre' is a unique fact and is the basis of all uniqueness in the manifestations of personality. Now this centre is, to Jung, a matter of inference, a logical necessity inherent in certain processes of the empirical consciousness, which he has observed. This centre has an obvious resemblance to the spirit or the soul principle of the yogic disciplines. But to them spirit or soul is an objective of experience and until it is experienced, yoga remains unsuccessful. Hence, it is not quite correct to compare yogic psychology with the metaphysical psychology of the West. Indian psychology is all empirical, only the term empirical is not taken as implying the experience of the normal waking consciousness, but all experience, normal as well as supernormal.

The attitude of taking conscious life as a whole and the refusal to limit the approach to the process of the waking consciousness has enabled Indian psychology to recognize the *bohirmukha manas* (the outward-directed mental consciousness) as only a part of our conscious life and discover besides it a field of the *samskāras*, the past experiences, and a large and wide realm of the superconscious, a field of consciousness marked by a higher degree of luminosity and integration or unity. These spheres are evidently interrelated and the problems of the one cannot be satisfactorily answered in terms of its own limited experience. The problems of conflict and integration of the waking consciousness surely have a relation to the superconscious, where integration exists as a fact. Indian psychology has been extremely happy in taking a larger approach to personality and its discovery of the dimensions of personality, in particular of the superconscious, which is of great promise so far as some of the most difficult problems of conflict and division of normal personality are concerned. The same has enabled it to give to the mental consciousness its place as a part in the whole of personality. In Western psychology this part has become the whole and thus arise many of its insoluble problems.

The third feature of the Indian approach can be mentioned as its emphasis on the supernormal and the possible of the human nature. This it does to such an extent that the normal and the actual human nature, which is the whole matter for Western psychology, seems to receive a scanty treatment. Indeed, we do not have the wealth of detail and classification of the normal processes in Indian psychology as we have in Western psychology. But the control, power and effective modification is more in Indian psychology. This is due to the fact that while it does not seem to have cared for the detailed conditions of the differentiations of mental processes, it has had a firm hold over the essential dynamism of them all. For example, the willing aspect of mind has been identified as involving impulse, habit, instinct, voluntary action, and then under each of them we have a wealth of detail. Indian psychology, as in particular represented in the Gītā, considers them all under the principle of desire. 'Desire' is to it a fragmentary willing, the willing of a part of our personality for a particular finite object. It is accompanied by a sense of want and deficiency and it seeks an external object or satisfaction. Further, desires are innumerable and they involve essentially a principle of opposition or dualism, *dwandwa*. Such is the picture of normal human life—an indefinite number of desires for all sorts of objects with an essential dualism existing among them. The problem presented by them is that of integration, how this state of multitudinous willing can be changed into a state of whole-willing. In answering this question Indian psychology is in an entirely happy and confident state. The individual must dissociate himself from the fragmentary willing of desires and seek to live and act out of a state of wholeness. That is the state of desirelessness, when described with reference to desires. Most Indian *sādhanās* and *yogas* are agreed on their reading of desire and the necessity of achieving for human living progressive integration and ultimately a state of felt and lived wholeness. They, however, have their distinctive means and methods for achieving it. We cannot say that Western psychology is equally confident as to the possibility of integration and wholeness and the means of achieving it. Now while Western psychology has a greater fullness of knowledge of the conative processes, Indian psychology is in possession of the essential key and the perspective, which gives it greater confidence in being able to answer to the essential problem of practical living, education and culture.

Similarly, on cognitive and affective aspects Indian psychology lacks vast detail, but it possesses the essential dynamism.

Life is not a static fact. It is a movement of growth. It is perhaps the appreciation of this fact that made Indian psychology look at personality as it is tending to become and not lay an exclusive sort of emphasis on what mental life actually is. At any rate much of the descriptive detail of Western psychology is due to the avowed motive to analyse and study it as it is. And that really means missing the essential movement of life and consciousness, its trend for growth.

Teleological determination or goal-seekingness is recognized in Western psychology as the essential attribute of mind as distinguished from matter. McDougall seeks to give to this characteristic the first place in his psychological studies and, therefore, chooses to call his standpoint purposivism. But it is interesting how his purposivism falls back upon the psycho-physical antecedents of instincts to explain the growth of the entire cultural life of the human adult. In contrast to this the purposivism of Indian psychology affirms the quality of wholeness of the superconscious as the true goal and all life is growth towards it and into it. Instincts are past determinations. They are not goals. They are adaptations already achieved, which must now be modified into the form of an integrated consciousness.

We have here in Indian psychology a purposivism of a challenging kind, a purposivism which throws other purposivisms into the category of mechanical determinations.

It is the distinctive ideas of causation of the East and West that have led to these differentiations. In the West the cause is the antecedent and so strong has been this idea that, when one thinks of a purpose, that too is sought to be reduced to an antecedent condition. In the East all growth is from or in something and it is towards something. One is the base, the other is the goal. The goal is also a fact of consciousness already existing, which exercises its own force and influence on the process of growth. The Upaniṣads describe the cosmos as an aśwatha tree with roots above. The cosmos as a process of growth considered from below consists of the *anna*, the *prāṇa* and the *manas* (matter, life and mind), but the process of growth has been essentially drawn out and determined by what is above it. The higher and the lower both co-operate in a process of growth and the higher is the true purposive factor and the lower and its conditions of working constitute the mechanical.

Indian thought has an essential truth on this point and the same gives a great strength of insight to Indian psychology so far as the growth of human personality is concerned.

These are a few most important general features of Indian psychology. The concept of the different dimensions of consciousness is almost innate to it. The waking consciousness carries with it the subconscious and the superconscious parts. An integralism is thus characteristic of all Indian psychology. However, at the hands of Sri Aurobindo, it receives an elaborate treatment, which enables Indian psychology to take the form of a well-developed integral psychology. This paper is no more than a broad characterization of the background of the psychological system of Sri Aurobindo.

16

RICHARD P. MARSH

The Organismic Psychology of Andras Angyal in Relation to Sri Aurobindo's Philosophy of Integral Nondualism

COMPARATIVE studies of Eastern and Western psychological and religious concepts often make references to the works of Dr C. G. Jung, the founder of analytical psychology. This is altogether proper. Dr Jung, as is well known, has undertaken various forms of psychological research with an inevitable appeal to students of Asian thought. He has, in addition, communicated the results of his research with a sensitivity and a resourcefulness which have added to their appeal.

Similarly, the achievement of Sri Aurobindo in creating the philosophy of integral nondualism, a remarkable blend of original thought with much that is first rate and enduring in both the Eastern and the Western traditions, has led to cross comparisons from the other side. In reading Aurobindo, one constantly experiences the shock of recognition. It is as though in Aurobindo one had rediscovered the West, or as if one had come across a new Dr Jung with a startling new vocabulary and a curiously vivid and massive style. So much of Jung is there, although cut to the pattern of a different idiom: the phenomenon of introversion, the concept of the collective unconscious, the relationship of ego to self, even in a sense the classification into psychological types—these and more are in Aurobindo, inviting comparison.

But scholars, in their attempts to spread enlightenment by tracing the parallels between these two giants, have tended to lose sight of the fact that the universality of Aurobindo's thought is such that echoes of it may be found in systems of Western psychology quite apart from Dr Jung's. If Aurobindo's insights into general human nature are valid—and this writer believes that they are—then inevitably the insights not merely of one but of many Western psychologists are bound to approach them sooner or later.

Many insights approaching those of Aurobindo have already occurred, in fact, among that large body of European and American psychologists who constitute what is sometimes loosely referred to as 'the organismic school'. The integralism of Sri Aurobindo and the organismic, holistic thinking of this school are radically related. This is not surprising in view of the fact that the organismic viewpoint has emerged as a reaction against earlier dualistic and pluralistic attempts to fragmentize the unfragmentizable individual.

In their recently published survey of contemporary personality theories, Calvin S. Hall and Gardner Lindzey have described the emergence of organismic psychology in these words:

Ever since Descartes in the seventeenth century split the individual into two separate yet interacting entities, body and mind, and Wundt in the nineteenth century, subscribing to the tradition of British associationism, atomized the mind by reducing it to the elementary particles of sensations, feelings, and images, there have been recurrent attempts to put the mind and the body back together and to treat the organism as a unified, organized whole. One notable attempt which has attracted a large following within recent years is known as the organismic or holistic viewpoint.[1]

That this attempt to restore wholeness where fragmentation has existed is perfectly in keeping with the thought of Sri Aurobindo is apparent to anyone who has read *The Life Divine* or any of Aurobindo's major works. It is also the thesis of this paper.

The similarity of organismic theory to integralism is evident from a survey of the chief tenets of the former. The essence of

[1] Calvin S. Hall and Gardner Lindzey, *Theories of Personality* (New York: John Wiley & Sons, 1957), p. 296.

organismic theory is that the human organism is a unity, a psycho-physical system in which the part and the whole are inseparable so that what affects the one affects the other as well. It sees the organism as a body-mind unit which, although it may be studied from one point of view by the physiologist, and from other points of view by the psychologist, the sociologist, the anthropologist, and the like, may not be studied successfully from any of these points of view in isolation.

Because of this preference for studying the individual in his totality, organismic theory stresses the integration and coherence of the normal personality rather than the disorganization of pathological states so commonly emphasized by many other theories—the Freudian, for example—which have taken disease as their starting point.

Likewise, because it prefers to start with the whole and proceed to the part, organismic theory may be contrasted to the behaviouristic and the stimulus-response systems of psychology, which prefer to start with isolated data—and which consequently often remain at the level of the part and so fail to attain to the level of the whole.

As a result of this emphasis on the organism in the round, organismic theory draws extremely close to integral non-dualism at a crucial point; it 'assumes that the individual is motivated by one sovereign drive rather than by a plurality of drives'.[1] To this sovereign motive, Dr Kurt Goldstein, one of the leading proponents of organismic theory, has applied the terms *self-actualization* and *self-realization*. The concept of self-actualization presupposes that there is at work within the individual a prior drift, an innate tendency towards wholeness, which operates in such a way that the individual normally moves towards the realization of his inherent potentials.

The individual in his developed form is thus not the result of a mechanical interaction with his environment. In part, to be sure, his development is a function of his environment. But the drive towards self-actualization is logically prior to the impact of the environment; consequently, the individual responds to his environment selectively. Therefore, unless the environment is hopelessly inadequate, the individual will

[1] *Theories of Personality*, p. 298.

194

select those elements in it to react to which will move him relentlessly in the direction of the self that he potentially is.

It is possible to see in this a parallel to the doctrine of *līlā* as developed by Sri Aurobindo, the doctrine of divine play which gives rise to the struggles of the isolated individual in the relentless upward thrust by which he co-operates with the awakening divinity within and eventually transcends his isolation in the attainment of the supramental self. It may also be apparent by now that organismic psychology is very much in harmony with some of the basic tenets of C. G. Jung and that Jung might well be classified among the organismic theorists of personality.

In point of fact, he has often been so classified, together with a host of other contemporary personality theorists. The list of names is long: not only Jung and Goldstein, but Angyal, Maslow, Lecky, Allport, Murray, Murphy, Rogers, Freud, and many others, despite radical differences, have in one sense or other an organismic orientation. Indeed, as Hall and Lindzey ask, 'Who is there today who is not a proponent of the main tenets of organismic theory . . . ?'[1] Some, however, have been identified so closely with organismic theory that they have received the label of organismic theorists *per se*.

Among these, none has developed a model of the personality which compares more startlingly with Sri Aurobindo's conception than has Dr Andras Angyal. Dr Angyal, formerly on the faculty at Yale University, is now in private practice as a psychiatrist in Boston. Perhaps he would be astonished to see his name linked with Aurobindo's, but consider for a moment his conceptualization of the personality. To convey his sense of the totality of the individual, Angyal has coined the word *biosphere*. The word refers to both the individual and the environment, 'not as interacting parts, not as constituents which have independent existence, but as aspects of a single reality which can be separated only by abstraction'.[2] It is apparent from this that Angyal's view of the personality is

[1] *Theories of Personality*, p. 329.
[2] Andras Angyal, *Foundations for a Science of Personality* (Oxford University Press, 1941), p. 100.

nondual with a vengeance, and to this extent at least it is similar to Aurobindo's. But consider further.

The biosphere is seen as a system of interlocking systems so arranged that any given sub-system of the biosphere is both the container of lesser systems and the contained of a greater system or systems. The interplay of the interlocking systems creates a tension which gives rise to the energy which is available to the personality. Moreover, the biosphere as a whole is characterized by a fundamental polarity which gives rise to its most fundamental energy. This polarity arises from the fact that the environment pulls in one direction and the organism in the other.

To these fundamental yet opposed pulls of the biosphere, Angyal has given the names of *autonomy* and *homonomy*, respectively. Autonomy is the relatively egoistic pole of the biosphere: it represents the tendency to advance one's interests by mastering the environment, by asserting oneself, so to speak, as a separate being. Homonomy is the relatively 'selfless' pole of the biosphere: it is the tendency to fit oneself to the environment by willingly subordinating oneself to something that one perceives as larger than the individual self. In place of the words autonomy and homonomy, Angyal has also used the terms *self-determination* and *self-surrender* to describe these opposing yet co-operating directional trends of the biosphere, and he has felicitously summed up the individual's relationship to them with the remark that, 'the human being comports himself *as if he were a whole of an intermediate order*'.[1]

It would be difficult to find a closer parallel to Aurobindo's way of thinking. For who can fail to hear in it a clear echo of Aurobindo's concept of the involution and the evolution—the involution by which the eternal Brahman buries itself in the dark centre of inconscient matter waking it to that separative consciousness that provokes the individual ego to realize its difference from all other individual centres, the evolution by which the consciousness reascends until the isolated, autonomous ego is aroused to the unitary awareness of its radical

[1] Andras Angyal, 'A Theoretical Model for Personality Studies'. In Clark E. Moustakas, ed., *The Self: Explorations in Personal Growth* (New York: Harper & Brothers, 1956), p. 46.

identity with all other centres of consciousness? The individual does indeed 'comport himself as if he were a whole of an intermediate order', because that is precisely what he is: related on the one side by *avidyā* or ignorance, in a principle of separateness, to a world of diversity and conflicting entities; related on the other, through *vidyā* or knowledge, in a principle of homonomy, to a world of unity and absolute, seamless integration.

Nor is it fanciful to push the comparison this far. While Angyal writes as an empirical scientist and therefore makes no conclusive statements about the reality of a divine principle, he specifically allows for, even emphasizes, the possibility. 'The superordinate whole' sought by the pull towards homonomy

> may be represented for a person by a social unit—family, clan, nation—by a cause, by an ideology, or by a meaningfully ordered universe. . . . Its clearest manifestation, however, is in the religious attitude and religious experience.[1]

Thus, for the individual at least, there is no limit to the trend towards homonomy except the limits of his own perception, awareness, and experience.

Moreover, it would appear to be only the limiting force of one's own perception, awareness, and experience that sets up the illusion of a difference, a tension, between the poles of self-determination and self-surrender. If the biosphere is dominated by the 'single sovereign drive' of self-actualization—and Angyal agrees with Goldstein that it is—how can there be any genuine split within it? It would be absurd to suppose that a self-actualizing individual could be the result of a compromise between, say, x per cent of autonomy and y per cent of homonomy. Actually, autonomy and homonomy, like heredity and environment, must be seen as presupposing each other and being therefore mutually essential. Then it would follow that the fully self-actualized person represents, not a mechanical compromise but an integral fusion of 100 per cent autonomy and 100 per cent homonomy which is at the basis of his self-actualization. This is evident in Hall and Lindzey's discussion

---

[1] *The Self: Explorations in Personal Growth*, p. 46.

of *self-expansion*, the equivalent in Angyal's system to self-actualization in Goldstein's:

Although autonomy or self-determination and homonomy or self-surrender may appear to be opposed to one another, they are really two phases of a more inclusive trend of the biosphere, that of *self-expansion* . . . the chief system principle of the biosphere.[1]

In other words, since the polar tendencies of the biosphere are merely 'phases of a more inclusive trend' they are not in reality opposed but rather they are aspects, conditions, of each other. Taken together, they constitute a single phenomenon: the movement towards self-expansion. Moreover, this tendency towards wholeness and the ascent towards supermind described by Aurobindo—what are these but the same nondual, bipolar process glimpsed from slightly different points of view? Angyal tells us that 'the human being comports himself as if he were a whole of an intermediate order'. This carries the clearest possible hint of Aurobindo's concept of the overmental consciousness: that global awareness which is separative in its action and unitary in its knowledge, tending simultaneously downward into the realm of the autonomous ego and upwards into the realm of homonomy and the eternal self. The double and simultaneous pull in opposite directions constitutes for Angyal the process of self-expansion by which the biosphere constantly differentiates, enlarges, and unifies itself. For Aurobindo it is the process by which individualization, universalization, and transcendentalization occur simultaneously, not as negations, but as functions, fulfilments, of one another. In his words:

We have . . . the transcendent and the cosmic, the universal and the individual . . . each member of these pairs is contained in its apparent opposite. The universal particularizes itself in the individual; the individual contains in himself all the generalities of the universal. . . . So too, the cosmic contains in all itself and in each thing in it the complete immanence of the transcendent. . . . The transcendent contains, manifests, constitutes the cosmos and by

[1] *Theories of Personality*, pp. 320–1.

manifesting it manifests or discovers, as we may say in the old poetic sense of that word, its own infinite harmonic varieties.[1]

For both Angyal and Aurobindo, therefore, the self has triple reference points. Angyal sees it as an intermediate system containing lesser systems and contained by a greater. Aurobindo sees it as involving a 'triple transformation' of mind to overmind to supermind.[2] This triplicity of the self, moreover, is reflected in still another parallel between the thought of these two men.

Angyal observes that the personality has three structural dimensions. The so-called *vertical* dimension, extending 'from overt behaviour at the surface of the biosphere down into the central core of the biosphere',[3] suggests the depth of personality characteristic of the fully transcendentalized individual in Aurobindo's system who has attained to a realization of the *paramātman* or transcendental self. The *transverse* dimension, consisting of 'the co-ordination of discrete acts into a larger, better integrated and more effective behaviour unit',[3] suggests the breadth of personality characteristic of the fully universalized person who has attained to the realization of the *jivātman* or the individual's pure spiritual self. And the *progressive* dimension, the directionality which results when 'a series of acts brings a person closer and closer to a final goal',[3] suggests the personal uniqueness of an individual who has attained to an effective working relationship with his *antarātman*, the inner, private self that leads one to his specific destiny.

But more even than in their agreement about the triple nature of the bipolar personality, Angyal and Aurobindo meet in their agreement about the distinguishing characteristics of the self-realized man. They are for Angyal the presence of mastery, resulting from fulfilment of the autonomous impulse, combined with the capacity to love and be loved which results from the satisfactory expression of the pull towards homonomy. Absence of mastery, in Angyal's view, leads to that peculiar feeling of powerlessness so characteristic of modern regimented man. The inability to love and be loved is the source of

[1] Aurobindo, *The Life Divine*, p. 342.   [2] *Ibid.*, Chapter XXV.
[3] *Theories of Personality*, p. 319.

neurotic anxiety, which in turn is not so much a 'mental phenomenon' as 'a state of limitation of life',[1] which narrows our lives to impoverished simulacra of what they might have been.

Love itself Angyal analyses in a manner astonishingly reminiscent of the central tenets of integral nondualism. It is based on a recognition of the value and otherness of the loved one combined with an experience of *sameness* with him.[2] This is Angyal's recognition of the phenomenon of identity-in-difference so emphasized by Aurobindo. The loved one must be 'other' in order to be loved rather than merely identified with, and yet also 'the same' as oneself in order not to be alien and therefore unlovable. This is similar to Aurobindo's conception of the relationship of the individual to the Eternal: between them there is both a gulf that separates and an identity that unites, the gulf and the identity related as adoration is related to rapture.

Aurobindo's vision of the fulfilled individual is similar to Angyal's, although it differs as a lightning flash differs from the spurt of a match. The light created by the one is supremely beyond that created by the other, yet the outlines of what they illuminate are similar. The 'gnostic being'[3] which Aurobindo conceives as the goal of evolution emerges as a sort of colossal, transcendentalized counterpart of the self-actualized individual described by Angyal. When he appears, he will exercise a total mastery as an autonomous individual absolutely unfettered by a reluctant environment and his capacity to love and be loved through his homonomous identity with the universe will be guaranteed by his status as

an infinite and universal being revealing . . . its eternal self through the significant form and expressive power of an individual and temporal self-manifestation.[4]

There will be no question of the anxiety which results from the separateness of the unloving and the unlovable. Inevitably, the gnostic being will

[1] Angyal, *op. cit.*, in *The Self*, pp. 46–7.   [2] *Ibid.*, p. 54.
[3] Aurobindo, *The Life Divine*, Book II, Chapter XXVII.
[4] *Ibid.*, p. 884.

act in a universal awareness and a harmony of his individual self with the total self, of his individual will with the total will, of his individual action with the total action.[1]

Thus, there will be simply no difference between his status as separate from others and his status as identical with them. The assertion of his autonomy will be identical with the assertion of his homonomy. His desires, individually, will correspond exactly to the universal intention, and he will love in the same rhythm as his breathing.

Love will be for him the contact, meeting, union of self with self, of spirit with spirit, a unification of being, a power and joy and intimacy and closeness of soul to soul, of the One to the One, a joy of identity and the consequences of a diverse identity.[2]

It will be out of this very condition of what might be called his absolute homonomy—that is, his diverse and loving identity with the One—that the limitless mastery of his absolute autonomy will arise. He will neither submit with impotence to the conditions of matter and social existence which frustrate the individual who has failed to achieve autonomy within the biosphere, nor will he impotently retreat from life and the world in the manner of the loveless and bewildered ascetic. Instead:

The gnostic being will take up the world of Life and Matter, but he will turn and adapt it to his own truth and purpose of existence; he will mould life itself into his own spiritual image, and this he will be able to do because he has the secret of a spiritual creation and is in communion and oneness with the Creator within him.[3]

Thus, the polarity of the biosphere which opposes autonomy to homonomy, dividing ego from self and necessity from freedom, will stand revealed, in its fullest sense, as a polarity which, in fact, combines rather than separates, or which separates in order only to combine. The integrally self-actualized being, therefore, instead of succumbing to the conditions of matter or retreating from those conditions

---

[1] Aurobindo, *The Life Divine,* p. 865.   [2] *Ibid.,* p. 874.   [3] *Ibid.,* p. 868.

altogether in a flight of transcendence, will freely manifest himself in endlessly varying forms, not so much self-actualized as self-actualizing, never 'completed' but creatively continuing, not 'having arrived' but always arriving.

To the biosphere, as Aurobindo would have seen it, what limits are possible? What can lie beyond self-actualization but the self-actualization beyond?

PART THREE

YOGA AND ETHICS

17

PITIRIM A. SOROKIN

The Integral Yoga of Sri Aurobindo
(1872–1951)

SRI AUROBINDO'S integral yoga is an attempt to give a synthesis of all the main yogas and of their philosophies. It endeavours to integrate into one system their valuable parts, as well as what is valuable in the Western science and religions. The main distinctive points of the integral yoga are as follows:

(1) Most of the surveyed yogas and their philosophies have a somewhat negative attitude towards the world of the senses and our empirical life. The manifold sufferings of our life are viewed by the yogas as 'conditioned by our entanglement either in the meshes of *prakṛti* (*Sāṅkhya*), or in the cobwebs of māyā (*Śaṅkara Vedānta*), or in the fetters of karma (*Buddhism*). The supreme goal of life must, therefore, consist in total liberation from Nature, in complete emancipation from the bonds of *prakṛti*, māyā, or karma.' 'The main endeavour of yoga has been to realize *mukti* or transcendental freedom by rising above the limitations of body, life, and mind which are supposed to be made of some alien or illusory stuff, and to rest permanently in that state of freedom on some lofty summit of spiritual attainment'[1] (absorption in Brahman, in nirvāṇa, or in 'kaivalya', the state of freedom from nature or *prakṛti* for ever and ever).

In difference from this, the integral or purṇa yoga views even the material nature as a lower form of the true reality—

[1] Chaudhuri, *Sri Aurobindo: The Prophet of Life Divine* (Calcutta: Sri Aurobindo Pathamandir, 1951), pp. 44–5.

the supermind—imperceptibly passing into a finer and finer form of the Divine. In the course of the evolution the matter tends to be increasingly divinized. The trend towards divinization of the whole material world is the main trend of world evolution. The *prakṛti* is not separated from the *puruṣa* by an unbridgeable chasm, but is a 'low-grade' manifestation of the Divine of which the *puruṣa* or self is the higher form. Respectively, the highest goal of a yogin is not simply an attainment of the transcendental *mukti* or freedom, but an active participation in the creative joy of the Divine and co-operation with it in the divinization of the empirical world and of the whole 'embodied life', here and now. As Chaudhuri aptly says, the goal is 'to live a life of divine activity after the attainment of individual liberation, so that Nature herself may be assisted in her liberation, that is, in the complete fruition of the creative urge concealed in her bosom. . . . Having reached the pinnacle of the supramental realization, the integral yogi is again to descend; he is to come to the point of his departure, to the physical consciousness, and he is to bring down there the light and power of the supramental Truth-Consciousness'.[1]

'Our Yoga', says Sri Aurobindo, 'is a double movement of ascent and descent; one rises to higher and higher levels of consciousness, but at the same time one brings down (the divine) power not only into mind and life, but in the end even into the body. And the highest of these levels is . . . the Supermind. Only when that can be brought down is a divine transformation possible in the earth-consciousness.'[2]

Integral yoga contends that the union with the divine supermind is possible not only in a spiritual trance or ecstatic

[1] Chaudhuri, *op. cit.*, p. 46.

[2] Sri Aurobindo, *The Riddle of This World*, pp. 2–3, and *The Life Divine*, pp. 34 ff., 232 ff. Passing by, it is to be noted that the idea of the descent of the liberated yogin back into the empirical world is not so new as Chaudhuri says. In Buddhist sūtra, the '*Laṅkāvatura*', we are told that there are two classes of 'the liberated' or 'enlightened' yogis: the Arhats who desire Nirvāṇa, or quiescent bliss only for themselves and want to stay in Nirvāṇa forever, and the Bodhisattvas who after attaining the true Buddhahood, do not desire Nirvāṇa's bliss just for themselves, and turn back or descend to assist humanity in its long road to the Enlightenment and Nirvāṇa. In Christianity, Jesus, the Virgin Mary, and some of the saints and the mystics also function in this role. They descend to humanity and help it in its salvation. The Son of God became man in order to help mankind in its divinization and

samādhi in which the waking consciousness fades out, but also in the state of a full waking consciousness as well. Its objective is not only and not so much a transcendental liberation of the individual, as it is the divinization of the whole embodied life and the collective liberation of mankind. The pūrṇa yoga strives to join hands with the evolutionary, creative effort of nature, through infusion of the eternal in the temporal, the supermind in matter. It endeavours to transform the empirical humanity into the divinized superman; to build progressively the 'kindgom of God' in this life, on this planet, here and now.

In conformity with this goal, the techniques of the integral yoga are integral also. They consist mainly in dynamic self-identification of every integral yogin with the supreme creative power—the supermind or the Divine Mother, as it is called metaphorically by Sri Aurobindo. This supreme creative power constantly guides (behind the scene) the course of the evolution of nature and man, and assists man's efforts to divinize himself. The integral yoga strives to help man's active union and co-operation with the creative Divine in the building of the divinized supermanhood on this planet. For that purpose the co-operation of man's aspiration from below and the supermind's grace from above is necessary.

The techniques of the pūrṇa yoga largely dispense with the posture and breathing exercises of hatha yoga and the rāja yoga, and to some extent with Patanjali's superhuman exercises in mental concentration and withdrawing of the senses.

Likewise, Integral Yoga does not believe that its objective can be reached exclusively through religious sentiment, rituals, and endless repetition of the prayers and mantras; or exclusively

salvation. One of the first acts of Christ after his bodily death was his descent into and liberation of the souls from the Inferno.

Similarly, the idea of the evolutionary divinization of the whole material and bodily world is also not quite new. Among other thinkers, Clement of Alexandria, N. F. Fedorov, and then V. Solovyev, developed it in as great detail as Sri Aurobindo. See N. F. Fedorov, *Filosofia obschevo dela* ('The Philosophy of Common Cause') (new edition, Kharbin, 1928–30) and V. Solovyev, *Lectures on God-Man*, 'The Justification of Good', and the 'Spiritual Foundations of Life' in his *Works* (in Russian) (St Petersburg, second edition, 1903), Vols. III, VIII; Eugéne de Faye, *Clément d'Alexandrie* (Paris, 1898), pp. 256–93.

through the moral force of nonviolence and good deeds; or by devotion and love; or wisdom and knowledge. Instead, its techniques require a sort of a synthesis of all these procedures; first, an unconditional opening and complete self-surrender to the supermind or 'the Divine Mother' and incessant co-operation with this cosmic creative power; second, 'psychization' and then 'spiritualization' of one's whole life—thoughts, words, and deeds. Third, for stilling the storms and tumult in our mental life the integral yoga prescribes effortful exercises to obtain successively four mental states: (1) quiet; (2) calm; (3) peace; and (4) silence. (This is not fundamentally different from the mental exercises of rāja yoga.) Fourth, its 'triple path' tries to integrate the separate ways of rāja yoga, karma yoga, jñāna yoga, and bhakti yoga; the path of wisdom and knowledge, of love and devotion, and of good deeds and work. It tries to enlist and to use the forces of thinking, feeling, willing, emotions, and actions. In brief, the integral yoga endeavours to unite into one philosophical, moral, and technical system most of the positive ideas and techniques of all the other yogas, as well as Eastern and Western philosophies, science, and techniques.

In this 'integration' lies its strong and weak points. Its strong points have been emphasized above; the main weakness is a sort of eclecticism that pervades especially the techniques of integral yoga. Rejecting as one-sided the techniques of other yogas, and trying to give its own system of techniques, the purṇa yoga hardly gives any of its own. It simply puts together, side by side, several techniques taken from other yogas. Neither its prescriptions of self-opening and self-surrender; nor of co-operation with the cosmic power; nor psychization and spiritualization; nor calming and stilling the bodily mind; nor the triple path, are new. They all are given and developed in other yogas, and in the techniques of various 'mystic ways' outside of India. For these reasons the integral yoga hardly contributes much that is original to this field.

On the other hand, by its ideological integration of several religious, philosophical, and scientific currents of the East and the West, Sri Aurobindo's 'philosophy' is a notable achievement in this age of considerable aridity in these areas. His attempts to put together various techniques of spiritualization and divinization of man and humanity also make an important contribution to the field of the techniques. After all, in some way the numerous diverse procedures have to be taken stock of, and somehow have to be unified into a system. If Sri Aurobindo only partly succeeded in this task, this partial success is already of some importance. The whole task is so gigantic that no single man can achieve it in its full totality. It is up to subsequent intellectual and moral seers to bring it nearer to its full fruition. So much about the integral yoga.

PERVERTED TECHNIQUES OF THE PSEUDO-YOGA LIBERTINES

Finally, in passing, the perverted techniques of the pseudo-yoga libertines may be mentioned. Once in a while, in a religious or ethical movement persons and groups appear that pervert the creed, the moral commandments, and the techniques of spiritualization or altruization for their own egoistic purposes. The objective result of such a perversion is not an altruization but a demoralization of respective persons and groups. Among the Indian 'denominations', the Tāntra or the cult of the Great Mother has been accused of such perversions. A more careful study has shown, however, that the accusations have been largely baseless, so far as the Tāntrika religion and practices are concerned.[1] If, however, now and then a few instances of perversion occur, such rare cases happen in many religious, political, and ethical movements. With this reservation, the following examples illustrate the pseudo-yoga techniques.

Among the Tāntrikas and in the sect of the Sahajiya in Bengal, a mystical eroticism in the form of the *maithuna* is supposed to be practised. Connected with their religious cult, a long ritual preparation takes place before the sexual act is permitted. The purpose of this preparation is to make the initiated a master of his senses and desires by the combined method of 'teasing and stimulating' his sex passion and teaching him at the same time to control it, especially at the highest

---

[1] Cf. on that Sir John Woodroffe, *Shakti and Shakta* (Madras–London, 1929), Chapter XXVII, *et passim*.

moment of the passion. This is achieved by the training of the initiated in a gradual approach to 'the selected woman' (*nāyikā*): during four months he should serve her as servant, sleeping in the same room, at her feet, and not touching her; then during the next four months he sleeps on her 'left side', then on her 'right side', then in embracing position. Finally, he is allowed to have sexual pleasure—in order to express Nirvāṇic beatitude —but he must control and stop the seminal emission, even to make (by his effort) the semen go back into his body. Otherwise, he is supposed to be damned to law of *karma*. All this is followed by some ideologies aiming to prove that by this technique his process of liberation is accelerated, that he receives some experience of remote resemblance to egoless bliss, and so on.[1] In connection with this *maithuna*, these groups have been accused of sex and other orgies. As mentioned, a great deal in these accusations is either baseless or represents a wicked misinterpretation of the socially sanctioned, religious, and moral rituals of marriage and sex relationships. A careful study of the sexual life of the Tāntrikas shows, if anything, a much purer and less loose sexual life among them than that among the populations of Western accusers.

Similar accusations have been made against many sects and movements in practically all countries, including the West: against the early Christians accused of 'nocturnal orgies' by the non-Christians; against the Manichaeans, the Montanists, the Priscillianists, the Cathari, the Waldenses, the Antinomians, the Brethren of the Free Spirit, and so on, up to the contemporary sects of the Khlysty, Scopzi and others. Most of these accusations have been again baseless. Once in a while, however, among these and many other groups there happen to be a few who have been guilty of libertinian perversion of their credos and rituals for satisfaction of their lusts and sexual abnormalities.[2]

Whatever 'ideological justifications' these libertines have offered, the objective result has been negative for our purposes: hardly any eminent altruist, or even spiritual leader, has ever emerged from these libertines. As a rule they seem to have

[1] See the details, literature, and sources in M. Eliade, *Yoga*, pp. 209, 212, 231 ff., 238, 243 ff.   [2] See on this Sir John Woodroffe, *op. cit.*, pp. 593 ff.

remained either outstanding egoists, or at best just ordinary persons neither too altruistic nor too egotistic, neither too religious and spiritual nor too atheistic and coarsely materialistic. All such techniques are unfit for altruization; more often than not they are definitely harmful from this standpoint. In spite of their ingenious ideologies, these perverted techniques demoralize and enervate, rather than integrate their practitioners. With this we may dismiss them.

GENERAL CONCLUSIONS ON THE YOGA TECHNIQUES

For the rank and file of human beings the techniques of Patanjali's rāja yoga are hardly accessible. Taken as a whole they far exceed the physical and mental capabilities of the overwhelming majority of human individuals. In a diluted form, however, a part of these techniques can be practised by the rank and file.

By a very few 'religious and moral athletes', the rāja yoga techniques can be fruitfully used for moral and spiritual transfiguration; however, even for these few not all of these techniques are equally good and efficacious. A combination of some of these techniques with those of the other yogas and the non-yoga procedures seems to be more practical for a greater part of even the religious and moral leaders.

For the ordinary human beings the techniques of the karma yoga and the bhakti yoga seem to be more suitable than those of the rāja yoga. The karma yoga techniques consist mainly in performance of good deeds and altruistic conduct. The Bhakti Yoga techniques are based mainly on deep devotion, self-surrender, and love of God. The jñāna yoga techniques are mainly intellectual; the karma yoga techniques are predominantly 'operational', based upon the retroactive effects of good actions upon the mind and conduct of the karma yogin; while the bhakti yoga techniques are preponderantly 'emotional and affective', powered by the fuel of devotional emotions and feelings. The techniques of good deeds and of intense devotion to God have been used by millions, while the exacting techniques of the rāja yoga have been practised only by very few individuals. The system of the techniques of each yoga contains in itself some of the techniques of other yogas. The integral yoga of Sri Aurobindo (and also the various techniques practised by Ramakrisha) deliberately attempts to unite the main techniques of all the yogas. In this point the integral yoga is on the right track. The techniques should vary in accordance with the character of the persons and groups undergoing altruistic transformation, as we have seen. In spite of this variation, all the efficacious techniques, and especially those applied to millions of the rank and file, are to be a unified mixture of the techniques of all yogas and of many non-yoga techniques. They have to contain some physical training, some intellectual concentration, meditation, and creativity, some emotional and affective self-discipline, and, finally, the operational performance of good deeds. Besides the supra-conscious, they have to use the physical, biological, intellectual, emotional, volitional, and actional forces of an individual to empower the drive of the transformation. In brief, the most efficacious system of techniques of altruistic transformation is always integral in this or that form. What sort of integration is best for what sorts of persons and groups has to be decided by the experience of the individual and by the wisdom of his moral counsellors.

18

RISHABHCHAND

The Philosophical Basis of Integral Yoga

THE integral yoga of Sri Aurobindo did not spring full-grown from any philosophical basis, like Minerva from the head of Jove. It is not the product of any philosophical thought and speculation. It is a natural outcome of Sri Aurobindo's spiritual realizations which, as the following quotations will show, converged upon an all-inclusive unity and integrality.

Sri Aurobindo's first decisive spiritual experience was of Nirvāṇa, but curiously enough, instead of being an end in itself, it opened doors upon higher experiences of an increasing comprehensiveness.

'. . . to reach Nirvāṇa was the first radical result of my own Yoga. It threw me suddenly into a condition above and without thought, unstained by any mental or vital movement; there was no ego, no real world—only when one looked through the immobile senses, something perceived or bore upon its sheer silence a world of empty forms, materialized shadows without true substance. There was no One or many even, only just absolutely That, featureless, relationless, sheer, indescribable, unthinkable, absolute, yet supremely real and solely real. This was no mental realization nor something glimpsed somewhere above—no abstraction—it was positive, the only positive reality—although not a spatial physical world, pervading, occupying or rather flooding and drowning this semblance of a physical world, leaving no room or space for any reality but itself, allowing nothing else to seem at all actual, positive or substantial. I cannot say there was anything exhilarating or rapturous in the experience, as it came to me—(the ineffable

Ānanda I had years afterwards)—but what it brought was an inexpressible Peace, a stupendous silence, an infinity of release and freedom. I lived in that Nirvāṇa day and night before it began to admit other things into itself or modify itself at all, and the inner heart of experience, a constant memory of it and its power to return remained until in the end it began to disappear into a greater Superconsciousness from above. But meanwhile realization added itself to realization and fused itself with this original experience. At an early stage the aspect of an illusory world gave place to one in which illusion[1] is only a small surface phenomenon with an immense Divine Reality behind it and a supreme Divine Reality above it and an intense Divine Reality in the heart of everything that had seemed at first only a cinematic shape or shadow. And this was no reimprisonment in the senses, no diminution or fall from supreme experience, it came rather as a constant heightening and widening of the Truth; it was the Spirit that saw objects, not the senses, and the Peace, the Silence, the freedom in Infinity remained always with the world or all worlds only as a continuous incident in the timeless eternity of the Divine.'[2]

It is clear from the above description that Sri Aurobindo's yoga tended from the very beginning towards an integrality. It did not follow the beaten track of either the yoga of knowledge or the yoga of love and devotion or that of will and action. Nor was it a mere synthesis of these different paths. It proceeded with a progressive inclusion and affirmation, a harmonization of the various, even contradictory, aspects of Reality, and hewed its way through many an unexplored region of Spirit to the supreme Truth-Consciousness which is the timeless origin of all creation and manifestation, and the meeting ground of all cosmic divergences and contradictions. Nirvāṇa led to the Divine, behind and above and at the heart of everything. He has vividly described his realization of the Divine in his famous Uttarpārā speech:

[1] Sri Aurobindo, *Sri Aurobindo on Himself and on the Mother* (Pondicherry: Sri Aurobindo Ashram, 1953), pp. 154 f.: 'In fact it is not an illusion in the sense of an imposition of something baseless and unreal on the consciousness, but a misinterpretation by the conscious mind and sense and a falsifying misuse of manifested existence.'   [2] *Ibid.*, pp. 153–5.

'. . . His strength again entered into me. I looked at the jail
that secluded me from men and it was no longer by its high
walls that I was imprisoned; no, it was Vāsudeva[1] who
surrounded me. I walked under the branches of the tree in
front of my cell, but it was not the tree, I knew it was Vāsudeva,
it was Sri Krishna whom I saw standing there and holding over
me His shade. I looked at the bars of my cell, . . . and again I
saw Vāsudeva. It was Nārāyana[2] who was guarding and standing
sentry over me. Or I lay on the coarse blankets that were given
me for a couch and felt the arms of Sri Krishna around me, the
arms of my Friend and Lover. This was the first use of the
deeper vision He gave me. I looked at the prisoners in the jail,
the thieves, the murderers, the swindlers, and as I looked at
them I saw Vāsudeva, it was Nārāyana whom I found in those
darkened souls and misused bodies.'[3]

Having realized the Divine everywhere, within himself and
without, Sri Aurobindo began his herculean ascent from level
to level of spiritual consciousness in quest of the plane which
permits of a simultaneous realization of the divine status and
the divine dynamism, the eternal divine repose and the eternal
divine movement, *pravṛtti* and *nivṛtti*, and which can, by
transforming the physical consciousness and the material body
of man, make him enjoy a complete and constant union with
the Supreme in his active life on earth. He ascended to the
higher mind, 'a mind of Spirit-born conceptual knowledge',
which is 'An all-awareness emerging from the original identity,
carrying the truths the identity held in itself, conceiving
swiftly, victoriously, multitudinously, formulating and by
self-power of the Idea effectually realizing its conceptions'.[4]
From the higher mind he rose to the illumined mind which is
not a mind of higher thought, but of spiritual light and vision.
'Here the clarity of the spiritual intelligence, its tranquil
day-light, and illumination of the Spirit: a play of lightnings
of spiritual truth and power breaks from above into the

---

[1] A name of Sri Krishna.
[2] The Divine dwelling in the heart of man.
[3] Sri Aurobindo, *Speeches* (Pondicherry: Sri Aurobindo Ashram Press,
1952), pp. 56–7.   [4] Aurobindo, *The Life Divine*, p. 835.

consciousness, . . . a fiery ardour of realization and a rapturous ecstasy of knowledge.'[1] Leaving the illumined mind, Sri Aurobindo ascended to intuition which has a fourfold power: a power of revelatory truth-seeing, a power of inspiration or truth-hearing, a power of truth-touch or *immediate* seizing of significance, and a power of true and automatic discrimination of the orderly and exact relation of truth to truth.[2] But here too Sri Aurobindo did not find the secret of the ultimate dynamic unity of the One and the many, of Spirit and Matter, of the transcendent silence and the universal movement. His next ascent was to the overmind, which is 'a power of cosmic consciousness' and 'a principle of global knowledge', in which 'the predominance of the centralizing ego-sense is entirely subordinated, lost in largeness of being and finally abolished; a wide cosmic perception and feeling of a boundless universal self and movement replaces it. . . .'[3] Speaking of the overmind, Sri Aurobindo says that most of the spiritual seekers who set out to discover the solution of the ultimate mystery of existence, stopped short at it, taking the torrential downpour of its massed lustres for the supreme light, the gnosis, of the creative, divine truth-consciousness. But the overmind failed to give Sri Aurobindo the all-harmonizing, all-transforming truth he was seeking. Its golden lid, as it is termed in the Iśa Upaniṣad, hid the face of the Truth.

The next stage of the epic ascent took Sri Aurobindo quite a number of strenuous years to reach. Passing through its two lower statuses, he attained at last to the summit of the truth-consciousness, called *rta-cit* in the Veda, and *vijñāna* in the Upaniṣad. It is the poise of Saccidānanda as the supreme Lord, Parameśwara, of the whole universe. It is the highest integralizing power and principle of existence. Sri Aurobindo calls it the Supermind. In its all-revealing sun-blaze, all problems of life disappear in integral knowledge, and life with its ever-developing diversity is viewed, not as an illusion or an unaccountable freak of chance or as necessity, but as a creative movement of the supramental force and a perennial field for the working out or realization of the infinite potentialities of Spirit. It must be noted here that at each step of the spiritual

[1] Aurobindo, *The Life Divine*, p. 839.　[2] *Ibid.*, p. 843.　[3] *Ibid.*, p. 844.

ascension of Sri Aurobindo's consciousness, there was a corresponding descent of the characteristic light and force of the plane attained, to change the consciousness and being of Sri Aurobindo into its own image. He had to pass through a series of conversions of his consciousness and transformations of his being. The descent of the supermind was the consummating movement. But as it was not a personal supramentalization that he was seeking for, but the ascent of the consciousness of humanity from mind to supermind as the next inevitable step of evolution, he had to wage a long war with the forces of ignorance and inconscience which still rule the earth-nature. The descent of the supermind into matter and the answering emergence of the supermind involved in matter can alone, he knew, bring about a radical transformation of the integral being and consciousness of man and the establishment of the life divine on earth.

The single secret of Sri Aurobindo's conquest of the truth-consciousness was a complete, unreserved, integral surrender of his whole being to the Divine and His supreme force—a surrender not only of the mind or the heart or the will and life's activities, but of every part of his being and every movement of his nature. The divine force, or, as Sri Aurobindo terms it, the Divine Mother, did the yoga in him, and led him to his goal.

We have reviewed at some length Sri Aurobindo's spiritual experiences and explorations in order to show that his integral yoga was a natural evolution out of them, and not out of any philosophical speculation. But nevertheless, like every other Indian yoga, it has a philosophical basis, and a very wide one at that, supporting its massive structure.

If we study the evolution of Nature deeply and comprehensively, passing beyond its biological aspect, we find that what she aims at is a continuous self-transcendence by the triple method of ascent, widening of the field and base, and integration. Her evolution is nothing but a progressive ascent from matter to spirit. All evolution presupposes an involution. According to the Veda and the Upaniṣad, what is involved here in unconsciousness is the Absolute, the superconscient Saccidānanda. From inconscience matter emerges as the first evolute, then a little of the submerged consciousness trickles out with life, and more of it with mind. But the human mind, which is a mind of ignorance, seeking for knowledge but not finding it, cannot be the last term of evolution. If the Superconscient with Its infinite knowledge, power and bliss are involved here, it must inevitably evolve. The next principle to evolve, according to Sri Aurobindo, is the supermind. During all the various stages of this graded evolution, one can very well perceive the intention and method of Nature. She does not reject matter when she rises to the play of life, but vitalizes it and raises it up into a sort of active and intimate alliance with life. Similarly, when she evolves mind and rises to the play of consciousness with thought and reason and imagination as its principal faculties, she does not cut out from herself matter and life as obstructive elements and a drag on her upward advance. She mentalizes matter and life both, so that a physical mind and a vital mind are developed out of that integration. The basic principle of the mind, which is consciousness or rather self-consciousness, permeates the whole organism, and the evolutionary being of man comes to have a vital ego and a physical ego as well as a mental one. It is, therefore, obvious that it is not Nature's way to renounce and annul the lower principle as soon as a higher one is evolved. She goes on lifting the lower into the higher, and both into the next higher, till she reaches Spirit, integrates to It and unites with It in a dynamic and creative unity all that she has evolved.

This process of the Divine Nature—for she is there directing from behind the frontal aspect of mechanical Nature—witnesses to the teleology of earthly evolution, which is an integral manifestation of spirit in matter. Viewed in this light, all life appears to be a stupendous, incalculable yoga of Nature.

'In the right view both of life and of Yoga, all life is either consciously or subsconciously a Yoga. . . . All life, when we look behind its appearance, is a vast Yoga of Nature attempting to realize her perfection in an ever-increasing expression of her potentialities and to unite herself with her own divine reality.'[1]

The aim of the integral yoga is identical with the secret aim of

[1] Sri Aurobindo, *On Yoga*, p. 4.

Nature in her evolution—it is the epiphany of the Supramental Divine in the material world by the self-transcending ascent of the consciousness of man and its transforming and integrating descent. But though the aim is the same, their methods are somewhat different. Nature's universal ascent is slow and leisurely, for she has to proceed tentatively, with many a detour and set-back, through the inconscience or subconscience of her evolutionary elements, as if she were groping her way in the dark. But yoga has this advantage that it enlists from the very start the conscious, willed and active co-operation of the individual; and this co-operation considerably accelerates the pace of evolution. The work of several lives can thus be accomplished in the course of a single life, or even a few concentrated years.

As an illustration of the dual movement of ascent and descent, which is common to both the integral yoga and the yoga of Nature, Sri Aurobindo traces the evolution of spirituality in India in the following words:

'. . . in India the reign of Intuition came first, intellectual Mind developing afterwards in the later philosophy and science. . . . The effect of the Vedic mystics revealed to them the things behind through a power of inner sight and hearing. . . . The Vedic age was followed by a great outburst of intellect and philosophy which yet took spiritual truth as its basis and tried to reach it anew, not through a direct Intuition or occult process, . . . but by the power of the mind's reflective, speculative, logical thought; at the same time processes of Yoga were developed which used the thinking mind as a means of arriving at spiritual realization, spiritualizing the mind itself at the same time. Then followed an era of the development of philosophies and Yoga processes which more and more used the emotional and aesthetic being as the means of spiritual realization and spiritualized the emotional level in man through the heart and feeling. This was accompanied by Tāntric and other processes which took up the mental will, the life-will, the will of sensations and made them at once the instruments and the field of spiritualization. In the Hathayoga and the various attempts at divinization of the body, there is also a line of endeavour which attempted to arrive at the same achievement with regard to living matter. . . . We may say therefore that the universal Consciousness after its descent into Matter has conducted the evolution there along two lines, one of ascent to the discovery of self and Spirit, the other of descent through the already evolved levels of mind, life and body so as to bring down the spiritual consciousness into these also and to fulfil thereby some secret intention in the creation of the material universe. Our Yoga [the Integral Yoga] is in its principle a taking up and summarizing and completing of this process, an endeavour to rise to the highest possible supramental level and bring down its consciousness and power into mind, life and body.'[1]

Another point to consider is the immanence of the Divine in the world. If we accept the world as a real creation of God, we have to admit that His immanence in it can have only one purpose behind it—an increasingly flawless expression of Himself; unless we choose to regard the Immanent only as a passive leaven or an agent for recruiting ripe souls and packing them off to the Transcendent. The hierarchy of the planes of consciousness and their distinctive principles, powers and instrumental faculties, if they have any teleological significance at all, confirm the hypothesis of the will of the Immanent to an integral self-manifestation in the world. The essential unity of the world and the harmony and organic correlation of its multitudinous elements and energies also argue an integral consummation.

In Indian philosophy there are three different kinds of liberation, each pursued separately to the exclusion of the other two. Those who aim at *sāyujya*, or a complete merger in the transcendent Brahman, follow the exclusive path of knowledge, using the intellect as the means of realization. Those who seek an intimate closeness to the Divine, *sāmipya* or *sālokya*, and a union and communion in an eternal relation of love and devotion, but not a self-abolition, follow the path of the heart's feelings and emotions turned exclusively to their Lover and Beloved. Those who seek union with the Divine in His Will and Power, seek to assume the nature of the Divine and enjoy its

[1] Sri Aurobindo, *Letters of Sri Aurobindo* (First Series) (Pondicherry: Sri Aurobindo Ashram Press, 1950), pp. 6–8.

dynamic freedom, *sārupya*. But man is an integer, or an organic
and composite entity, every part of which has an undeniable
right to a total and dynamic union with the Divine from whom
alone it is originally derived. The integral yoga aims at a
complete fusion of the three liberations.

In the Upaniṣad, Ātman or Brahman is described as having
a fourfold poise—the poise of the waking self, *jāgrat pāda*; the
poise of the dream self or the subliminal self, *swapna pāda*; the
poise of the sleeping self or the blissful, creative self, *suṣupti
pāda*; and the ineffable, transcendent self, *tūriya pāda*. The
four poises together constitute the integrality of Brahman. In
later Vedānta, the tūriya or the unthinkable transcendent
alone was regarded as Reality, and the other three poises of
Brahman were negated and dismissed as illusion. The integral
yoga envisages this fourfold integrality as its goal.

According to Indian philosophy, the soul lives simultaneously
in five sheaths which are called *koṣas*. The first two of these are
the immortal sheaths of the soul so long as it remains in the
world of manifestation; they are the sheaths of *vijñāna* and
ānanda, supramental knowledge and supernal bliss. The other
three are the temporal sheaths of mind, life and matter. In
each sheath the soul presides as a *puruṣa* or being, which is a
self-projection or self-formation of its central essence of entity.
The Upaniṣad speaks of these *puruṣas* and traces the evolution
of the soul from the physical to the vital, from the vital to the
mental, from the mental to the supramental, and from the
supramental to the *pnruṣa* of bliss or *ānanda*. Each of these
Puruṣas seeks its individual perfection and fulfilment in an
integral manifestation of the Divine. To eliminate the three
lower formulations of the soul, the material, vital and mental,
and aim at the exclusive fulfilment of the higher two, or to
eliminate all the five and shoot into the featureless Absolute,
cannot certainly be an integral fulfilment of the soul in the
world of God's self-expression. To fulfil God in the world is the
mission of the soul. The simultaneous perfection and fulfilment
of the five *puruṣas* or the composite being of man is the aim of
the integral yoga of Sri Aurobindo.

To realize a complete union with the Divine means to be one
with Him in all the poises of His being, in all the modes of His

nature, in all the states of His consciousness, in all the worlds of His self-expression and in all the infinite powers and principles through which He veils and reveals Himself. His utmost transcendence, His universal immanence and His individual presence in the heart of every being and every thing have to be simultaneously embraced in an active and dynamic union as well as in an eternal silence and repose, if he wants to realize the Divine integrally.

One of the main strands of the philosophical basis of the integral yoga is the indivisible unity of God, Man and Nature; of Being and Becoming. To cut oneself off from the becoming in order to enter into the Ineffable is a unilateral movement which denies all spiritual reality and significance to man and nature. An integral philosophy of existence must reckon with both being and becoming, for if being is real, its becoming, though mutable, is equally real.

'It is possible for the soul in the Becoming to know itself as the Being and possess the Becoming, to know itself as Infinite in essence but also as the Infinite self-expressed in the finite, the timeless Eternal regarding itself and its works in the founding status and the developing motion of Time-eternity. This realization is the culmination of the Becoming; it is the fulfilment of the Being in its dynamic reality. This too [along with the truth of the eternal stillness of the Being] must be part of the total truth of things, for it alone gives a full significance to the universe and justifies the soul in manifestation; an explanation of things that deprives cosmic and individual existence of all significance cannot be the whole explanation or the solution it proposes the sole true issue.'[1]

To be as perfect on earth as God is perfect in heaven, to be one with the Divine not only in His being but also in His nature, to fulfil His will on earth, and to realize in active life the triple formula of the Upaniṣad—Brahman is in all, all are in Brahman, and all are Brahman—this is the object of the integral yoga of Sri Aurobindo. It is an integral approach to the integral Reality.

[1] Aurobindo, *The Life Divine*, p. 588.

19

HAJIME NAKAMURA

Practice of Selfless Action

THE integralism of Sri Aurobindo has little been known to the Japanese in general. When the writer of the present paper stayed in America, he came to take notice of the fact that some leading scholars in America had stimulated the interest of intellectuals in Aurobindo, which was rather surprising to the Japanese visitor. A report by him to this effect was published in the *Indogaku Bukkyōgaku Kenkyū* (i.e. Journal of Indian and Buddhist Studies—Vol. I, No. 1, July 1952, edited by the Japanese Association of Indian and Buddhist Studies, Tokyo, pp. 209, 213–14). It was not known that so many intellectuals were to be attracted by the thought of Aurobindo. Recently Professor Koshiro Tamaki of Tokyo University, Tokyo, discussed his philosophy very briefly in *A History of Indian Ethical Thought* (in Japanese) (edited by H. Nakamura, Tokyo, Gakugeishobo, 1958). Some Japanese have come to hear the name of Aurobindo through Japanese translations of Romain Rolland's works. On the occasion of the UNESCO Symposium attached to the IXth International Congress for the History of Religions, Tokyo 1958, the writer of the present paper read in his paper 'The influence of Eastern Culture on the West' as follows: 'The tendency to appreciate Indian civilization which is the rage among some highly Westernized Japanese intellectuals, is chiefly due to the influence of Romain Rolland. . . . The thought of Aurobindo Ghosh is now propagated by the American Academy of Asian Studies group in San Francisco and Professor Herbert in Switzerland.'

This, so far, is almost all that has been said about Aurobindo in the academic circle of Japan. Japanese scholars knew so little about the gospel of Aurobindo that they would refrain from saying anything to English-reading people who know much of it. The writer wants to deal with only one thing which is relevant to Aurobindo.

Briefly speaking, Aurobindo aimed at the discovery of the fundamentals of life and existence and of the true methods which could lead to fulfilment and perfection of man and his culture. His messages sound very convincing, as if he were speaking words of revelation with full confidence. It is very difficult to analyse and review his sayings until one has grasped the whole body of his abstruse and profound thought. In so far as the writer has come to know, it seems that some main points of his thought were especially based upon the Bhagavadgītā on which he so enthusiastically elaborated. According to it, the aim of human life can be fulfilled by selfless actions, although so many things are taught in the Gītā. The writer wants to review the passages which lay such stress upon selfless action in the Gītā first, and then compare the ideas therein with that in Mahāyāna Buddhism.

The battle of the Bhāratas which forms the main story of the Mahabhārata was fought between a hundred princes of the Kuru people and the five princes of the King Pāṇḍu. They were related to each other as cousins. However, they had to fight. The two nearly related but hostile clans, after disputes extending over many years, made ready for open combat, and advanced against one another with the forces and allies on either side on the plain of the Kurus in the neighbourhood of modern Delhi. On the field of the Kurus the ranks of the two rival armies drew up against each other, and all was prepared for the opening trumpet blast. When they were about to begin fighting, Arjuna, a prince who was the son of the King Pāṇḍu, felt himself very sad on his deplorable destiny. Although Arjuna was a famous archer of that race, he hesitated to begin the fight at the sight of his near relatives in the hostile army; he did not know what he should do; his mind whirled. Being unable to distinguish the right from the wrong, Arjuna, in despair, turned to his friend and charioteer, Kṛṣṇa. He confided his inner agony to his charioteer who was in reality none but an incarnation of Viṣṇu, the highest god. He saw there relatives, comrades and friends, teachers and pupils arrayed in both the armies. At the sight of these he was overcome with great compassion. His limbs failed; his mouth was parched; his body was shaken and his hair stood on end. He became very dubious about the significance of this battle. 'I never perceive any good in slaughtering my own people in battle.'[1] . . . 'How can we ever be happy by killing our own people?'[2] . . . 'I desire neither victory nor empire nor even any pleasure: of what avail to us is empire, of what avail are enjoyments and even life itself?'[3] 'Alas: we are resolved to commit a great sin, in that we are ready to slay our kinsmen to satisfy our greed for the pleasure of a kingdom!'[4] Arjuna, suffering from agony, cast aside his bow and arrow and sank down on his chariot seat, his mind being overcome with grief.

He was, however, recalled to a sense of his duty by Kṛṣṇa. To Arjuna, who was thus overwhelmed with pity, and whose troubled eyes were filled with tears, Kṛṣṇa spoke these words: 'In this crisis, O Arjuna, whence comes such lowness of spirit, unbecoming to an Aryan, dishonorable! Do not yield to unmanliness! It does not become you. You have been mourning for those who should not be mourned for.'[5] 'It is most desirable for a warrior to sacrifice himself in a righteous war. You should not avoid battle. Considering your own duty you should not waver; for to a warrior nothing is better than a righteous war.'[6] I.e. there exists no greater good for a warrior than a battle enjoined by duty. 'Happy are the warriors for whom such a war comes of its own accord as an open door to heaven.'[7] 'But if you refuse to wage this righteous war, then renouncing your own *dharma* and honour, you will certainly incur sin.'[8] 'People will tell your infamy forever. And to a man who has been honoured, dishonour is worse than death.'[9] The proper duty of a warrior consists in fighting to the last at any cost. In order to fulfil his own duty, everything else should be given up. The only way to be chosen by a warrior is to fight. 'Regarding alike pleasure and pain, gain and loss, success and defeat, prepare yourself for battle. Acting in this way you will incur no sin.'[10]

[1] Sir S. Radhakrishnan, *The Bhagavadgita* (London: Allen & Unwin Ltd., 1948), I, 31.   [2] *Ibid.*, I, 37.   [3] *Ibid.*, I, 32.   [4] *Ibid.*, I, 45.
[5] *Ibid.*, II, 11.   [6] *Ibid.*, II, 31.   [7] *Ibid.*, II, 32.
[8] *Ibid.*, II, 33.   [9] *Ibid.*, II, 34.   [10] *Ibid.*, II, 38.

H

Here we shall cite an admonition given to warriors in ancient Japan just for comparison. 'There is nothing important except the relationship between lord and retainer. We will never waver, even if we should be admonished to do something else by Shakyamuni, Confucius or the Effulgent God [i.e. the foremost ancestor of Emperors]. Let us be doomed to hell, or let us be punished by gods, we have nothing to do in mind but to serve for our feudal lord whole-heartedly! If we go astray on this point, we shall be misled by banal doctrines of Shintoism or Buddhism. We are sure that Buddhas and gods will approve our attitude.'[1] In the feudal age of Japan loyalty or the genuine or sincere attitude to the feudal lord was more esteemed than religious reasons, whereas in ancient India warriors wanted to justify their engagement in wars on religious grounds.[2]

According to such a conception of duty in the Gītā, every action should centre on the fulfilment of his own duty. 'To action alone, you are entitled, never to its fruit. Never let your motive be the fruit of action, nor let there be any attachment to non-action.'[3] A man should perform an obligatory action only because it ought to be done, and renounce all attachment to the fruit.[4] 'The action that is obligatory and is done without love or hate by one who desires no fruit and who is free from attachment—that action is said to be of *goodness*.'[5] This verse we can explain as follows: man should do his duty simply because it *is* his duty, and with perfect indifference to the results, whether they are favourable or not. This doctrine is called 'the Way of Practice of Selfless Action' (karmayoga). It reminds us of Kant's categorical imperative. The ethical principle in this doctrine of *karmayoga* requires that the individual should continue carrying on his usual duties and activities of life as before, but with a new attitude of detachment from their fruits or results, i.e. from the possible gains or losses that they will entail.

Against the view that all action should be abandoned, since

---

[1] *Hagakure*, Chapter II.

[2] We shall refrain from getting into details on the Way of Warriors, *Bushidō*, of the ancient Japanese. With regard to the Indian replica, cf. M. Winternitz: *A History of Indian Literature*, Vol. I, published by the University of Calcutta, 1927, pp. 385–7.

[3] *The Bhagavadgita*, II, 47.   [4] *Ibid.*, XVIII, 9.   [5] *Ibid.*, XVIII, 23.

it leads to bondage, the Gītā asserts that actions of worship, gifts and penance should not be abandoned. 'Actions of worship, gift and austerity are not to be given up, but should be performed. For verily, actions of worship, gift, and austerity purify the wise.'[1] But they should be done without selfish attachment or expectation of rewards. 'Even these works, however, should be done without attachment and desire for fruit.'[2] 'It is indeed impossible for an embodied being to renounce action entirely. But he who renounces the fruit of action [i.e. reward], is regarded as one who has renounced.'[3] From the viewpoint of a modern thinker the purport of the teaching is explained as follows: 'When we do our work, plough or paint, sing or think, we will be deflected from disinterestedness if we think of fame or income or any such extraneous consideration. Nothing matters except the good will, the willing fulfilment of the purpose of God.'[4] A man cannot remain inactive even for one moment, and all actions have some measure of defect. Therefore, we must say that work prompted by one's own nature is not harmful as a whole. 'One should not give up the activity suited to one's own nature, even though it may be defective; for all undertakings are enveloped by defects, as fire by smoke.'[5]

In the world there are two kinds of people. Some are absorbed in contemplative life, while others are engaged in social activity. The latter are superior to the former. 'The renunciation of works and their unselfish performance both lead to the soul's salvation. But of the two, the unselfish performance of works is better than their renunciation.'[6] 'Do your allotted action, for action is superior to inaction. And even the bare maintenance of your body will not be possible if you remain inactive.'[7] As daily ethics the fulfilment of one's own duty is stressed. 'Better is one's own duty, though imperfectly carried out, than the duty of another carried out perfectly. One does not incur sin when one does the duty ordained by one's own nature'.[8] On this point we are reminded of Plato's saying: 'One man should

---

[1] *The Bhagavadgita*, XVIII, 5.　　[2] *Ibid.*, XVIII, 6.
[3] *Ibid.*, XVIII, 11 (cf. IV, 20; 21).　　[4] *Ibid.*, p. 119.
[5] *Ibid.*, XVIII, 48.　　[6] *Ibid.*, V, 2.
[7] *Ibid.*, III, 8 (cf. XVIII, 7: 48).　　[8] *Ibid.*, XVIII, 47.

practise one thing only, the thing to which his nature is best adapted.'[1] It was asserted that in a well-ordered state one should do one's own business.[2]

Such a way of practice is the *karmayoga*, or it is simply called *yoga*. 'He who in action sees inaction, and action in inaction, is wise among men; he is a yogin, and has accomplished all his work.'[3]

We find a similar saying in China also. Lao-tzu says:

> It acts without action, does without doing
> finds flavour in what is flavourless,
> Can make the small great and the few many
> requites injuries with good deeds,
> Deals with the hard while it is still easy,
> With the great while it is still small.[4]

This saying answers to the attitude of the man of stabilized mentality.[5]

This conception of *yoga* was inherited and developed by Aurobindo. He says: 'Yoga is a generic name for the processes and the result of processes by which we transcend or shed off our present modes of being and rise to a new, a higher, a wider mode of consciousness which is not that of the ordinary animal and intellectual man. Yoga is the exchange of an egoistic for a universal or cosmic consciousness lifted towards or informed by the super-cosmic, transcendent Unnameable who is the source and support of all things."[6]

The Gītā was expounded by Aurobindo, and his exposition was translated by Professor Jean Herbert into French. How far the notion of practice of selfless action in the Gītā was incorporated and developed in the philosophy of Aurobindo must be made clear by further investigation.

The ideal of selfless action has highly been esteemed in

---

[1] Plato's *Republic*, 433; The Dialogues of Plato translated into English by B. Jowett, Vol. I (New York: Random House, 1937), 696.

[2] (Charmides, 161).   [3] *The Bhagavadgita*, IV, 16.

[4] *Tao Tê Ching*, LXIII.

[5] Sthitaprajña described in Radhakrishnan, *The Bhagavadgita*, p. 126.

[6] *Science and Culture: A Selection of Passages from the Writings of Sri Aurobindo and the Mother*, compiled by Indra Sen (Pondicherry: Sri Aurobindo Ashram, Aditi Kāryalaya, 1951), p. 60.

Buddhism also. Especially the emphasis has been put on the altruistic inclinations and activities. From the outset the Bodhisattva strives towards a plane where there are no differences between his ego and his neighbour's; he identifies his ego absolutely and entirely with that of others. And yet he should not have the conceit that he has helped, or has been helping others. Help or service should be done without attachment. 'Here, O Subhūti, a Bodhisattva should think thus: As many beings as there are in the universe of beings—be they egg-born, or born from a womb, or moisture-born, or miraculously born; be they with form, or without; be they with consciousness, or without consciousness, or with neither consciousness nor no-consciousness—as far as any conceivable universe of beings is conceived; all these should be led by me into Nirvāṇa, into that realm of Nirvāṇa which leaves nothing behind. And yet, although innumerable beings have thus been led to Nirvāṇa, no being at all has been led to Nirvāṇa. Why? If in a Bodhisattva the consciousness of a "being" should take place, he would not be called a "being destined for enlightenment" (bodhi-sattva).'[1] If a Bodhisattva should be self-conceited that he has helped others, then he is not a real Bodhisattva. A famous poem composed by an Indian, and cited and recited frequently by Chinese and Japanese Buddhists, runs as follows:

The donator, the donatory and things donated should be thought of without attachment in the past, present and future. We are firmly settled in the highest state of mind. Thus we worship all the Buddhas of the ten Directions.[2]

This poem is called the Poem of Purity of the Three. It means that without attachment alone the above mentioned three can be pure, without defilement. This attitude derives from the fact that the practice of Mahāyāna is firmly based upon the standpoint of the Void (sūnyatā).

From the consideration set forth above, we are led to the

[1] *Buddhist Texts from Japan*, ed. F. Max Mueller (Oxford: Clarendon Press, 1881), Anecdota Oxoniensia, Aryan Series, Vol. 1, Part 1, Sec. 3.
[2] *Daijo-Honsho-Shimjikan-kyo*, Vol. 1, *The Taisho Tripitaka*, ed. J. Takakusu and K. Watanabe (Taisho: Issaikyo Kankokai, 1924), Vol. 3, p. 296b.

conclusion as follows: the ideal of selfless activity was advocated by both the Gītā and Mahāyāna Buddhism. The philosophical basis of the one may be fundamentally different from that of the other. The ethics of the Gītā is based upon the traditional conception of *Brahman* with theistic modifications, whereas Mahāyāna is based upon the conception of the Void which is peculiarly Buddhistic. We do not minimize the fundamental difference. However, in the spirit of selfless action they coincide; practically there is no difference.

It might be too absurd to jump from the Gītā and Mahāyāna which came into existence about 2,000 years ago straight down to Aurobindo of the present age. The writer will refrain from drawing any conclusion from this short investigation. However, we should not deny the validity of the fundamental ethical principle which might be called *dharma* that never changes in the changing, transient human life, and that has been propounded in various ways by great thinkers of humankind.

20

ANILBARAN ROY

Gītā, the World Scripture

As the tension of the crisis in human world-destiny increases, 'the feeling that there is no other solution than the spiritual cannot but grow and become more imperative under the urgency of critical circumstance'.[1] So says Sri Aurobindo in the concluding chapter of *The Life Divine*. But people have as yet no clear idea of spirituality, and they readily mistake it for religion or morality. Religion, however, as it is commonly understood and practised, has not much spirituality in it, though, like morality, it can serve as a preliminary preparation if pursued rightly. Religion is a thing of creed and dogma; people accept certain beliefs and practise certain prescribed rites and ceremonies as a matter of custom and convention. Though practised all over the world from very ancient times, religion has not essentially changed human life and society; in many respects, man still continues to be the barbarian though under different guises; the so-called civilization has created more ills than it has cured. 'A total spiritual direction given to the whole life and whole nature can alone lift humanity beyond itself.'[2] The Gītā teaches us how to do this practically, though the core of its teaching has not yet been fully understood or followed. People go to the temple, church or mosque, offer prayers and worship according to rule and custom and think they have done all that is necessary. But this by itself does not take us very far. The temple or church is only a symbol; we have to find and see Kṛṣṇa or Christ eternally seated within our heart and establish a conscious and living relation with Him, shaping all our life

---

[1] Aurobindo, *The Life Divine*, p. 939.   [2] *Ibid.*, p. 938.

and action in a constant union with the Divine—that is what is true spirituality. Kṛṣṇa described in the Gītā as seated in the chariot of Arjuna in the battlefield of Kurukṣetra (which is really the field of life which is a continuous battle), dispelling all the doubts of Arjuna, removing his weakness and fear, giving him the strength to do his divinely appointed work in the world is a vivid illustration of the ways of God to man. God is not a being sitting only in some distant heaven, to whom our prayers may or may not reach. He is very near to us and is the closest friend who will never fail us if we sincerely put our trust in Him. A regular perusal of the Gītā will impress these spiritual truths deeply in our mind and our whole life will be moulded by them.

The Gītā is pre-eminently the Śāstra or scripture for the modern age in so far as it lays the philosophical foundation for the unification of the human race. There are other great scriptures in the world, but the difficulty is that they contain many things which conflict with modern knowledge and modern ideas; that is why the men of our time have their faith shaken in spirituality and God. But without God there is no meaning and no fulfilment in life; that is being realized more and more as the crisis in world affairs is deepening, and people all over the world are searching for a saving light. The Gītā is a great depository of that light; there is nothing in it which conflicts with modern knowledge, while it gives a conception of God which satisfies the soul and a discipline which all can accept and follow and proceed towards God-realization. 'Truth', says Sri Aurobindo, '. . . is one and eternal', but it 'expresses itself in Time and through the mind of man; therefore every Scripture must necessarily contain two elements, one temporary, perishable, belonging to the ideas of the period and country in which it was produced, the other eternal and imperishable and applicable in all ages and countries. . . . In the Gītā there is very little that is merely local or temporal and its spirit is so large, profound and universal that even this little can easily be universalized without the sense of the teaching suffering any diminution or violation; rather by giving an ampler scope to it than belonged to the country and epoch, the teaching gains in depth, truth and power. . . . Thus it dwells on the ancient Indian system and idea of sacrifice, as an interchange between gods and men—a system and idea which have long been practically obsolete in India itself and are no longer real to the general human mind; but we find here a sense so entirely subtle, figurative and symbolic given to the word "sacrifice" and the conception of the gods is so little local and mythological, so entirely cosmic and philosophical that we can easily accept both as expressive of a practical fact of psychology and general law of Nature and so apply them to the modern conception of interchange between life and life and of ethical sacrifice and self-giving as to widen and deepen these and cast over them a more spiritual aspect and the light of a profounder and more far-reaching Truth.'[1]

At the same time we must guard against the error committed by many modern commentators on the Gītā who make it a mere gospel of humanism and social service. Service of humanity is the modern ideal preached by the West and no doubt its achievements have been considerable. Known as the 'religion of humanity', it was a mental creation of the rationalist thinkers of the West who made it a substitute for the formal spiritualism of ecclesiastical Christianity. One has only to compare human life and thought and feeling a century or two ago with human life, thought and feeling in the period preceding the two world wars to see how great an influence this religion of humanity has exercised and how fruitful a work it has done. Writers like Nietzsche vehemently attacked the orthodox religions, as they had no faith in humanity and its future; they looked with gloom and sorrow on earthly life and bade men to suffer all the ills of life hoping for a better life after death. The religion of humanity, on the other hand, '. . . to some degree humanized society, humanized law and punishment, humanized the outlook of man on man, abolished legalized torture and the cruder forms of slavery, raised those who were depressed and fallen, gave large hopes to humanity, stimulated philanthropy and charity and the service of mankind, encouraged everywhere the desire for freedom, put a curb on oppression and greatly minimized its more brutal expressions'.[2] All this is on the right line and tends to human progress. But with all its idealism it could not prevent

---

[1] Sri Aurobindo, *Essays on the Gita* (Pondicherry: Sri Aurobindo Ashram, 1949), pp. 4–6.   [2] Sri Aurobindo, *The Ideal of Human Unity*, p. 312.

the two world wars and it brought forward, as a sort of reaction, Nazism and Communism, both of which in their own ways are negations of the religion of humanity. If this new religion has to fulfil its brilliant promise, we must see and cure its radical defect. Its fundamental idea that mankind is the godhead to be worshipped is an intellectual concept and in spite of its appeal it cannot counteract the opposing tendencies in human nature. Thus the Nazis easily substituted the German race for mankind to be worshipped and respected and served by all. Until the religion of humanity rises above the intellectual level and finds a spiritual basis, it cannot entirely prevail over its own principal enemy. 'That enemy, the enemy of all real religion, is human egoism, the egoism of the individual, the egoism of the class and nation.'[1] In the ego, we regard ourselves as different from all other beings in the world and feel justified in aggrandizing ourselves at the expense of others. But this ego is only our superficial self, a point of reference created by our mind; under its influence we identify ourselves with the body, life and mind, but these do not constitute our true self, they are rather its instruments for self-manifestation. It is this recognition of true self as something beyond our body, life and mind that constitutes the essence of spirituality. Generally people do not make any essential distinction between mind and spirit; thus in German and French, the same word means both spirit and mind. Science has created the impression that matter is ultimate reality, that life and mind have somehow appeared in it and that what is called spirit is nothing but a refined function of mind. As the liver secretes bile, so the brain secretes thought, and as the flower blooms on the plant so it is only the mind which blooms as the spirit which has no independent reality. 'One might as well on the same lines have concluded that electricity is only a product or operation of water and cloud matter, because it is in such a field that lightning emerges; but a deeper inquiry has shown that both cloud and water have, on the contrary, the energy of electricity as their foundation, their constituent power of energy-substance: that which seems to be a result is—in its reality, though not in its form—the origin; the effect is in the essence pre-existent to the apparent

[1] *The Ideal of Human Unity*, p. 313.

cause, the principle of the emergent activity precedent to the present field of action.'[1]

Spirituality emerging in mind is the sign of a power which itself has founded and constituted life, mind and body and is now emerging as a spiritual being in a living and thinking body. This emergence has not yet gone very far, that is why men in general cannot have any clear conception of the spirit. But science is no longer an obstacle in the path of the discovery of the spirit, rather scientific thought is clearing the way for such discovery, though science by itself cannot achieve that discovery as that is not within its scope. 'Physical research aims not to disclose a real existence of things from "behind" the appearance world, but rather to develop thought systems for the control of this appearance world.'[2] It is spiritual research which aims at disclosing the reality behind appearances and the Gītā is pre-eminently a book of such spiritual research. It begins with the description of the self of man as being something not mutable or destructible like the body. 'This is not born, nor does it die, nor is it a thing that comes into being once and passing away will never come into being again. It is unborn, ancient, sempiternal; it is not slain with the slaying of the body.'[3] The spirit is not only not the body, it is not also the vital operations and the mind and the intelligence with which we ignorantly identify ourselves. 'Supreme, they say (beyond their objects), are the senses, supreme over the senses the mind, supreme over the mind is the intelligent will: that which is supreme over the intelligent will, is he (the Purusha).'[4] When we discover this, our true self, we see that our body, life and mind are only its instruments, and we can have full mastery over them, and that is the true meaning of liberation or salvation. All evils of life arise from the fact that we have no control over ourselves and our passions and desires. The ordinary method of practising self-control by following certain mental and moral rules, such as the ten commandments of the Christians and the *pancha śilas* of the Buddhists, do not take us very far, as we violate these rules in spite of ourselves. Thus Arjuna asks in the

---

[1] Aurobindo, *The Life Divine*, p. 759.
[2] Pas and Jordan, *Physics of the 20th Century*.
[3] *Gītā*, II, 20.   [4] *Ibid.*, III, 42.

Gītā, what is this in us that drives a man to commit sin, as if by force, even against his own struggling will? Thus all men become sinners as if by necessity, and the wages of sin is death. That is the true lesson of the parable of Christ's calling for a person who has never committed any sin to throw the first stone at a fallen woman. It is not by practising outer austerity that we can get rid of desire, which is the root of all sins in our nature. Only when we see in us the self which is beyond the mind and life can we root out all desires from our nature and enter into the eternal kingdom of peace and bliss. The Lord says to Arjuna in the Gītā: 'Thus awakening by the understanding to the Highest which is beyond even the discerning mind, putting force on the self by the self to make it firm and still, slay thou, O mighty-armed, this enemy in the form of desire, who is so hard to slay.'[1]

It may be objected that to find the self or the spirit is not an easy thing and cannot be put forward as a practical solution of man's difficulties. Even if it be so, there is no other solution, for to hope for a true change of human life without a change of human nature is an irrational and unspiritual proposition. 'It is to ask for something unnatural and unreal, an impossible miracle'[2] and the first condition of changing our nature is to find our true self, the spirit, and allow that to shape our life and action. The spirit is not something far and distant but it is within us and in the course of evolution it is slowly emerging, as life before emerged in matter and mind in life. But man can hasten this natural process of evolution by conscious effort and that is what is meant by yoga in India, of which the Gītā is an authoritative scripture, yogaśāstra. '. . . the mental human being is not aware of a soul in him standing back from the mind and life and body, detaching itself, seeing and controlling and moulding their action and formation; but, as the inner evolution proceeds, this is precisely what can, must and does happen—it is the long-delayed but inevitable next step in our evolutionary destiny.'[3]

When one discovers the spirit within him, he realizes that in his true being he is one with God and all other fellow human beings and that is the solid spiritual basis of human unity. Only then, and not before, can love become the law of life and peace

[1] Gītā, III, 43.   [2] Aurobindo, The Life Divine, p. 938.   [3] Ibid., p. 760.

and harmony be established permanently on earth. Only then the religion of humanity will find its firm and true basis and justification. 'For that essentially must be the aim of the religion of humanity, as it must be the earthly aim of all human religion, love, mutual recognition of human brotherhood, a living sense of human oneness and practice of human oneness in thought, feeling and life, the ideal which was expressed first some thousands of years ago in the ancient Vedic hymn and must always remain the highest injunction of the Spirit within us to human life upon earth.'[1] There must be a discipline by which this spiritual religion of humanity '. . . can be developed by each man within himself so that it may be developed in the life of the race.'[2] All our philosophy, science, art, politics, economics, education should have its essential aim to help man to discover his true self. The required spiritual discipline will be found elaborately given in the Gītā when we read it with the help of Sri Aurobindo's luminous interpretation, which brings out its inner significances in a way which brings them home to the modern mind. In order to follow this discipline, one should start with an adequate conception of God that is as complete as possible. He is the creator and ruler of the world, for whose sake all forces and all beings live and work. He is unfolding the universal play in His own being for His self-delight; nothing happens in the world without His will, nothing can resist the fulfilment of His divine plan which is to lead all creatures to immortality and the joy of the god-life. He is the supreme and loving friend of all. All these truths about God are expressed as follows in the Gītā: The Lord says: 'When a man has known Me as the enjoyer of sacrifice and *tapasyā* (of all askesis and energisms), the mighty lord of all the worlds, the friend of all creatures, he comes by the peace.'[3] With this conception of God fixed in the mind, one should learn to love and serve Him in all ways, *sarva-bhāvena*. For this one need not take the help of a priest or go to a temple or a holy place, but should daily devote some time to silent meditation and also worship the Divine in a simple manner as indicated by the Lord Himself in the Gītā: 'He who offers to Me with devotion a leaf, a flower,

---

[1] Aurobindo, *The Ideal of Human Unity*, p. 313.
[2] *Ibid.*, p. 323.   [3] *Gītā*, IX, 24, and X, 3.

a cup of water, that offering of love from the striving soul, is acceptable to Me.'[1] The Gītā does not require that one should renounce the world or life in order to realize the Divine, but insists that all necessary work in the world, *sarva-karmāni*, should be done with resolution and zeal, and it should be offered as a worship to the Divine. 'Whatever thou doest, whatever thou enjoyest, sacrificest, whatever thou givest, whatever *tapasyā* of the soul's will or effort thou puttest forth, make it an offering unto Me (that is, do all these things in a spirit of worship).'[2]

Desire, anger and greed, the greatest enemies of men, should be controlled, that is, nothing should be done under their influence. All actions should be decided in the light of calm reasoning until one unites himself directly with the Divine and becomes a conscious instrument of His will and power.

As an aid to their discipline, one should regularly study the Gītā with the help of Sri Aurobindo's soul-stirring interpretation and also do social service not as a charity, but as a worship of the Divine who is seated in all beings. 'The Yogin,' says the Lord, 'who has taken his stand upon oneness and loves Me in all beings, however and in all ways he lives and acts, lives and acts in Me.'[3] By serving our fellow men disinterestedly as a means of worshipping God, we shall realize our oneness with all, we shall find the one Self in all beings and that is the foundation of true love. 'A spiritual oneness which would create a psychological oneness not dependent upon any intellectual or outward uniformity and compel a oneness of life not bound up with its mechanical means of unification, but ready always to enrich its secure unity by a free inner variation and a freely varied outer self-expression, this would be the basis for a higher type of human existence.'[4]

---

[1] *Gītā*, IX, 26.   [2] *Ibid.*, IX, 27.   [3] *Ibid.*, VI, 31.
[4] Aurobindo, *The Ideal of Human Unity*, p. 323.

21

JAY R. McCULLOUGH

The Integral Approach in Sri Aurobindo and Jacob Boehme[1]

FROM time to time and from age to age, there have arisen men of far-reaching vision and deep insight into that which may be termed the realm of spirituality. The degree and approach toward integrality of this vision and insight appear to be varied, and the reports given by these witnesses of the experienced Fact also exhibit an apparent variability, strained as they have been through the individual capabilities of the seer-sages and the cultural-semantic environment within which they developed. We need not marvel, however, at this divergence, for that is within the realm of logical expectation. What truly is remarkable is the factor of *identity* running through the evidence like an eternal organ-point upon whose body play and dance the ever-changing Kāli-figures of fugue and counterpoint which, as accidents, embellish it—and even these 'figures' exhibit recurrent patterns and nuances of similarity. Examples of this similarity-in-difference are many, and any choice of personalities as subjects for a discussion involves a certain amount of arbitrary decision; for the 'seed of grandeur'[2] eternally is buried

---

[1] For simplicity and as a matter of personal preference the view-point of, and translations from, the works of Boehme are from Howard H. Brinton, *The Mystic Will* (New York: The Macmillan Co., 1930). Brinton bases his references upon the Schiebler edition of Boehme's works, in seven vols., Leipzig, 1843.

[2] Aurobindo, *Savitri*, p. 6:

> 'Ablaze upon creation's quivering edge,
> Dawn built her aura of magnificent hues
> And buried its seed of grandeur in the hours.'

Howard H. Brinton, *op. cit.*, p. 118, a quotation from Boehme, *The Threefold Life*, 6, 5: 'If you make a little circle as small as a grain of seed, so the whole birth of the eternal nature is therein and also the Trinity.'

within the flux of time and the fruits born of its eternal evolvement, through and as the manifold, are rich, varied and far-flung.

Any attempt to portray within the limited framework of a short article the spiritual genius of two men such as Jacob Boehme and Sri Aurobindo, carries with it the necessity to speak in generalities, in headlines which cannot bear the light of accurate comparison. An academic, comparative study, however, is not the purpose here. The aim, rather, is to indicate in an appreciative manner certain meaningful harmonics which may serve to yoke in integrality the views of the relatively untutored sage of Görlitz and the richly endowed and highly educated seer-philosopher (ṛṣi) of Pondicherry, separated as they are by time, geography and the conceptual imagery involved in cultural and personal differences. In addition, there is no wish to posit any thesis of causality as existing between the two points of view, nor to draw any definite conclusions as to the comparative values of the two philosophies.

Both the voluntaristic mysticism of Boehme and the integral idealism of Sri Aurobindo portray a cosmic drama wherein the ineffable basis of supreme Reality is involved as a darkly buried seed of unseen and unseeing light which evolves by the triple play of opposites (sharing here with other philosophical systems the motif of thesis, antithesis and synthesis) through its inseparable forms and ever higher levels or planes of manifestation which emerge from the murky depths of the 'unconscious' into the clear awareness and concrete experience of transforming divine light, power, or truth-consciousness. In each case, however, the ascent of the spirit to transcendence is not the end or final resting place of the journey. It is but the median-station, the illuminative point of transformation. Neither in Boehme nor in Sri Aurobindo is there a place for world denial or the obliteration of the true individuality of man. Each sage, in his own way, refuses to negate an apparent dualism by overtly abolishing one of the terms. Each, again in his own way, affirms not only the divine triune ground itself, but the world and the individual as well, not in the purely egoical sense, but integrally emergent as all-of-a-piece with and fulfilled in Reality itself. For Boehme the soul is reborn from darkness to light, yet the 'limitation' is not banished but becomes transmuted, as it were, through the fiery experience in the light as a meaningful vehicle or basis for the light's free manifestation. In a somewhat similar vein Sri Aurobindo in another fashion expresses not only the primal descent of the triune Divine into cosmic being, even unto the lowest reaches of materiality, but the ascent of man from egoity through levels of wider life, mind and spirit toward the Divine. Furthermore, he envisions a transforming centre of experience 'where mind and supermind meet'[1] which permits the liberating descent of that supermind through men to matter itself, transmuting and integrating all as a form of divine existence, consciousness-force, and bliss.

Thus both views of the cosmic drama may be said to pertain to the way of alchemy. Sri Aurobindo asks, 'By what alchemy shall this lead of mortality be turned into that gold of divine Being?'[2] and gives the answer by establishing as the heart of his yoga the pivotal, yet all-embracing, supermind as that which alone may transmute all of manifestation into life divine. Boehme wrote during a period of transition from the old traditional Hermetic philosophy to the beginnings of modern scientific thought. After Boehme, the two strains of German idealism and scientific methodology began their great flow into the present, but Boehme himself tended to express his vital and voluntaristic mysticism in the philosophical language and conceptual patterns of spiritual alchemy fused with certain elements of neo-platonism, gnosticism and the kabbala. Here the *prima materia*, the as yet unconscious possibility of embodiment, is acted upon and in turn interacts with the divine power at the 'heart of things',[3] the philosopher's stone or saviour. Thus there is set into motion from within a redemptive process to be traced through progressively higher 'stages' from the chaotic strife of materiality to the utmost perfection both of man and nature. Man, sharing with each element of nature its microcosmic-macrocosmic identity relationship, plays a deci-

---

[1] D. S. Sarma, *The Renaissance of Hinduism* (Benares: Benares Hindu University, 1944), p. 327, a quotation from Sri Aurobindo.

[2] Aurobindo, *The Life Divine*, p. 48; also cf. *Brihadāraṇyaka Upaniṣad*, I, 3, 28. [3] Brinton, *op. cit.*, p. 86.

sive part in carrying out the plan of salvation both in nature and himself. Through the ego-consuming fires of 'self-renunciation'[1] a new centre, the living stone of transformation, is found and the power of the stone is made to descend with its transmuting light through man and nature, even unto '. . . the darkness' depths'.[2] For Sri Aurobindo, also, the ego of and by itself is powerless both to effect the illuminative experience and the descent of transforming force. The true self of man, however, is not the ego but is the 'secret Purusha within'[3] us, the jīvātman as an undivided portion and eternal living power of the supreme Personality itself. It is the power of this true and original centre of man, the Self which lies 'in the heart of every being',[4] which *offers* the ego-surrender and the opening. It is this centre which 'evolves' or ascends into the harmonizing supermind experience of freedom and enlightenment and it is this same 'perfecting experience' which allows and permits the divine transmuting power or *śakti*[5] to descend through and as the now perfected centre of realization which may act as a conscious instrument for world transformation.[6]

It is to the core-centre wherein the seemingly dual movements of enlightenment and transformation are made possible that we must look for the very heart and spirit of the insight-philosophies of both sages. In Boehme's pattern or doctrine of the Seven Nature Forms that centre is the median-point, the Fourth Form or Transition Point where man's transformation is accomplished and, through him, the world-transformation into the Kingdom of Heaven is to be achieved. In Sri Aurobindo's pattern of being and becoming, the involution into matter of the ineffable Supreme, the nondual but three-in-one Saccidānanda, through the mediation of Supermind (the fourth or median-point) manifests the lower triune hemisphere of the mental, the vital and the physical as veritable harmonics of that omnipresent and absolute pure Existent (Sat) inseparable from absolute

---

[1] Brinton, *op. cit.*, p. 233. Cf. *tapoyajña* and *ātmasamarpaṇa*. Also *Gītā*, 18, 65–6.   [2] *Sāvitrī*, p. 5.

[3] Aurobindo, *Essays on the Gītā*, p. 201.   [4] *Gītā*, 10, 20.

[5] Brinton, *op. cit.*, pp. 183–202 (cf. the *Divine Virgin Sophia* of Boehme).

[6] Cf. the ideal of mahāpurusha as Chakravartin—also the chintamani, the transforming Stone or Jewel which turns all things toward the will of the Supreme.

Consciousness-Force (Cit) and absolute Delight or Bliss of Existence (Ānanda). In both patterns the *real* nonduality of the 'above' and the 'below' is figured—one from the background of the Emerald Tablet of *Hermes Trismegistus* and the other from the less cryptic integral insight of the *Vedas* and *Upaniṣads*. The coincidental movements of man's rise or ascent to total awakening and the descent of that transforming light-power into nature itself is traced upon the framework of these two rather similar pattern-forms.

In Sri Aurobindo the long journey of the soul[1] working upward through the dual form of its desire-self or surface expression encounters in its emergence and development recurrent dual stresses which are to be resolved by means of a higher and inner synthesis at each stage of its progress. Throughout the upward unfoldment and manifestation of the Divine, the story of opposition and its reconciliation, 'the stuff of which life is made', the solving of the fundamental discords arising anew on each level of existence, is a basic, cyclical theme.[2] The conflict between passive matter and the creativity of life is harmonized in the living world through the union of the material and the vital. Life and mind are united in the animal kingdom when mind is embodied in living matter. The manifestation of man makes possible a meaningful harmony between the sense mind and rational mind, and the opposition between the present level of man and the spirit is to be worked out in the human laboratory by the energies of superman. Just as a lotus works upward from the ooze of a lake bed through the opaque and murky veil of the surrounding waters, the mind as

---

[1] The psychic being or true, inner subliminal consciousness.
Savitri, p. 27:
> 'A spirit that is a flame of God abides
> . . . .
> Immortal in our mortal poverty.'

[2] *Ibid.*, p. 159: 'A contradiction founds the base of life:
The eternal, the divine Reality
Has faced itself with its own contraries;'

Ibid., p. 206: 'For Contradiction is her nature's law'.

Ibid., p. 381: 'A riddle of opposites is made his field:'

Also see *The Life Divine*, pp. 76–7; and Sri Aurobindo, *Letters of Sri Aurobindo* (Bombay: Sri Aurobindo Circle, 1947), pp. 14–15.

a microcosm bearing within it the image of the macrocosm works upward through higher mind (the truth thought), the illumined mind (the more immediate and intuitive truth light), the intuitive mind (the immediate perception of the image of true knowledge and action) into the highest reaches of the global or cosmic consciousness of overmind, past the transparent veil of the 'golden lid' marking the limit of the lower hemisphere into the fourth and central point of the journey, the *vijñānam* or supermind, the source and fountain-head of evolvement and transformation. Here all veils are removed and the interdependence of the two dynamic movements made manifest so 'That the eyes of the Timeless might look out from Time and world manifest the unveiled Divine'.

Boehme, in his doctrine of the Seven Nature Forms, depicts the ascent through the first three forms unto its culmination in the fourth, the point of transition and transformation, the centre for the return or descent back into nature.[1] In this pattern Boehme, in line with his vitalistic background, accentuates the dynamic volitional element. Here, also, the stress between two opposing wills of the primary, unseeing and unconditioned 'Abysmal Will' underlying the nature forms, finds its expression in nature. Seen from the 'outside' this activity or will is nature manifesting itself in all things, a force of attraction, repulsion and 'rotation' which, by resolving its series of inner conflicts, breaks through the 'bonds of nature into the higher consciousness'. Thus begins the evolving drama of Will striving within the processes of contradictions to know itself.[2] Two opposing types or ways of knowing, therefore, are (1) this negative, in-going, subjective point of view (*verstand*), a one-pointed will toward identity-knowledge, a 'resigned will' directed toward the infinite and ultimate primal unity of the

---

[1] These seven nature forms are interwoven in a basic manner throughout all of Boehme's major works, particularly in the *Aurora*. They are stressed in Brinton, *op. cit.*, pp. 131–66 and 232–54.

[2] In his *Essays on the Gītā*, p. 202, Sri Aurobindo states that the will in nature is only a partial, modified reflection of the will of the free Self. It is that reflection in successive moments of time and is only imperfectly conscious. 'But the Will within, exceeding the moments of Time, knows all these, and the action of Nature in us is an attempt, we might say, to work out under the difficult conditions of a natural and egoistic ignorance what is foreseen in full supramental light by the inner Will and Knowledge.'

Abyss from which multiplicity arises and, (2) that out-going objective will (*vernunft*) directed in a 'positive', rational and logical manner toward knowing the external and historical, the multiple which finds its universal term in the unity, a self-assertive action (in contradistinction to the self-surrendering action of *verstand*) to grasp and control multiple phenomena rather than reality-in-itself. From the interpenetrations and reconciliations of these flows arises meaning within both man and nature—for here the stresses separating man and nature-centred wills are dissolved through the experience which witnesses the meeting of *vernunft* in its logical development from the multiple to the unity, with *verstand* in its *understanding* of the unity which, in its freedom, bears within it all possibility of multiplicity. The element of *exclusiveness*, though, the out-going will manifested in crystallized philosophical and religious concepts or systems which oppose any reconciliation, must be eliminated. 'Throw away your outer reason', says Boehme, 'so is your will God's will and God's spirit will seek you in you.'[1] Thus the dual temporal will is resolved, progressively, through appropriate stages toward a common goal, the one eternal will which also is the source. Reason, far from being abolished, is now the 'dwelling, the localization in space and time', of the *verstand*,[2] the outward, inseparable and nondual expression of the deeper inward insight. The objectification or determination of the will[3] arises from a process of 'imagination' or creative visualization mutually reactive with the will's inner contractions, and the recurrent poises of reconciliation or temperature of the determinate will form life stages of a progressive higher unity unfolding from the will's opposition to itself. Although described linearly, this movement is to be conceived as a circular process of the threefold will in thesis, antithesis and synthesis.

The divine imagination or plan of creation arising from the first creative movement was personified by Boehme as a wisdom or 'inherent structure' known as the Virgin Sophia—

---

[1] Brinton, *op. cit.*, p. 125; cf. *Gītā*, 18, 66.

[2] *Ibid.*, *op. cit.*, p. 101; cf. *Iśa Upanishad* 1.

[3] *Ibid.*, *op. cit.*, p. 109. Here Brinton parallels Schopenhauer's 'objectification of the will' with Boehme's 'imagination'. See also pp. 76, 77, 108, 118, 141, 197 and 220.

that which is discovered through the will's primal objectification of itself and which is projected in the out-going will as
determinitive of all action.[1]

The stage now is set in the drama of life as it follows the
'upward spiral' through Boehme's pattern of the seven forms.
Prior to nature and its first form the divine Absolute as
Ungrund,[2] the eternally ineffable and undifferentiated 'God' as
the groundless, indeterminate will (the Father) is an activity
('a will to seek itself') which divides circularly into opposites,
the in-going 'conceived will' as the Son wherein the *Father*
knows himself, and the out-going will-to-project creatively
through the Son as the Spirit, thus forming an esoteric, ideal
or subjective trinity. This unmanifested trinity of possibilities
becomes in the seven forms a manifested, objective trinity
within which the primordial 'Father' becomes the dark or as
yet unknown world of nature and the ideal 'Son' the light
world wherein the 'Father' is known. Through Boehme's seven
nature forms, the eternal unmanifested will is realized objectively both in the modes of the visible and the invisible, the
temporal and the eternal.[3] While presented logically in
sequence they are in reality interdependent with each other
and with the absolute will. Outwardly (*vernunft*) they form
the appearance of the physical, and inwardly (*verstand*) they
appear as the vital, dynamic and universal will-of-life itself.
The internal, then, is mirrored in the external which, 'in the
property of the generation of all forms' becomes a 'signature'[4]
of the inward Spirit.

For the purpose of a rough correlation, the functions of the
first three forms of Boehme, in which the physical predominates,

---

[1] Cf. the thirty-six *Tantratattvas*. See Sir John Woodroffe and P. N.
Mukhyopadhyaya, *Mahamaya* (Madras: Ganesh & Co., 1929), pp. 209–20,
and Woodroffe, *The Garland of Letters* (London: Luzae & Co. Ltd., 1951),
pp. 89–98.   [2] Cf. 'Creation Hymn', *Rig Veda*, 10, 129.

[3] Cf. the seven chakras of Kundalini Yoga, with the anāhata (hridpuruṣa)
as the fourth padma; the seven lokas and their relation with the Gāyatrī;
Katha, 6, 1; *Gītā*, 15, 1–3; *Mundaka*, 2, 1, 8.

[4] Brinton, *op. cit.*, p. 99 (from Boehme's *Signatura Rerum*, 1, 3).

Cf. lines from *Sāvitrī*, p. 86:

'. . . the signature and fiery seal
Of Wisdom on the dim Power's hooded work
Who builds in Ignorance the steps of Light.'

may be likened unto those of Sri Aurobindo's lower hemisphere, while the last four of the forms may be said to bear some correspondence to the upper hemisphere comprising Supermind and Saccidānanda, the integrator and transformer of the lower. The first of the seven nature forms is that of Contraction, the physical manifestation of unseeing Desire.[1] It is the primal desire or in-going *will-to-be*, the creative fiat contracted upon itself or *attracted* to itself, the origin of individuality and the darkness of separateness. This contraction cannot exist of and by itself, for it needs an opposing force. This, the second form, Expansion, is conceived in and by the frustration of the first as its outgoing reflex will grasping toward an impossible freedom outside of the Self. The tension resulting from the interaction of two equally opposing forces, this being torn between two conflicting wills, generates further frustration and darkness which, through the turning of desire upon desire (inward and outward) creates Rotation, the third form. Here is the wheel of life and death, of *saṁsāra*, turning hopelessly in existential anguish and rent by two desires seeking self-satisfaction. We approach, here, a twofold possibility of choice, either to deny one of the desires in a flight either from the world or the Spirit, or to find an integral meaning through a higher synthesis which (and here we borrow the terminology of Sri Aurobindo) unites an inward, introversive, self-opening into the depths of the subliminal (compare Christ's descent into hell) with the extroversive 'free soaring into the sky of the superconscious'.

Sri Aurobindo places Supermind in the intermediate or fourth place (*tūriya*) between the triplicity of world manifestation and the trinity of Saccidānanda. As such it is the connecting or unifying link between the absolute and the relative 'worlds' and it alone has and is the sovereign power of transformation. Similarly, Boehme's fourth nature form[2] is

---

[1] Cf. Greek Eros and Indian Kāma as the first of the Gods; also *Rig Veda*, 10, 29: 'Thereafter arose Desire in the beginning. Desire the primal seed and germ of spirit.'

[2] Suzuki describes the Zen-experience as 'Buddhahood, in which all the contradictions and disturbances caused by the intellect are entirely harmonized in a unity of a higher order'. Quoted by R. H. Blyth, *Zen in English Literature* (Tokyo: The Hokuseido Press, 1948), p. 5.

called the 'Transition Point', the place of rebirth into light, the principle of transmutation, where 'spirit acquires body and body acquires spirit' and life-manifestation arises to integral self-consciousness. At and through this point the dark lower ternary, the first three forms, becomes the higher, fiery ternary, the last three forms. Within this nondual point, however, Boehme speaks of three planes which have been called: (1) the sinking down to the point, or the resigned will, (2) the point or the abyss, and (3) the rising beyond the point, culminating in the integral realization of the Kingdom of Heaven or the seventh form.[1] Within this fourth form or point in the evolutionary process, there may be traced, then, an inward movement toward the depths of Being, a descent, as it were, into a 'hell' wherein the resigned and surrendered outer, subjective unity is shredded into anguished multiplicity; yet, in the deepest depths of this descent, there is found, if a surrender be complete, not 'hell' but the Absolute itself as the primal abyss. It is at this point, the core centre, that a new unity is fused out of the fractured many, an integral unity which flows outward or which rises to the transforming power and realization of the many in the one and the one in the many.

The 'sinking down to the point', also called the 'resigned will' or 'the cross', is related harmonically to the lower ternary of nature or self-will which first must be resigned or crucified in order to be reborn. In the first three forms the will has exercised its egoistic freedom to be bound and frustrated. Now, on the cross of acceptance or surrender through an equally free act of resignation it endures, if the resignation be perfect, the anguish or hell of ego-effacement and sinks deep into the fundamental subjectivity, the abyss or absolute will—the ineffable void (as in *śūnyatā*) from where it came.

This point (comparable to the Indian *bindu*, which is also the endless expanse of the ocean or *sindhu*), the neutral and static abyss of eternal freedom, the absolute will of the omnipotent Godhead, is the single portal through which man and all of

---

[1] Brinton, *op. cit.*, pp. 143–53. The triple movement within the fourth form is encountered throughout Boehme's works, particularly in the *Aurora, The Forty Questions, The Threefold Life, Signatura Rerum, The Six Points, Clavis*, and *Predestination*, according to Brinton.

manifestation pass to rebirth. Being infinite, the point also is boundless. As the centre and source of all meaning, it transforms relative ignorance-knowledge to truth-knowledge. It is the crossing point[1] from a partial view to 'God's view'. Here, following the agony of the 'sinking', life has descended beyond death to reach the uttermost depths of the ineffable absolute will to find therein true life itself, a transformed substance shining in its own light. The soul and nature, forced by the fruits of frustration into total acceptance-surrender, has gone within, has sunken into God as the abyss which, so to speak, meets it in a union of total completion. This union, however, is not one of an annihilation of individuality but, rather, is eternal freedom itself where the manifold, the many, experiences in clear awareness not only the mutual interdependence of its parts but also their essential and original harmony through the abstract, ideal wisdom of God, the Virgin Sophia.

Poised as it is between the two triads, 'where light and darkness divide',[2] the centre of the fourth form, this point or abyss, also is the point of freedom, the point of choice between the ternary of darkness and the ternary of light, between a return to dark ignorance or a conscious participation as an instrument of the divine in the transforming descent of the light into nature. If the darkness dominates the will, the surrender is not true and complete and the approach to the abyss is experienced as hell, spiritual rebirth fails to take place, and there is a return to the first three nature forms. If the light of transformation dominates the will, it becomes unitive, at one with the absolute will of the abyss which, from within, remains the fundamental unitive basis of all nature, just as it is prior to the evolvement of the seven forms. The reborn will now return to nature, not on its periphery, but from within, from the very ground of nature itself. Here it is in living identity with nature, based on the synthesis of a perfect freedom and an understanding, compassionate harmony. The will now sees with the eye of the eternal rather than the

[1] Cf. Mahāyāna Buddhism's doctrine of *Prajñāpāramitā* as the 'Crossing to the Other Shore'.

[2] Brinton, *op. cit.*, p. 146. See also p. 247. Cf. note 3, p. 225, *supra*.

temporal, and, in a flash of integral identity-knowledge, perceives the lower ternary, from within, as changed or transformed into the higher ternary, for the higher eternally is the lower seen integrally.[1] No change in substance is indicated, for the first three forms do not lose their identity as such; they now are seen in their true light as the unmanifested material basis, internally harmonized through the point of absolute will, for the higher ternary.

The subjective, static, mystical vision is not the end of the cycle, for the will has received a vision of the possibility of its fulfilment in the transforming process which grows out of the abyss. The vision now must be embodied, the transforming power experienced in the core centre of the fourth form now is brought into the realm of dynamic actuality and the living earth transfigured through the touch of divine life. From the abyss the integrative movement is 'upward' and the stage called 'rising up beyond the Point' is reached, for it is fulfilment itself, a fulfilment realized in the higher ternary which emerges from the fourth form. This ternary is: (5) Love, (6) Expression, and (7) the Kingdom of Heaven, and through the transfiguring power generated in the abyss, expresses eternal nature and its infinite love and wisdom. This is the new world, the new life as an incarnate resurrection of the old. Particularity is not abolished but becomes, instead, the body for the new transformation within an organic self-consciousness. The entire complex of the seven forms in this integral union compose eternal Nature, Absolute Will fully realized and objectified. This may be thought of as comparable, in its way, to the full descent of the Spirit in the Aurobindonian pattern and its culmination in the life divine. In this harmonization of the seven forms, man's will springs from a new centre, for it has become the will of God, and divine life is known, not through the outward rational knowledge, but by inward identity-knowledge (*verstand*). 'God must become man', says Boehme, 'man must become God, heaven must be one with the earth

---

[1] Brinton, *op. cit.*, p. 234. See also pp. 137, 146, 150, 213, 228, 239.
Such as the immediate, spontaneous, all-embracing satori of Zen, the non-verbal, nondualistic experience of the identity of Nirvāṇa and Saṁsāra.

and the earth must become heaven. Wouldst thou make heaven out of earth, then give the earth the food of heaven.'[1] When the will of man is merged inwardly with the light of the divine Will, man becomes an instrument of God's freedom, creating outwardly as God creates. Man, the new man, does not spurn the outer world of men and nature but acts as a divine means for its redemption, directing the inner divine light (met in the fourth nature form as a flash), 'into the dark places of the world'[2] and raising them to higher levels *in* the light *by* the light. It is by love, creatively determinate, that, in the words of Brinton, 'The whole comes down into nature as a harmonizing influence and the three struggling forces of nature, contraction, expansion, and rotation, are transformed into the last three nature forms, love, expression, and eternal nature, which incarnates the living God. Nature is now in temperature, for the parts act under the influence of the whole.'[3] The fifth form, Love (cf. Kripā and the Bodhisattva ideal), the transformation of 'attraction' (form 1) through the freedom of the abyss (form 4), is the cohesive or in-going power of the spiritual or higher ternary just as 'attraction' holds together the lower ternary. The sixth form, Expression (cf. Prajñā and the Bodhisattva ideal), arises through the union of 'expansion' (form 2) and the freedom of the abyss (form 4). It is associated with speech (logos, sphota, vāk), tone, sound, and understanding as *expressions* of love, harmonically extending it beyond the confines of cohesion. The seventh form, the Kingdom of Heaven, is the Diety incarnate, the will fully matured and integrated, the positive, crowning goal of the inseparable sevenfold process which, as eternal nature, the perfection of life, is the true synthesis of the one and the many. Reminiscent of the Īśa Upaniṣad, Boehme speaks of this as the 'substance of spirit which the spirit of God wears as a garment and within which He reveals Himself, otherwise His

---

[1] Brinton, *op. cit.*, p. 241, a quotation from Boehme's *Signatura Rerum*, 10, 48. Cf. *Sāvitrī*, p. 43: 'God found in Nature, Nature fulfilled in God.' Concerning the concept of 'food', cf. *Durgā* as *Annapurnā*, also *Annam Brahman* in *Brihadāraṇyaka Upaniṣad*, 5, 12; *Taittiriya Upaniṣad*, 2, 2, 3, 1, 3, 10, 2–6; *Taittiriya Brahamana*, 2, 8, 8.   [2] *Ibid.*, p. 222.

[3] *Ibid.*, p. 221. For a further consideration of 'temperature' as Harmony or Integrality, see pp. 145–52, 233.

form would not be known'.[1] But this is not the end, for the pattern of the mystic will is one of an eternal spiral. The entire cycle is to be reflected upon itself as the wisdom-mirror (Virgin Sophia) of a new manifestation of the Spirit, a continuation of the play between the internal and external within the pattern of thesis, antithesis and synthesis. It is this play which revolves in timeless, creative repetitions in the upward spiral toward the light which is its centre.

This all-too-inadequate sketch of Boehme's system as projected upon equally sketchy sections from the pattern of Sri Aurobindo's integral yoga admittedly has stressed the similarities existing between the visions of these two men of spiritual genius, for in the similitude itself lies that which bears witness to the thrilling universality of a message which spans and unites two cultures seemingly separated by time and geography. In the academic world of purely rational philosophic system-building such a similarity might tend to lessen the value of uniqueness so prized by some facets of traditional Western scholarship. In the case of spiritual insight, however, similarity well may be one of the hall-marks of that thread of unity integrating the outwardly varied records of spiritual experience left by seers throughout all ages and in all lands. It well may be said, and with a certain amount of justification, that the sage of Pondicherry pursued his wisdom deeper into the Truth and brought back into the everyday world a more comprehensive transformation. We also may say that the spirit of traditional Indian metaphysic served as a far richer cultural medium for the development and growth of such an all-embracing insight. But that, in this instance, is not the point. It is the light of similitude which casts its beam of illumination upon the one 'seed of grandeur' from which a tree of many branches and infinite leaves has grown, and the infinite variety of differences (and admittedly there are many profound differences existing in and apparently separating the two spiritual experience-patterns) provides charmingly interesting academic investigation problems which might serve

[1] Brinton, *op. cit.*, p. 156, a quotation from Boehme in *The Threefold Life*, 5, 50. See *Iśa Upaniṣad* 1.

to point up the rich possibilities inherent in any consideration of the many-in-the-one.

Experience of the *nondual* supreme Reality may be expressed in infinite and varied ways, and there appears to be no absolute justification for a claim that any one particular way or pattern, or one general mode of formulating patterns, constitutes the *only* way or *sâdhanā*. By this it is not at all to be inferred that each way is to be thought of as just as 'good' or 'true' as any other. It does imply, however, that in the play of similitude there is a basis for an inner similarity which unites the differing views of reality-experience, views which on their periphery appear even diametrically opposed and which show little or no 'sameness' in their approach. By this it is to be suggested that 'systematic' *sâdhanās* in themselves, no matter how integrally formulated, do not exhaust the possible ways by which the one and many are *fully* experienced as not being different in reality. In every formulation involving thesis, antithesis and synthesis, the synthesis itself may become a new thesis which engenders its own antithesis *ad infinitum*, and even the concept of transformation or transmutation as a supreme force integrating the opposites of materiality and spirituality may incur the semantic danger of re-establishing the One through the practical absorption of its opposition. Patterns, words, charts and philosophies in and by themselves, no matter how exact and intricate their make-up, cannot *contain* the Fact-vision of the seer himself. The greatest similitude may well be the integral and all-embracing Fact *behind* the pattern. The experience of the Fact, patternless, void and uncharted, but fully evident in the smallest fact of the everyday world, is the supreme witness. It is only when we have come face to face with this Fact that we can communicate truly with the sages of Görlitz and Pondicherry.

PART FOUR
LITERATURE

22

K. D. SETHNA

The Poet of Integralism

THE term 'integralism', in our treatment of Sri Aurobindo the poet, the wielder of an intense art-form, must go beyond the discovery of a special spiritual experience and vision which we may designate by it. It must connote primarily an integral style, an integral word-power to match that experience and vision. But this style and this word-power cannot be defined just by saying that the former is one which commands with consummate versatility divers modes and attitudes of speech and that the latter seizes articulately on all possible objects with a vivid intimacy as well as with a large sense of their interrelations within a world-harmony. We have also to speak in terms of 'planes' of expression. For, no matter how high or wide or deep the state of consciousness, how supra-intellectual the mystic's realization, the poetic expression may take the mould of the mere mind's manner of utterance, the moved imaginative speech proper to the plane distinguished by Sri Aurobindo as the creative intelligence which is no more than a particular intensified operation of the same mental conscious-ness we find in the bulk of human activities. Most poetry is written from the creative intelligence, though the founts of it are more inward, more secret than those of our habitual mental life. Rarely do those founts deliver not only the significance but also the very word and rhythm native to their greater inwardness and secrecy. Poetic integralism would lie in an expression springing straight from the highest, widest, deepest fount of spiritual experience and vision instead of getting shaped in the mere mind or even predominantly in the intermediate planes whose lights and shadows play in the usual universe of poetry.

How the style and word-power of the creative intelligence differs from the Aurobindonian expression which we may consider poetically integral can be concretely seen if we compare a few phrases collected from several sections of *Paradise Lost* with a few from the opening of Sri Aurobindo's epic, *Sāvitrī: A Legend and a Symbol*. Milton apostrophizes the Divine Spirit:

> Thou from the first
> Wast present, and with mighty wings outspread
> Dovelike sat'st brooding on the vast abyss
> And mad'st it pregnant.[1]

He also addresses the original spiritual Light:

> Bright effluence of bright essence increate!
> . . . .
> Before the Heavens thou wert, and at the voice
> Of God as with a mantle didst invest
> The rising world of waters dark and deep,
> Won from the void and formless infinite.[2]

About the advent of this illumination, we may quote him further in the verses:

> But now at last the sacred influence
> Of light appears, and from the walls of Heaven
> Shoots far into the bosom of the Night
> A glimmering dawn.[3]

He has depicted too an ethereal revelation, an entrance to God's grandeur, in the illumined distances:

> The work as of a kingly palace-gate,
> With frontispiece of diamond and gold
> Embellished; thick with sparkling orient gems
> The portal shone, inimitable on Earth
> By model, or by shading pencil drawn.[4]

[1] Milton, *Paradise Lost*, Book I (Macmillan & Co. Ltd., 1934), lines 19–22.
[2] *Ibid.*, Book III, lines 6, 9–12.   [3] *Ibid.*, Book II, lines 1034–7.
[4] *Ibid.*, Book III, lines 505–9.

Now look at *Sāvitrī*:

> The huge foreboding mind of Night, alone
> In her unlit temple of eternity,
> Lay stretched immobile upon Silence' marge.
> Almost one felt, opaque, impenetrable,
> In the sombre symbol of her eyeless muse
> The abysm of the unbodied Infinite;[1]
>
> . . . .
>
> A long lone line of hesitating hue
> Like a vague smile tempting a desert heart
> Troubled the far rim of life's obscure sleep.
> Arrived from the other side of boundlessness
> An eye of deity pierced through the dumb deeps;
>
> . . . .
>
> Intervening in a mindless universe,
> Its message crept through the reluctant hush
> Calling the adventure of consciousness and joy
> And, conquering Nature's disillusioned breast,
> Compelled renewed consent to see and feel.
> A thought was sown in the unsounded Void,
> A sense was born within the darkness' depths,
> A memory quivered in the heart of Time
> As if a soul long dead were moved to live:[2]
>
> . . . .
>
> Into a far-off nook of heaven there came
> A slow miraculous gesture's dim appeal.
> The persistent thrill of a transfiguring touch
> Persuaded the inert black quietude
> And beauty and wonder disturbed the fields of God.
> A wandering hand of pale enchanted light
> That glowed along a fading moment's brink,
> Fixed with gold panel and opalescent hinge
> A gate of dreams ajar on mystery's verge.[3]

The passages from Milton are blank verse in a philosophico-religious mood conveying strongly-cut imaged ideas in a tone of exalted emotion with the help of words that have a powerful stateliness and a rhythm that has a broad sweep. But Milton's substance, as Sri Aurobindo has pointed out in a letter, 'is,

---

[1] Aurobindo, *Sāvitrī*, p. 3.   [2] *Ibid.*, pp. 2–3.   [3] *Ibid.*, pp. 3–4.

except at certain heights, mental—mentally grand and noble'[1] and his 'architecture of thought and verse is high and powerful and massive, but there are usually no subtle echoes there, no deep chambers: the occult things in man's being are foreign to his intelligence.'[2] He may employ certain turns resembling Sri Aurobindo's and there is the largeness of breath which seems to make his suggestions break through the intellectual grip, yet on attending closely we miss the sheer spiritual vision going home to us with a vibrant vastness and stirring up in us an intuitive sense of mystical realities. Something in the rhythm remains unsupported by the sight and the word. God, Light, Infinity, Heaven do not reveal their own body, as it were, and do not utter themselves in their own tongue: they are reflected in the mental imagination and given forceful speech there. But because of the rhythm the critical ear is likely to be deceived about the mostly intellectual-imaginative quality of Milton and it is with this possibility in view that Sri Aurobindo, for all his admiration for the poetry of *Paradise Lost*, has warned a disciple-poet who wanted to write authentically of the supra-intellectual: 'The interference of this mental Miltonic is one of the great stumbling-blocks when one tries to write from "above".'[3]

What Sri Aurobindo here terms writing from 'above' is generally spoken of by him as 'overhead' poetry and described as an inspiration that is felt in yogic experience to be descending from some ether of self-existent consciousness extended boundlessly beyond the brain-clamped human mind. This overhead inspiration can come even when one is not a practising mystic, but then it manifests like a shining accident and is a rare note; Milton himself at times catches it suddenly and at least in one line he has it, according to Sri Aurobindo, at its highest pitch:

Those thoughts that wander through Eternity.[4]

Sri Aurobindo distinguishes a fourfold gradation of the

[1] Sri Aurobindo, *Life, Literature and Yoga* (Pondicherry: Sri Aurobindo Ashram, 1952), p. 38.
[2] *Letters of Sri Aurobindo*, third series (Bombay: Sri Aurobindo Circle, 1949), pp. 118–19.　　　　[3] Aurobindo, *Life, Literature and Yoga*, p. 38.
[4] Milton, *Paradise Lost*, Book II, line 148.

overhead planes as having acted so far in the world's literature on a few occasions: higher mind, illumined mind, intuition, overmind. On all these planes the experience of the Infinite is automatic and there is a light of direct knowledge of the universe's fundamental being and becoming. But the light varies in intensity. The higher mind is like a broad clear day revealing through a spiritual rather then intellectual thought the divine substance and its multiform activity: it is, as it were, the arche-type of the mental Miltonic, the plane active behind Milton's grand style but unable to send its own spiritual stuff of thought in an authentic shape and motion through his genius. The illumined mind is more a luminous seeing than a luminous thinking: it is a play of spiritual sight, the divine secrecies are disclosed through a crowd of colourful yet subtle images in a swift or slow design with thought as a subordinate element. One may say it is the plane active behind Shakespeare's leap and coruscation and felicitous ingenuity of the life-force but mostly translated into vivid passion and sensation and idea-impulse instead of being transmitted in its multi-toned seerhood of divine values. Intuition is not what usually passes by that name, a quick abbreviated movement of thought itself or a rapid seizing through the vital drive: it is a profound penetration into the essence of things by a spontaneous inner intimacy on a superhuman level. It differs from the illumined mind in that it is a flash by which divine realities bare themselves rather than are bared by a flood of illumination thrown upon them. Heart-beat upon essential heart-beat of Truth is felt more than Truth's opulent limb-gesture and robe-undulation. Intuition is at work behind the revealing reticence that is the Dantesque utterance, only, the style of the decisive sparing stroke in *La Divina Commedia* mostly converts into a mental incisiveness the sheer piercing Truth-touch. Even in that touch, however, the direct knowledge is not complete; the whole sense of the divine being and becoming is not caught in pure identity. The entire directness is really the privilege of the supermind, the sovereign truth-consciousness that is the special dynamic of the Aurobindonian yoga, but a radiant representative of it is possessed by the overmind which is what the world has hitherto known as the extreme Godhead. Also, the overmind vision, word and rhythm are at once intense and immense to the utmost. The line of poetry charged with them carries vastly a movement as if from everlasting to everlasting— thought, image, expression, vibration bear a value and a form in which all the qualities of the other planes fuse in something diversely ultimate and variously transfigured by an inmost oneness with the cosmic harmony and with the supracosmic mystery. The voice of the overmind is the *mantra*, the eternal word spoken of and sought for by the Vedic Ṛṣis.

The typical mark of the passages quoted from Sri Aurobindo is the general overhead atmosphere breathing one or another level, either distinctly or in combination, and everywhere a lift towards the *mantra*, culminating now and again in that sovereign speech itself. The higher mind inspiration passes distinctly through

> The huge foreboding mind of Night, alone[1]

and mixes with that of the illumined mind in

> An eye of deity pierced through the dumb deeps[2]

and is replaced completely by it with

> A slow miraculous gesture's dim appeal.[3]

The illumined mind works up to the intuition in the phrases about the 'gold panel and opalescent hinge'[4] fixed by the wandering hand of dawn-glamour, and blends exquisitely with the intuitive revelation in

> A gate of dreams ajar on mystery's verge.[5]

We may note also something of the ineffable amplitude that is the overmind's power in all the lines, a pervading influence which perhaps looms out most undeniably in another verse:

> The abysm of the unbodied Infinite.[6]

It is not always easy to distinguish the overhead style or to get perfectly the drift of its suggestion. There must be as much

---

[1] Aurobindo, *Sāvitrī*, p. 3.   [2] *Ibid.*, p. 5.   [3] *Ibid.*, p. 5.
[4] *Ibid.*, p. 6.   [5] *Ibid.*, p. 6.   [6] *Ibid.*, p. 3.

as possible a stilling of ourselves, an in-drawn hush ready to listen to the uncommon speech; and we must help the hush to absorb successfully that speech by repeatedly reading the poetry aloud, since it is primarily through the rhythm that the psychological state with which overhead verses are a-thrill echoes within us, quickening the eye to open wider and wider on spiritual secrecies and the brain to acquire a more and more true reflex of the transcendental that is the truth of things, waiting for manifestation.

The truth of things, however, need not always be concerned with the occult and spiritual and we should by ready to perceive the overhead utterance, even the *mantra*, in a delineation of earthly matters. Of course, Sri Aurobindo could not be loyal to his revelatory mission if *Sāvitrī* did not give wide scope to the occult and spiritual themselves, and with the vision and rhythm proper to the summits, seek to poetize them—either

> The superconscient realms of motionless peace
> Where judgment ceases and the word is mute
> And the Unconceived lies pathless and alone,[1]

or the domains of divine dynamism, either the solitary Unmanifest or the 'Wisdom-Splendour, Mother of the universe'—

> O radiant fountain of the world's delight
> World-free and unattainable above,
> O Bliss who ever dwellst deep hid within
> While men seek thee outside and never find[2]

either the levels and beings of the mid-worlds or the mysteries and travails of cosmic evolution, like that dreadful commerce of Sāvitrī with one to whom Sri Aurobindo gives no name:

> One dealt with her who meets the burdened great
> . . . .
> Assigner of the ordeal and the path
> Who uses in this holocaust of the soul
> Death, fall and sorrow for the spirit's goods,
> The dubious Godhead with his torch of pain
> Lit up the chasm of the unfinished world
> And called her to fill with her vast self the abyss.[3]

[1] Aurobindo, *Sāvitrī*, p. 39.   [2] *Ibid.*, p. 390.   [3] *Ibid.*, p. 21.

Yes, *Sāvitrī* would hardly be the unique poem that it is if it did not try in passages like these to bring home to us the Unknown as it is in itself. However, it is a poem of many layers and no mean part of its excellence lies in its deploying the imponderables of sight and sound and remaining intensely spiritual even when its innumerable ranges and changes are not ostensibly concerned with spirituality. It is legend as well as symbol, a story with many scenes and levels of development at the same time that it is instinct with a mystical light. That light itself plays over many regions and does not fail to cover most aspects of world-thought.

There is a variety not only of matter but also of style in *Sāvitrī*. The double phenomenon may be illustrated in several ways. The Homeric note of simplicity and depth is struck:

> But Narad answered not; silent he sat,
> Knowing that words are vain and Fate is lord.[1]

The Virgilian accent of dignity and poignancy reaches us:

> His words were theirs who live unforced to grieve
> And help by calm the swaying wheels of life
> And the long restlessness of transient things.[2]

Homer and Virgil combine in an Aurobindonian *tertium quid:*

> Bear: thou shalt find at last thy road to bliss.
> Bliss is the secret stuff of all that lives.[3]

The descent as of a beatific Beatrice into the Inferno, untouched by its flames, is felt with a typical Dantesque brevity of suggestion at the end:

> His steps familiar with the lights of heaven
> Tread without pain the sword-paved courts of hell;
> There he descends to edge eternal joy.[4]

There are glimpses of Nature's moods, coming with a powerful haunting evocation as in that transference into English of a phrase of Vyasa:

> some lone tremendous wood
> Ringing for ever with the crickets' cry,[5]

[1] Aurobindo, *Sāvitrī*, p. 480.   [2] *Ibid.*, pp. 484–5.
[3] *Ibid.*, p. 514.   [4] *Ibid.*, p. 668.   [5] *Ibid.*, p. 437.

or with an exquisite profundity that hints at the whole secret of art-expression:

> I caught for some eternal eye the sudden
> Kingfisher flashing to a darkling pool.[1]

Glimpses of the human situation mix often with those of natural objects, as in that simile cosmically sublime in its sweep:

> As a star uncompanioned moves through heaven
> Unastonished by the immensities of space,
> Travelling infinity by its own light,
> The great are strongest when they stand alone.[2]

The inner strength of the great is also made intimately vivid in that gesture of Sāvitrī when, confronting Death's subtle arguments and refusing to employ the frail artifices of Reason, which are vain because always open to doubt, she chooses to match all fate with the nude dynamism of her heart and soul in a terrific line which we may term, in a phraseology popular today, superexistentialist:

> I am, I love, I see, I act, I will.[3]

Here is an utterance deriving its force and resolution from deeper layers of being than the famous close in Tennyson's poem about Ulysses and his comrades:

> Made weak by fate and time, but strong in will
> To strive, to seek, to find, and not to yield.[4]

Those deeper layers render Sri Aurobindo's line more effective art than also Shelley's memorable words put into the mouth of Rousseau's ghost in his *Triumph of Life*:

> Before thy memory,
> I feared, loved, hated, suffered, did and died.[5]

The insufficiency of the mere reason as compared either to

[1] Aurobindo, *Sāvitrī*, p. 458.   [2] *Ibid.*, pp. 522–3.   [3] *Ibid.*, p. 671.
[4] *Poems of Tennyson*, 1830–1870 (Oxford University Press, 1943), p. 183.
[5] Carlos Baker, ed., *The Selected Poetry and Prose of Percy Bysshe Shelley* (New York: Modern Library College Editions, 1951), p. 349.

the inner soul's moved perception or to the puissant supra-
intellectual sight is pictured with an inspired conceit the
Elizabethans or the Metaphysicals would have welcomed with
a whoop:

> A million faces wears her knowledge here
> And every face is turbaned with a doubt.[1]

As unexpectedly striking and happy, though in a different key
of inspiration, is the simile applied to the truth-direct ways of
the higher harmonies of consciousness to which Sāvitrī's father
Aśwapathy climbed:

> There was no gulf between the thought and fact,
> Ever they replied like bird to calling bird.[2]

The felicity and the novelty that are prominent features of
Sri Aurobindo's style in *Sāvitrī* take at times a compact,
strangely figured epigrammatic form heightened as well as
enlightened the more by being immediately followed by a verse
of simple surprise:

> Earth's winged chimeras are Truth's steeds in Heaven,
> The impossible God's sign of things to be.[3]

Ancient motifs and motifs of our own day are equally caught
up by the integral inspiration. Even modern totalitarianism is
seized in its essence in the occult figure of it that from demoniac
planes behind earth precipitates amongst us the Hitlerite
power and propaganda:

> A bull-throat bellowed with its brazen tongue;
> Its hard and shameless clamour filling space
> And threatening all who dared to listen to truth
> Claimed the monopoly of the battered ear;
> A deafened acquiescence gave its vote,
> And braggart dogmas shouted in the night
> Kept for the fallen soul once deemed a god
> The pride of its abysmal absolute.[4]

---

[1] Aurobindo, *Sāvitrī*, p. 285.   [2] *Ibid.*, p. 371.
[3] *Ibid.*, p. 60.   [4] *Ibid.*, p. 245.

Even the new physics that has replaced the classical concepts in which 'all was precise, rigid, indubitable' enters the poetry:

> Once more the world was made a wonder-web,
> A magic's process in a magical space,
> An unintelligible miracle's depths
> Whose source is lost in the Ineffable
> ....
> A quantum dance remained, a sprawl of chance
> In Energy's stupendous tripping whirl
> ....
> The rare-point sparse substratum Universe
> On which floats a solid world's phenomenal face.
> Alone a process of events was there
> And Nature's plastic and protean change
> And, strong by death to slay or to create,
> The riven invisible atom's omnipotent force.[1]

But here too the accent is recognizably Aurobindonian. The overhead breath flows everywhere and in the last line we have its art at top pitch. The craftsmanship of that line is superb, with its dense humming sound dextrously mixed with other expressive vibrations, and all moving in a metre packing fourteen syllables and a predominantly anapaestic run into a scheme of five strong stresses which are helped to beat out clearly as well as to contain the overflowing music by massed consonants in several places. The four 'i' s and the four 'o' s suggest at once penetration and expansion, the latter as if from an all-round fastness. The 'v' in 'riven', pronounced as it is with the upper teeth touching the lower lip, aids the sense of cutting that is in the word, while the 'v' in 'invisible' not only supports and increases the cutting suggestion but also hints by occurring in that particular word and in the midst of several syllables successively short in quantity the marvellous carrying of the power of fission into the mystery of the infinitesimal that constitutes the unseen atomic nucleus. Then there are the two 'm' s with their movement of lip-closure corresponding to the closed secrecy that is being spoken of and they are preceded and followed by the labials 'b' and 'p' respectively

[1] Aurobindo, *Sāvitrī*, pp. 288-9.

267

which correspond to the initial motive of breaking open the closed secrecy and to the final accomplishment of that explosion. The hard strokes of the three 't' s mingle a further nuance of breaking. The 'f' of 'force' picks up again the fission-power of the 'v' s and completes it with its own acute out-loosening sound accompanied by the somewhat rolled sibilance at the end. The sibilance itself, giving clear body to the softer sound of the pair of 's' s earlier in the line achieves the idea of a full escape of the power that was so far not sweeping out of the charmed circle, as it were, of the atom's vibrant energy.

Indeed, the craftsmanship of the line is superb, but its success is different from what most poets might have attained, for it is due to the choice and collocation of particular words so as to create a particular rhythm embodying the vision-thrill of an overhead consciousness. One could be grandly resonant or else deploy a crowded colourful strength and prove a perfect poet thereby, yet fail to charge one's utterance with that vision-thrill—especially when it is a question of infusing into verses about apparently non-mystical subjects the very *enthousiasmos* of the *mantra*. Sri Aurobindo succeeds everywhere because he not only is familiar both as mystic and artist with the magnitudes and intensities of our subliminal and supraliminal being, but has also endeavoured to lay on the poor dust of the outer self 'the high Transcendent's sunlike hands'. Man's earth-born heart is never forsaken by him and it is shown, on the one side, the misery with which it falls short of the Infinite, and, on the other, the apocalyptic fulfilment here and now that is possible to it. And the fulfilment is again and again depicted in terms which go home to us and which set forth in a colossal clarity the eternal in the movements of time. For, Sri Aurobindo did not write his epic of 23,813 lines with the disposition of either a sworn surrealist wedded to the obscurely entangled or a strict symbolist cherishing a cult of the glimmering elusive. Behind the poet in him is the master of the integral yoga whose work, however distant on occasion from familiar experience, was to enlighten and not to puzzle and who, for all his roots in India's hoary past of spirituality, was yet a modern among the moderns and the seer of a new mystical progression, a collective advance in dynamic consciousness from mind to supermind, a whole

world evolving Godwards and breaking the fetters not only of
political or social tyranny but also of mortal ignorance. A
democracy of the Divine liberating the human was his goal, as
in those words he puts into the mouth of his Sāvitrī:

> A lonely freedom cannot satisfy
> A heart that has grown one with every heart:
> I am a deputy of the aspiring world,
> My spirit's liberty I ask for all.[1]

[1] Aurobindo, *Sāvitrī*, p. 728.

23

ARABINDA BASU

The Integration of Spiritual Experience

ALL problems of life are problems of harmony. This is the key-note of Sri Aurobindo's *weltanshaüung*. His world-view neces-sarily includes a practical ideal of life. For an integral philosophy must be not only a statement about the nature of Reality but must also give concrete direction for the realization of an abso-lute value. Otherwise its title to being integral will be false. Similarly the ideal of life in such a philosophy must be realizable. If not, it will not be a truly harmonious philosophy. According to Sri Aurobindo, at any rate, a philosophy, the principles of which cannot be tested and proved right and true in experience, is barren. It may be brilliant in its dialectic and a marvel of system-building. But it cannot be described as integral. Sri Aurobindo's own philosophy lays great stress on reconciliation between different points of view, between theory and practice, between metaphysic and ethic in the broad sense of the realization of a spiritual ideal.

This does not mean that the philosophy of Sri Aurobindo is syncretic. No, it is rather the unfoldment of a central vision which subsumes under it the viewpoints of different philo-sophies. It is integral in the sense that the basic truths of most of the important systems of thought find their proper places in its own scheme of the truths of existence and life. For one thing the integral idealism of Sri Aurobindo is a truly spiritual philosophy. Its material is provided by a developing pattern of spiritual experiences and realizations. When we say spiritual experience, we do not exclude the experience of senses and the intellect. For however much they may distort and fall short of the spiritual view of things, Sri Aurobindo's concept of Spirit is such that it is the creative force of the Spirit that becomes all that appears as non-spiritual. It is true that the Spirit is not hemmed in by the body, life-force and the mind. But it is the power of the Spirit which sustains these apparently non-spiritual elements of our nature. Spirit itself is free from the limitations, both existential and functional. The Spirit is eternal, uncreated, self-become, being and consciousness and self-existent delight. As consciousness, it is self-revealing. In other words, it is self-consciousness. This capacity of the Reality for self-consciousness is called consciousness-force (cit) by Sri Aurobindo. It is this consciousness-force which manifests itself as centres of the Spirit's self-knowledge and self-enjoyment. These sparks of the Spirit-flame, these centres of the conscious Reality, are the individual selves.

The individual selves are the intermediate links between the inalienable unity of the Divine and the multiplicity of this world in which unity is almost a chimera. The jivātman, the individual self, is not involved in the evolutionary world. Something of its essence, a portion of its being as it were, is the conscious soul here on the earth. At the beginning it is hidden in the sheaths of the body, life-force and mind and as such ineffective. But it awakens to its spiritual nature and destiny. It can however realize its relationship with the Reality in diverse manner. The different religions of the world and the many spiritual philosophies within the fold of Hinduism are partial expressions and rational statements respectively of one or more of these experiences of the nature and ultimate destiny of the evolving soul in its approach to the supreme Reality. In the integral philosophy of Sri Aurobindo, all manner of realizations are set forth in a systematic way; the spiritual seeker must have all these different realizations if he wants to know God in all his aspects. The total realization must include elements of knowledge, love and will. One must know the ultimate Absolute, love the divine Lord and Master, and surrender one's will to the supreme Will. This however is not a new ideal in Indian philosophy. The originality of Sri Aurobindo lies in this, that he considers this reconciliation of different types of realization to be the basis of the integral experience which he himself advocates. The soul having realized God has to found the life divine on earth. The trans-

formation of nature and life in the world is the realization
which he proposes as the integral ideal of man. That is the
consummation.

In this brief article we shall essay a brief exposition, mostly
in Sri Aurobindo's own words, of the spiritual saga of the
individual soul as presented in his *Last Poems*. The individual
soul is the most important category in Sri Aurobindo's system
of spiritual pragmatism from the point of view of the actual
realization of the implications of his metaphysic. For the
individual soul is the repository of all experiences, both
spiritual and non-spiritual. It is the soul that is steeped in the
mire of matter, it is the soul again which rises to the supernal
heights of the Divine.

This brings us to the question of the nature of man. In the
poems under study, Sri Aurobindo unfolds the philosophy of
the psychic being in terms of his own experience, as the representative individual soul, as it were.

> I am a centre of Thy golden light
>   And I its vast and vague circumference,
> Thou art my soul great, luminous and white
>   And Thine my mind and will and glowing sense.
>
> Thy spirit's infinite breath I feel in me;
>   My life is a throb of Thy eternity.[1]

Nay, more. Our poet declares

>   And yet I know my footprints' track shall be
>   A pathway towards Immortality.[2]

But let us follow the soul's journey from the starting point,
i.e. from his ordinary human status. What is man?

> A trifling unit in a boundless plan
>   Amidst the enormous insignificance
>   Of the unpeopled cosmos's fire-whirl dance,
> Earth, as by accident engendered man.
>
> A creature of his own grey ignorance,
>   A mind half-shadow and half-gleam, a breath
>   That wrestles, captive in a world of death,
> To live some lame brief years.[3]

[1] Sri Aurobindo, *Last Poems* (Pondicherry: Sri Aurobindo Ashram, 1952),
p. 28.   [2] *Ibid.*, p. 5.   [3] *Ibid.*, p. 47.

He is only

> a transience of the eternities.[1]

And yet there is something in man which defies mere transience.

> I with repeated life death's sleep surprise;
> I am a transience of the eternities.[2]

But is man's destiny just to be drowned in the sleep of death and again rise on the crest of life? Is he only fated to enjoy a little respite in a ceaseless flux? Not so, for the poet says that there is

> . . . a divinity within,
>   A consciousness in the inconscient Night,
>   To realize its own supernal Light
> Confronts the ruthless forces of the Unseen.[3]

Indeed,

> There are two beings in my single self.
>   A Godhead watches Nature from behind
> At play in front with a brilliant surface elf,
>   A time-born creature with a human mind.[4]

What is the nature of the two beings? One of them is spiritual, the other purely human which knows nothing of its divine origin.

> Tranquil and boundless like a sea or sky,
>   The Godhead knows himself Eternity's son.
> Radiant his mind and vast, his heart as free;
>   His will is a sceptre of dominion.
>
> The smaller self by Nature's passions driven,
>   Thoughtful and erring learns his human task;[5]

Because of these two beings man is a despot of the contraries. In the spheres of knowledge, will and emotions, he sways between the true and the false, strength and weakness, right and wrong, pleasure and pain. He even feels himself in contact

---

[1] Aurobindo, *Last Poems*, p. 43.   [2] *Ibid.*, p. 43.
[3] *Ibid.*, p. 47.   [4] *Ibid.*, p. 21.   [5] *Ibid.*, p. 21.

with God and yet in his nature contradicts the divinity within.

> I am greater than the greatness of the seas
>   A swift tornado of God-energy:
> A helpless flower that quivers in the breeze
>   I am weaker than the reed one breaks with ease.
>
> I harbour all the wisdom of the wise
>   In my nature of stupendous Ignorance;
> On a flame of righteousness I fix my eyes
>   While I wallow in sweet sin and join hell's dance.
>
> My mind is brilliant like a full-orbed moon,
>   Its darkness is the caverned troglodyte's.
> I gather long Time's wealth and squander soon;
>   I am an epitome of opposites.[1]

The soul, however, discovers its deathless being and that new knowledge opens the way to the transcendence of this duality.

> I have discovered my deep deathless being:
>   Masked by my front of mind, immense, serene
> It meets the world with an Immortal's seeing,
>   A god-spectator of the human scene.
>
> No pain and sorrow of the heart and flesh
>   Can tread that pure and voiceless sanctuary.
> Danger and fear, Fate's hounds, slipping their leash
>   Rend body and nerve—the timeless Spirit is free.
>
> Awake, God's ray and witness in my breast,
>   In the undying substance of my soul
> Flamelike, inscrutable the almighty Guest.
>   Death nearer comes and Destiny takes her toll;
>
> He hears the blows that shatter Nature's house:
> Calm sits he, formidable, luminous.[2]

The poet now feels that

> There is a need within the soul of man
>   The splendours of the surface never sate;[3]

[1] Aurobindo, *Last Poems*, p. 43.   [2] *Ibid.*, p. 25.   [3] *Ibid.*, p. 13.

His contact with the Guest, even though not yet very close, enables him to withstand the ordinary sensations of life.

> I am held no more by life's alluring cry,
>   Her joy and grief, her charm, her laughter's lute.
>   Hushed are the magic moments of the flute,
> And form and colour and brief ecstasy.
>
> I would hear, in my spirit's wideness solitary
>   The Voice that speaks when mortal lips are mute:
>   I seek the wonder of things absolute
> Born from the silence of Eternity.[1]

The soul's aspiration for things of eternity is a process which is fulfilled in the experience of liberation. The poet feels his identity with the unnameable Reality, he becomes what before time he was:

> My mind, my soul grow larger than all Space;
>   Time founders in that vastness glad and nude:
> The body fades, an outline, a dim trace,
>   A memory in the spirit's solitude.
>
> . . . .
>
> In the thrilled happy giant void within
>   Thought lost in light and passion drowned in bliss,
> Changing into a stillness hyaline,
>   Obey the edict of the Eternal's peace.
>
> Life's now the Ineffable's dominion;
> Nature is ended and the spirit alone.[2]

The self's infinity is now his status.

> I have become what before Time I was.
>   A secret touch has quieted thought and sense:
> All things by the agent Mind created pass
>   Into a void and mute magnificence.
>
> . . . .
>
> A momentless immensity pure and bare,
> I stretch to an eternal everywhere.[3]

[1] Aurobindo, *Last Poems*, p. 13.   [2] *Ibid.*, p. 31.   [3] *Ibid.*, p. 20.

The timeless Self, however, says one of the Upaniṣads, desired for a second, it willed, it went forth. This is the movement of the Self's conscious-force as will to be the world. This is the Absolute as the lord and master of whom this world is the habitation. Our poet as the aspiring soul has realized his identity with the worldless Self. The next step in his journey is the experience of unity with the divine Lord.

> He is in me, round me, facing everywhere.
>   Self-walled in ego to exclude His right,
> I stand upon its boundaries and stare
>   Into the frontiers of the Infinite.
>
> Each finite thing I see is a façade;
>   From its windows looks at me the Illimitable.
> In vain was my prison of separate body made;
>   His occult presence burns in every cell.
>
> He has become my substance and my breath;
>   He is my anguish and my ecstasy.
> My birth is His eternity's sign, my death
>   A passage of His immortality.
>
> My dumb abysses are His screened abode;
> In my heart's chamber lives the unworshipped God.[1]

His unity with the omnipresent reality enables him to expand his consciousness to embrace everything in the world. Cosmic consciousness is now his natural way of seeing.

> I have wrapped the wide world in my wider self
>   And Time and Space my spirit's seeing are.
> I am the god and demon, ghost and elf,
>   I am the wind's speed and the blazing star.
>
> All Nature is the nursling of my care,
>   I am its struggle and the eternal rest;
> The world's joy thrilling runs through me, I bear
>   The sorrows of millions in my lonely breast.

[1] Aurobindo, *Last Poems*, p. 35.

> I have learned a close identity with all,
>   Yet am by nothing bound that I become;
> Carrying in me the universe's call
>   I mount to my imperishable home.
>
> I pass beyond Time and Life on measureless wings,
> Yet still am one with born and unborn things.[1]

All life is now unified in him and he feels the throb of every heart.

> I housed within my heart the life of things,
>   All hearts athrob in the world I felt as mine;
> I shared the joy that in creation sings
>   And drank its sorrow like a poignant wine.[2]

This expansion of the poet's consciousness does not however mean that his individuality is abolished. His inner being grows as the soul of love and yearns for the Beloved. With knowledge is wedded love, with identity of the Absolute is married the adoration of the Lord.

> Because Thou art All-beauty and All-bliss,
>   My soul blind and enamoured yearns for Thee;
> It bears Thy mystic touch in all that is
>   And thrills with the burden of that ecstasy.
>
> Behind all eyes I meet Thy secret gaze
>   And in each voice I hear Thy magic tune:
> Thy sweetness haunts my heart through Nature's ways;
>   Nowhere it beats now from Thy snare immune.
>
> It loves Thy body in all living things;
>   Thy joy is there in every leaf and stone:
> The moments bring Thee on their fiery wings;
>   Sight's endless artistry is Thou alone.
>
> Time voyages with Thee upon its prow
> And all the future's passionate hope is Thou.[3]

---

[1] Aurobindo, *Last Poems*, p. 9.   [2] *Ibid.*, p. 10.   [3] *Ibid.*, p. 38.

This last line brings in the point of hope as an essential thing in Sri Aurobindo's philosophy. The soul widens its experience of God as the guide of life and in the world. The time has come for the poet to see and participate in God's great plan of the world. He is calm and tranquil and prepares himself to accept the will of God.

> I dwell in the spirit's calm nothing can move
>> And watch the actions of thy vast world-force,
> Its mighty wings that through infinity move
>> And the Time-gallopings of the deathless Horse.
> . . . .
>
> All this I bear in me, untouched and still
> Assenting to Thy all-wise inscrutable will.[1]

We have seen before that the poet's aspiring soul has realized its unity with the transcendent and the universal aspects of Reality. But now the devotee in him flowers out as the divine worker. He surrenders himself to God and prepares to do His will here on the earth.

> O Thou of whom I am the instrument,
>> O secret Spirit and Nature housed in me,
> Let all my mortal being now be blent
>> In Thy still glory of divinity.
>
> I have given my mind to be dug Thy channel mind,
>> I have offered up my will to be Thy will:
> Let nothing of myself be left behind
>> In our union mystic and unutterable.
>
> My heart shall throb with the world-beats of Thy
>> love;
>> My body become Thy engine for earth-use;
> In my nerves and veins Thy rapture's streams shall
>> move;
>> My thoughts shall be hounds of Light for Thy
>> power to loose.
>
> Keep only my soul to adore eternally
> And meet Thee in each form and soul of Thee.[2]

[1] Aurobindo, *Last Poems*, p. 7. [2] *Ibid.*, p. 23.

This love for the Divine, the surrender to the Master, makes our poet equal in all circumstances. He feels the presence of God in everything and always and thus is able to practise the dedicated service of God.

> I face earth's happenings with an equal soul;
>   In all are heard Thy steps: Thy unseen feet
> Thread Destiny's pathways in my front. Life's whole
>   Tremendous theorem is Thou complete.
> . . . .
>
> In this rude combat with the fate of man
>   Thy smile within my heart makes all my strength;
> Thy Force in me labours at its grandiose plan,
>   Indifferent to the Time-snake's crawling length.
>
> No power can slay my soul; it lives in Thee.
> Thy presence is my immortality.[1]

The poet soared with measureless wings to the heights of the Absolute which cancelled Nature. There was a stage in his experience in which Nature was ended and there was the Spirit alone. But now a deeper and wider insight reveals to him the sovereignty of God.

> Now more and more the Epiphany within
>   Affirms on Nature's soil His sovereign rights.
> My mind has left its prison-camp of brain;
>   It pours, a luminous sea from spirit heights.
> . . . .
>
> Nature in me one day like Him shall sit
> Victorious, calm, immortal, infinite.[2]

The assurance given in the last two lines is possible because the inconscient, which betrays no sign of consciousness at all and is the immediate origin of all things in the world, is really nothing but a veil of God.

> The darkness was the Omnipotent's abode,
> Hood of omniscience, a blind mask of God.[3]

[1] Aurobindo, *Last Poems*, p. 24.   [2] *Ibid.*, p. 26.   [3] *Ibid.*, p. 8.

Indeed there is a hidden plan which now unfolds before the awakened sight of the poet.

> However long Night's hour, I will not dream
>   That the small ego and the person's mask
> Are all that God reveals in our life-scheme,
>   The last result of Nature's cosmic task.
>
> A greater Presence in her bosom works;
>   Long it prepares its far epiphany:
> Even in the stone and beast the godhead lurks,
>   A bright Persona of eternity.
>
> It shall burst out from the limit traced by Mind
>   And make a witness of the prescient heart;
> It shall reveal even in this inert blind
>   Nature, long veiled in each inconscient part,
>
> Fulfilling the occult magnificent plan,
> The world-wide and immortal spirit in man.[1]

The soul now hears a silver call. To it is revealed a godhead of things to be realized.

> There is a godhead of unrealized things
>   To which Time's splendid gains are hoarded dross;
> A cry seems near, a rustle of silver wings
>   Calling to heavenly joy by earthly loss.
> . . . .
>
> As rain-thrashed mire the marvel of the rose,
> Earth waits that distant marvel to disclose.[2]

The poet's intrepid soul armed with God's might makes an assignation with the night. It is not so much a struggle, this journey through the darkness is rather a pilgrimage.

> I made an assignation with the Night;
>   In the abyss was fixed our rendezvous:
> In my breast carrying God's deathless light
>   I came her dark and dangerous heart to woo.

---

[1] Aurobindo, *Last Poems*, p. 4.　　　　　[2] *Ibid.*, p. 45.

I left the glory of the illumined Mind
  And the calm rapture of the divinized soul
And travelled through a vastness dim and blind
  To the grey shore where her ignorant waters roll.

I walk by the chill wave through the dull slime
  And still that weary journeying knows no end;
Lost is the lustrous godhead beyond Time,
  There comes no voice of the celestial Friend,

And yet I know my footprints' track shall be
A pathway towards Immortality.[1]

The pilgrim of the night now passes through a luminous abode and previsions the upward evolutionary ascent of the creative Force. From the inconscient blossoms forth the secret, sleeping, dormant consciousness. Out of matter blooms forth the divine soul.

I passed into a lucent still abode
  And saw as in a mirror crystalline
  An ancient Force ascending serpentine
Of the ascending spirals of the aeonic road.
Earth was a cradle for the arriving God
  And man but a half-dark half-luminous sign
  Of the transition of the veiled Divine
From Matter's sleep and the tormented load
Of ignorant life and death to the Spirit's light.
  Mind liberated swam Light's ocean-vast,
    And life escaped from its grey tortured line
I saw Matter illumining its parent Night.
  The soul could feel into infinity cast,
    Timeless God-bliss the heart incarnadine.[2]

The rule of the Spirit over nature first manifests itself as a change of the very senses of the poet. Hearing and sight and taste undergo a radical change. This presupposes a descent of the golden light, the supramental consciousness into the poet's brain.

[1] Aurobindo, *Last Poems*, p. 5.   [2] *Ibid.*, p. 48.

> Thy golden Light came down into my brain
>   And the grey worms of mind sun-touched became
> A bright reply to Wisdom's occult plane,
>   A calm illumination and a flame.[1]

The light comes down through his throat and his heart, the centres respectively of expression and the psychic being, to nether regions. Even the earth is bathed by it.

> Thy golden Light came down into my feet
> My earth is now thy playfield and thy seat.[2]

The transformation of the senses is expressed categorically:

> Surely I take no more an earthly food
>   But eat the fruits and plants of Paradise!
> For Thou hast changed my sense's habitude
>   From mortal pleasure to divine surprise.
> Hearing and sight are now an ecstasy,
>   And all the fragrances of earth disclose
> A sweetness matching in intensity
>   Odour of the crimson marvel of the rose.
> . . . .
>
> The body burns with Thy rapture's sacred fire,
> Pure, passionate, holy, virgin of desire.[3]

The pilgrim of the night now arrives at a new island on which the supramental sun streams down its vivifying, transforming rays of immortality. The poet soars into the very heart of the sun and sees the revelations of the new world to be. The power surrounds him when he comes back to the earth bringing like Prometheus from heaven the flame of transformation into the womb of the earth. Nature is no longer the field of opposites, the cavern of darkness and a denial of God. The epiphany of the collective God founds the life divine in the transformed field of human nature.

> I have sailed the golden ocean
>   And crossed the silver bar;
> I have reached the Sun of knowledge
>   The earth-self's midnight star.

[1] Aurobindo, *Last Poems*, p. 11.   [2] *Ibid.*, p. 11.   [3] *Ibid.*, p. 42.

Its fields of flaming vision,
  Its mountains of bare might,
Its peaks of fiery rapture,
  Its air of absolute light,

Its seas of self-oblivion,
  Its vales of Titan rest,
Because my soul's dominion,
  Its Island of the Blest.

Alone with God and silence,
  Timeless it lived in Time;
Life was His fugue of music,
  Thought was Truth's ardent rhyme.

The Light was still around me
  When I came back to earth
Bringing the Immortal's knowledge
  Into man's cave of birth.[1]

[1] Aurobindo, *Last Poems*, p. 33.

24

JUDITH TYBERG

The Drama of Integral Self-Realization

(*The Spiritual Message of* Sāvitrī)

SRI AUROBINDO'S *Sāvitrī* is an epic poem of high spiritual challenge in the yoga of integral self-realization it presents. Its spiritual conception is so all-encompassing, so integral that it gives birth to a power which transforms life on earth to a life of divine activity rather than leading to an escape from life. The epic is the mantric expression of this great seer-sage's inner findings and conquests, leading to his vision of an age of truth-consciousness and immortality. It portrays in living drama the daring climb within of a king-soul through progressive states of consciousness to nirvāṇic heights and beyond to summits ne'er reached before. The poet reveals how at meditation's peaks at one with God, where many cease their search, he becomes aware of a Presence, God's consciousness, power and bliss, which he calls the Divine Mother. He relates how this creatrix of boundless love and wisdom-splendour comes down to earth to transform darkness into light, the unreal into the real and death into immortality.

The famous *Mahābhārata*[1] legend of 'Sāvitrī and Satyavān', the story of 'Love Conquers Death', is made the basic symbol of this mystic scripture of 'Divine Life on Earth'. The legend tells of the noble and virtuous king Aśwapathy performing all kinds of austerities in order that God might be pleased and grant him a child to uphold his kingdom. After eighteen years the goddess Sāvitrī, wife of the Divine Creator, issues forth

[1] From the Pativratā Māhātmya Parva in Chapters 291–7 of the *Āranyaka Parva*.

from the sacrificial flames and promises the king a radiantly
spiritual daughter to spring from her own being.

The child is born and is named Sāvitrī. She grows up like
unto the 'Goddess of Beauty' herself in embodied form and is
blessed with godlike qualities. When she reaches maturity,
kings and princes, overwhelmed by her divine character, dare
not ask her hand. So her father sends her forth to seek her own
lord. Her heart finds Satyavān, the faithful son of Rājā
Dyumatsena, a blind and exiled king who lives in a forest
hermitage.

When Sāvitrī comes to declare her love to her father, she
finds him in conversation with Nārada, the great heavenly
sage. When Nārada hears Sāvitrī's words he warns that
Satyavān, though endowed with all high qualities and with
honour constant as the pole star, is destined to die in a year.
The parents try to persuade their daughter to choose another,
but in vain. Nārada advises the father, however, to allow
Sāvitrī to marry Satyavān. So the princess is married and lives
a simple quiet life in the forest. She pleased all with her tender
service, self-denial, evenness of temper, her skill and gentle
speech and her love for Satyavān.

But night and day Nārada's prophetic words are present in
her mind. She speaks of them to no one. When the appointed
day for Satyavān's death approaches, Sāvitrī fasts and prays
and on the fated day she begs permission to follow her
husband into the forest in order to see the blossoming woods
through which he passed daily. Never having petitioned
anything previous to this day, she is granted her request.
Satyavān goes ahead to make way for her and soon comes to
where he stops to cut wood for the home-fire.

After a few strokes Satyavān falls smitten with pain and
Sāvitrī, stricken with grief, sits and holds his head in her lap.
Suddenly she beholds Yama, the god of death, standing before
her with a noose in hand. She rises and asks why he had come
himself instead of sending one of his emissaries as was his
custom. Yama tells her that this prince is endowed with such a
sea of virtue and accomplishment and beauty that he is too
worthy to be borne away by anyone but the god of death
himself. Then Yama takes the soul of Satyavān and proceeds

southward. Sāvitrī, undaunted, follows him. Time and again Yama turns to stop her but with wise and appealing words she moves him to grant one boon after the other, save the life within his hand. Still she continues to follow him, right into his dark cave, until finally her devotion and unparalleled love and wisdom move Yama to return the soul of Satyavān. Sāvitrī hastens to the woods where her lord's body lay and woos the soul back into consciousness and together they return to their home and all the boons promised by Yama are fulfilled.

Adapting this legend as a symbol for a great living spiritual experience, Sri Aurobindo changes king Aśwapathy's sacrificial asceticism into the *tapasyā* or conscious spiritualization of an aspiring soul of humanity. Sāvitrī is not only the incarnation of a goddess but divine grace born in answer to Aśwapathy's longing for help in bringing some living form of God on earth to relieve it of its burden of inconscience. The marriage of Sāvitrī and Satyavān is the divine linking of their lives for the raising of the world and man to God and the bringing of God to earth to transform it into an abode of divine delight.

Sri Aurobindo first gives a panoramic vision of the character and mighty events of the momentous day of divine conquest. Dramatically he opens the epic with a description of the dawn of the day destined for Satyavān's death and makes it the symbol of the dawn of the spiritual tomorrow which is to usher in an age of truth-consciousness and immortality. How this wondrous dawn appears to humans with 'time-born eyes'[1] and how it affected Sāvitrī awaiting her mighty struggle with death is compared. Telling verses give the key to the source of Sāvitrī's power to rise above her lone grief and the thoughts oppressing her mind. Her godlike character and sensitive nature are set forth and reveal the source of her power and will in the battle with death.

As the significant day of death arrives, Sāvitrī is pictured preparing within, struggling with the burdens of her *karmic* past, seeking the aid of her purified will to help her disown the trails and legacy of past selves which were 'a block on the immortal's road'.[2] As she reviews her past we hear the radiant

[1] Aurobindo, *Sāvitrī*, p. 8.　　　　[2] *Ibid.*, p. 15.

prologue to this day, her twelve months' life in the secluded beauty of the woodlands where there was 'deep room for thought and God'.[1]

Striking verses tell of how when faced with the death of Satyavān her 'heart stood in the way of the driving wheels' of the 'engines of the universe',[2] how she kindled her divine strength, how pain assailed her divinest elements, and how the truth of her divinity within 'broke in in a triumph of fire', and empowered her to smite 'from Death's visage its dumb absolute' and 'burst the bounds of consciousness and Time'.[3]

After this survey of the mighty moments of the epic the poet takes up the sequence of events in accordance with the original legend commencing with a description of the spiritual steps taken by Aśwapathy for his soul's release. We learn how through inner concentration and a steady will he keeps his consciousness in his supernature and is helped in turning his 'frail mud-engine to heaven-use'.[4] To free himself from ego and its finiteness, from mind's limits and 'the lines of safety reason draws'[5] is his task.

Then we are told how 'these large wide-poised upliftings' whose peace the 'restless nether members tire of'[6] are made to endure, how the spirit's power gradually transforms the darker parts of man's being, even the body's cells, and makes them feel the need and will to change in order that 'this immense creation's purpose'[7] may not fail. What he must check crowding through mind's gates under 'forged signatures of the gods',[8] what the silences of his being reveal, and what priceless riches he finds in the deep subconscient as his being becomes transfigured, all are here described.

The secret knowledge follows, giving out the grandiose meaning of our lives, the story of the climb of the god-spark through the kingdoms of the earth to Godhood, how the spirit-guardians of the silence of the Truth work in the vicissitudes of our lives, what the true sources of our beings are, who the cosmic managers are, and how the secret God within makes himself felt in our lives. But still unexplained problems made

---

[1] Aurobindo, *Sāvitrī*, p. 17.　　[2] *Ibid.*, p. 24.　　[3] *Ibid.*, p. 25.
[4] *Ibid.*, p. 29.　　　　　　　[5] *Ibid.*, p. 31.　　[6] *Ibid.*, p. 40.
[7] *Ibid.*, p. 41.　　　　　　　[8] *Ibid.*, p. 44.

Aśwapathy plunge into 'unplumbed infinitudes'[1] in order to find the key to what could join spirit and matter, join what is now parted, opposed and twain and fulfil the oneness that was the stamp of Being.

So Aśwapathy moves into the freedom and greatness of his spirit, dares 'to live when breath and thought were still'[2] and steps into that magic place where all is self-known, where the riddle of the world 'grew plain and lost its catch obscure'.[3] In magnificent poetry we follow him as he rises, leaving earth-nature's summits below his feet. We are made to feel the ecstasy, might and sweetness of God's mystic power, as he is drawn from his loneliness into God's embrace.

As he climbs his sealless eye uncovers a series of graded kingdoms twixt life's poles through whose 'organ scale of consciousness' souls move. Up this stairway of worlds he starts and enters into another space and time. With Aśwapathy we travel and become acquainted with the nature of these spheres and their godheads. Here Sri Aurobindo unveils occult cosmogony in grandiose and vibrant detail in a clarity of language that only direct experience can utter. To read of these inner states of ourselves, also the pattern of the universe to be seen within, below, without, above, is to more fully understand ourselves.

Aśwapathy crosses out of this gross material world into a subtle material existence where the patterns of our forms are found; then into planes of pure life-force, where in the lower regions, 'an unhappy corner of eternity',[4] the little cravings of earth's beings and a motley mass of lower vital creatures abound; while in its higher regions live the higher emotions, desires and aspirations, where unattained ideas are beings and kings. Then lower into the dangerous nether regions of nescience with its brood of hate and selfishness along with this explorer we go to find the causes of the failure of the desire-worlds to fulfil themselves. There we see the twists of Nature. Further below into Hell we penetrate with this warrior-adventurer who keeps 'a prayer upon his lips and the great Name'[5] to protect him from its terrors and demoniacal creatures. What

[1] Aurobindo, *Sāvitrī*, p. 79.   [2] *Ibid.*, p. 84.
[3] *Ibid.*, p. 86.   [4] *Ibid.*, p. 171.   [5] *Ibid.*, p. 238.

scenes of horror and yet grim majesty are portrayed! Even to
'the hidden heart of Night',[1] the absolute denial of Truth and
Being, this spirit-soul dives, where the 'hypocrite blooms',[2] a
'spiritless blank Infinity',[3] a home of the dark powers, 'a studio
of creative Death'[4] and a dire place of torture. Passing through
the suffering of its blackest pit, while treasuring 'between his
hands his flickering soul'[5] Aśwapathy discovers that the
highest secrets are locked in these abysmal depths.

Then up into the paradises of the gods of life and hope, we
are made to feel the sweetness and joys of this state. But this
too he quickly leaves, journeying on to find something higher,
that which makes all one; for to remain within the limits of
desire's satisfactions delays the discovery of that immortal
One who gives all one could desire and more. The kingdoms
and godheads of the little mind show him their ceaseless
analytical workings and we are introduced to the three dwarfs
of mind: habit, desire and reason. Then to the more luminous
planes of greater mind, where few are guests, he enters and
finds them a plane which God uses as a bridge to send his forms
of truth to man. Inspiring are the lines outlining what could
be ours if we opened the gates leading to this shining corridor
of mind.

Next Aśwapathy ascends to the blissful heavens of the Idea,
the home of the source of our spiritual longings wherefrom we
hear 'the flutings of the Infinite'[6] which rouse the soul from
its depths. From this beautiful realm where mind's radiant
flower-children dwell he enters into the silence where the Self
of mind, the witness lord of nature, has his secret base.
Aśwapathy watches the motive-thoughts of this thinker, but
this firmament of abstract thought he observes is a finder
only, but not a knower or a lover.

Seeking for an escape from these limits the king-soul goes
through a brilliant opening carried by a mysterious sound
into the Soul of the world. Here the poet describes the
universal harmonies, sympathies and wisdom of this cosmic
consciousness, home of souls in spiritual sleep between lives on
earth. We learn how souls plan there in this 'fashioning chamber

[1] Aurobindo, *Sāvitrī*, p. 249.   [2] *Ibid.*, p. 251.   [3] *Ibid.*, p. 249.
[4] *Ibid.*, p. 256.   [5] *Ibid.*, p. 261.   [6] *Ibid.*, p. 316.

of the worlds'[1] the adventures of their new lives. The watching eye of this spiritual traveller sees there his own soul, and now, soul-conscious, becomes aware of the 'Two-in-One',[2] the cosmic Father-Mother absorbed in deep creative joy, and learns of their works and powers. In awe he falls before this unveiled Goddess, knowing he is nearing the heart of things. Now our hero-soul steps into a realm of boundless silence 'where all are different and all is one'.[3] The plenitudes of wisdom found there are spread before us.

Next on creation's heights this tireless seeker arrives where only a formless Form of Self is left. There appears the Godhead of the whole with 'his feet firm-based on Life's stupendous wings'.[4] The utter aloneness, stillness and inscrutability of this God with diamond gaze rejecting from itself world and soul is powerfully set forth. Still this 'consciousness of unshared immortal bliss'[5] did not satisfy him. He sought in this absolute silence 'an absolute Power',[6] for he knew that a huge extinction is not God's last word, that the escape into this glad divine abyss is not the crown of the Self's mission or the Self's power, or the meaning of this great mysterious world. Verses of challenge ring forth to the soul who might seek the end of his being in *nirvāna*.

Passages pregnant with deep meaning then flow forth from the poet as he narrates the drawing near of the Divine Presence behind the Godhead, that Luminous Heart which Aśwapathy had been yearning for with the passion of his soul. Here was the Glory of God, the Divine Mother of All. Soul-stirring is his prayer to the Mighty Mother after having torn 'desire up from its bleeding roots' and 'offered to the gods the vacant place'.[7] The poet depicts the transformation that comes over Aśwapathy as his heart meets the Divine Mother and describes the vision that comes to him of the new creation to dawn on earth, bringing with it a harmony of all contraries. Splendid and prophetic passages! Suddenly the Divine Mother rises in him and speaks in his heart's chambers, warning him not to make too soon the immeasurable descent, and revealing her miraculous powers. But Aśwapathy, who has now beheld this wondrous

---

[1] Aurobindo, *Sāvitrī*, p. 333.   [2] *Ibid.*, p. 334.   [3] *Ibid.*, p. 340.
[4] *Ibid.*, p. 348.   [5] *Ibid.*, p. 349.   [6] *Ibid.*, p. 353.   [7] *Ibid.*, p. 360.

Mother, pleads with a heart grown vibrant with love for all: 'Incarnate the white passion of thy Force'.[1] The beauteous Immortal's consent and her promise to come down to earth is one of the lofty mantric passages of the epic. So to change Nature's doom Sāvitrī is born. Exquisite poetry recounts her childhood, the gradual growth of the flame within her, the call to her divine quest and the meeting of the two young lovers.

Then we hear Nārada, the heavenly sage, not only announcing to Aśwapathy, the father of Sāvitrī, the fated death of Satyavān but giving out with singular force the laws and ways of *karma*, fate and pain, and the mystery of why great souls suffer.[2] Like the despondency of Arjuna in the Bhagavad-Gītā, the ordeal of the foreknowledge of Satyavān's death and her heart's grief are shown to be the beginning of Sāvitrī's yoga, her union with God. With the poet we watch her struggles with forces of indifference and inertia, with the senses, desire and the restless brain, against truth mixed with poison, and against weakness of heart. The strong charge of her soul in response to her request: 'Speak to my depths, O great and deathless Voice, Command, for I am here to do thy will',[3] is the spiritual charge for every soul seeking to serve the Divine and conquer darkness.

Next we are given a picture of what Sāvitrī sees when she looks into herself and seeks her soul. Closing the door to the God within are serpents of temptations of all kinds, limitations luring to the easier paths of the all-negating absolute, to escape from the battle with life and to *nirvāna*. How she answers these and pushes them away is told. On seeking the occult fire within, three soul-forces appear: the Mother of Divine Pity, the Mother of Might and the Mother of Wisdom. Each relates her various form and work in the world. Finally the poet chants of Sāvitrī's finding of her Secret Deity.

But soon the portentous yet promising day of Satyavān's death arrives and it is portrayed in verses of poetic pathos. At the moment of death Sāvitrī enters the mystic lotus in her head, 'a thousand-petalled home of power and light'[4] and rises

---

[1] Aurobindo, *Sāvitrī*, p. 391.   [2] *Ibid.*, pp. 471–523.
[3] *Ibid.*, p. 540.   [4] *Ibid.*, p. 647.

to meet the dreadful God, the limitless denial of all being. The two oppose each other, Woman and universal God of Death. The poem shows Satyavān moving with Death into the silence beyond and Sāvitrī casting off her sheaths and entering into the trance of her soul in order to stay with Satyavān. At the brink of the shadow-world Death peals forth his abysmal cry ordering her to go back. But silent, she dares enter into the eternal night with them. Death warns her to go no further and depicts his home of dark immensity and the helplessness of all in his power. After his ruthless speech Sāvitrī answers what to her is a black lie of night and declares her spirit's power can resist him and then demands and challenges Death to give what Satyavān desired in his life for his parents. Death smilingly yields but demands her return to earth lest she be destroyed. But Sāvitrī boldly states her powers which like fire can destroy him. Death in mocking verses cries forth that he is the originator and destroyer of all. Sāvitrī then meets scorn with scorn and in dynamic poetry proclaims the wondrous might of her God's will and love. Death refutes all her statements, claiming his power can deny them all, make all things vain.

Sāvitrī's soul continues to wrestle with Death and to ridicule his words of reason. Death challenges her to seek to *know*, for knowledge kills love. Quickly comes her response that the nature of love gives birth to knowledge. Drifting along with them as they move into the land of Nought, we hear the debate continue, hear them pit all the contraries of life against each other, and we hear from Sāvitrī the very reason of Death's existence. Death peals forth a long proclamation how he cancels all life's golden truths. To his dangerous music this warrior-maiden gives a picture of what her God of Love has done and will yet accomplish and dares Death to produce a greater God to captivate her soul. Death sneeringly interprets her words as hallucinations of the mind and gives an oration on the deceptions of mind and raises unconsciousness as the pinnacle of all. Sāvitrī answers in Death's own words, calling him the dark-browed sophist of the universe masking divinity with his dance of death. She sings forth in glorious poetry the occult spiritual miracle of God's wonders from a tiny seed, and then again in lines of majestic power speaks of her assured triumph, of her love as stronger than his bonds of death.

The dark King, still trying to discourage her, ironically speaks of her fantasy of truth, saying that truth is hard as stone. Back and forth sparkle the words of the debate. Death uses subtle reason and arms himself with all man's faltering searches, his limiting spiritual goals, and exaggerated and imperfect understanding of truth to prove the futility of God's power, but Sāvitrī, 'delivered from all twilight thoughts',[1] with a heart of truth answers his lures. Here Sāvitrī chants lyrics of Nature's miracles, of the wonders of the Infinite and of the limitless powers of a soul integrally surrendered to God.

Death, suspecting her to be the Mother of the Gods embodied, challenges her to show a body of living truth, for has matter ever been able to hold truth? Sāvitrī tells Death who he really is and warns him he will cease to be when he touches the embodied truth supreme, and then reveals her being all one with God. Death, still unconvinced, makes his last stand in support of his blind force and dares Sāvitrī to reveal the power of the Divine, for many have truth but who has the power to radiate it? Then is given a picture of Sāvitrī as she becomes transformed into a divine being with all her *cakras* or lotuses of power scintillating. The most powerful speech of all follows and Sāvitrī exhibits her living power of truth and proves that death is needed no more. Death is shown gradually vanishing and finally defeated, eaten by light.

In the silences of the beyond Sāvitrī and Satyavān are alone.[2] Into the avenues of the Spirit they roam happily. But even there voices rise enticing them to come to a blissful home away from the battles of life, but Sāvitrī again meets the test with strength. With sun-words she replies that she was born on earth to dare the impossible, that imperfect is the joy not shared by all. Then God, knowing Sāvitrī now to be absolutely at one with his diamond heart, rings forth the final joyous paean of the divine transformation that shall be on earth and sends Sāvitrī as his power and Satyavān as his soul back to earth to change this earthly life to a life divine.

---

[1] Aurobindo, *Sāvitrī*, p. 716.   [2] *Ibid.*, pp. 753–800.

Sāvitrī falls like a star to earth[1] and Satyavān invisibly drawn soars past her. They reunite on earth and the epic closes unveiling the age-long secret deep-guarded in the stillness—the promise of a greater dawn.

Iti mayā śrutam—Thus have I heard—

Thus have I heard the revelation of *Sāvitrī*, Sri Aurobindo's epic poem, truly an apocalypse of the treasuries of spiritual experience and of the perfect divine existence.

[1] Aurobindo, *Sāvitrī*, pp. 803-14.

PART FIVE

MISCELLANEOUS

25

SWAMI SIVANANDA

Sri Aurobindo:
The Consummate Expression
of the Indian Spirit of Synthesis

Down through the centuries, with the exception of certain distinctive periods in Indian cultural history which constrained and fostered the development by isolation of one or the other aspects of the synthetic thought embodied in the rich and many-sided philosophic and spiritual traditions of the country, India had always borne the insignia of uniqueness for its irresistible and brilliant tendency towards a comprehensiveness of experience and thought.

Whether it is yoga-śāstra (science of self-realization) or arthaśāstra (economics) or āyurveda (science of medicine) or jyotiṣa (astrology) or simple forms of religious experience, we can always be given the awareness of having been taken by surprise and immense delight at the power and persuasiveness with which it comes home to us with the utility of a message which reveals at once a synthesis in its conceptions and a comprehensiveness in its techniques of actual practice, and this feature of distinctiveness for integrality it owes to the soil in which it has taken its origins, the soil of the Vedas, the background of the Upaniṣadic experience and endeavour, the wide-ranging experience of the Indian spiritual realization.

But then, as has already been hinted, there were times and trying periods in the vicissitudes of the history of this ancient land of India, which necessitated and encouraged lop-sided developments and compartmental monopoly in the organic many-limbed body of Indian cultural thought . . . and it remained for a number of stalwart saints, mystics and men of God in mediaeval India and the India of recent past, whose last and most impressive instance in the synthesis of experience in a diversity of religion has been Sri Ramakrishna.

And it needed the supreme cultural genius of a Sri Aurobindo, the like of whom the spirit and the creative vision of India alone can create, to give a yet bolder or rather the boldest manifestation to a synthesization of insights in philosophic, cultural and religious or spiritual wisdom and experience and to an invaluable integral conception of the triple Reality that the inquiring reason and metaphysical awareness of man encounters in creative endeavours against the facts and events of experience and reflection. Sri Aurobindo is indeed the consummate expression of the spirit of synthesis inherent in Indian culture.

Apart from the greatness we discern and admire in the uniqueness of the philosophic experience and statement of Sri Aurobindo, there is one thing more which needs and claims our recognition and consequent admiration, the fact that the methodology Sri Aurobindo had requisitioned as a means to his grasp of the fundamental facts of existence, of the great values of integral life, of the nature of the Divine in the human individual, the Divine in the universe and the Divine in its own timeless eternity and transcendentality, was constituted by no mere power of speculative reason, no mere philosophic vision, no building upon what has been handed over to him as his heritage, but by the intuition, the new brand of intuition, the integral insight that he had obtained in the seclusion of Pondicherry, in experience of the supernormal factors in the spiritual world, in an experimenting richness of personal *sādhanā* and *siddhi*.

With a joy that only a mother who has borne a genius-babe can know, India is proud of Sri Aurobindo and the phenomenon of his extraordinary contributions; but the profit accruing from the gifts of Aurobindo is not only its own, it is of all the world! May the spirit of Aurobindo shower its choicest blessings upon all mankind!

26

T. M. P. MAHADEVAN

The Significance of Sri Aurobindo

SRI AUROBINDO will ever be remembered as a *mahā-yogī*, a *pūrṇa-yogī*, a great teacher of integral *yoga*. Though he started his public life as a patriot, his patriotism was of a unique kind. It was no narrow nationalism that moved him as a pioneer in the movement for India's freedom. His conception of the motherland was not that of a geographical component of the globe 'spotted with hills and lined with rivers and shaded with plains'. His vision of India was that of a spiritual heritage whose powers had to be liberated for the lasting benefit of the whole of mankind. And the method of liberation lay, as he said, and as it has been worked out completely and in such great detail by Mahātma Gāndhi, in supplanting *kṣatriya-tejas* or brute force, by *brahma-tejas* or soul force. When the time came for retirement from active politics in response to an inner call, Sri Aurobindo was prepared for it, because he knew that the path which was opening out before him led to wider horizons and loftier realms.

On April 4, 1910, Sri Aurobindo arrived at Pondicherry, not as a political refugee, as it was wrongly imagined in some quarters then, but as a spiritual pilgrim, determined to scale the heights of *yoga*. In the famous Uttarpārā speech, he makes mention of the way he was attracted to *yoga*. This is what he says: 'When I approached God at that time, I hardly had a living faith in Him. The agnostic was in me, the atheist was in me, the sceptic was in me, and I was not absolutely sure that there was a God at all. I did not feel His presence. Yet something drew me to the truth of the Vedas, the truth of the Gītā, the truth of the Hindu religion. I felt there must be a mighty truth somewhere in this *yoga*, a mighty truth in this religion based on the Vedānta.' So, from atheism and agnosticism to God-realization—what a rapid and great march it was! And this grand march he made in the atmosphere of an *āśrama* which arose where he was. The realization of yogic experience which came to him was not for his private enjoyment; it was meant for all, as, according to him, the goal of spirituality is 'the flowering of the Divine in collective humanity'.

In *The Life Divine* and in numerous other works, Sri Aurobindo has expounded his philosophy of *yoga*. In exquisite language clothed in poetic beauty, he gives us not only intimations of the immortal life but also sketches the method by which that life is to be gained. Adopting the well-known Vedāntic term, Sri Aurobindo calls the ultimate reality— *Saccidānanda*. '*Saccidānanda*', he says, 'is the unknown, omnipresent, indispensable term for which the human consciousness, whether in knowledge and sentiment or in sensation and action, is eternally seeking.' In the very description of Reality as *Saccidānanda* we posit three entities and unite them to arrive at a trinity. We say, 'existence, consciousness, bliss', and then we say, 'They are one'. This is not all that is to be said of Reality. *Sat, cit* and *ānanda*, which Sri Aurobindo translates as the pure existent, consciousness-force and the delight of existence, constitute, along with the fourth principle, viz. supermind, the higher hemisphere of Being. The lower hemisphere consists of mind, life and matter. While in the higher hemisphere knowledge reigns, in the lower, ignorance rules. But it should be noted that mind, life and matter are only subordinate powers of the divine quarternary. Mind is a subordinate power of the supermind; life is a subordinate power of the energy aspect of *Saccidānanda*; and matter is a form of being which is to be traced to the existence aspect of *Saccidānanda*. Together these seven constitute the sevenfold chord of Being. All of them are essential to cosmic creation. 'The higher trinity is the source and basis of all existence and play of existence, and all cosmos must be an expression and action of its essential reality.'

There is a double movement at work in Reality, declares

Sri Aurobindo—a descent and an ascent. 'The Divine descends from pure existence through the play of Consciousness-Force and Bliss and the Creative medium of Supermind into Cosmic being; we ascend from Matter through a developing life, soul and mind and the illuminating medium of Supermind towards the Divine Being.' These two movements are, in fact, complementary to each other; there is no contradiction between them. The ascension enables the divine descent; the descent fulfils that for which the ascension aspires and which it makes inevitable. In the past, saints and sages have risen from the lower levels to the higher. But they did not attempt, says Sri Aurobindo, to bring the supermind down into the consciousness of the earth and make it fixed there. This is a consummation devoutly to be desired; this is the life divine—the *satyayuga*, the new heaven and new earth. And the way that leads to the goal is 'integral *yoga*'—the yoga in which all the powers of being 'will be combined and included in the transmuting instrumentation'.

There have been rival views in Indian thought as to the nature of ultimate Reality. There was, for instance, the great *Śaṅkara* in classical times who taught that Brahman is *nirguṇa*, devoid of characteristics though not characterless, and that the world is only an illusory appearance. It is a disputed question as to which of these philosophical views or spiritual visions is the ultimate. But as Sri Aurobindo himself says in a paper contributed to the Silver Jubilee Volume of the Indian Philosophical Congress, 'Whether the workings of the Spirit in the universe are a reality—or only a half reality, self-descriptive *Līlā* or illusory *Māyā*, whether it be an action of the Infinite Energy, *Śakti*, or a figment of some secondary paradoxical consciousness in the Eternal, *Māyā*, life as an intermediate reality is nowhere denied by any school of Indian thinking'.

All the saints and sages of India, teachers of philosophy and prophets of religion, are agreed that the goal of life is spiritual perfection. 'The peculiarity of the Indian eye of thought is', in the words of Sri Aurobindo, 'that it sees or searches everywhere for the Spirit, and the peculiarity of the Indian will in life is that it feels itself to be still unfulfilled, not in touch with perfection, nor justified in any intermediate satisfaction so long as it has not found and does not live in the truth of the Spirit.' The greatest homage that we can pay to Sri Aurobindo is to resolve not to rest until we reach the goal which is spiritual perfection.

27

S. K. MITRA

The Nineteenth-Century Upsurge

WHILE the critical eighteenth century was the indirect cause of the decisive event that changed India's political destiny, the century that followed witnessed the beginnings of tremendous movements whose consummation in the twentieth was one of the greatest events in all history. The nineteenth century was the veritable seed-time of mighty ideas that took shape in the next. It was indeed for the whole world 'a century of hope', as F. S. Marvin would say, for which evolutionary Nature had been at work in the previous century through wars and revolutions. Her aim in the nineteenth century appeared to be to prepare the mind of the race for its regeneration into a new consciousness that would lead to and sustain a fresh adventure of the world's soul towards a greater and grander fulfilment in the future. To this adventure mankind is being impelled largely by the very problems it itself created in the nineteenth century. This is one of Nature's ways to realize her aim in human evolution.

The nineteenth century saw the birth, growth and expansion of remarkable political and cultural movements in Europe and other parts of the world. They helped forward the cause of human progress as nothing else had done before. Large ideas, vast thoughts, wonderful visions stirred the heart and soul of man and he began to feel that a new world was about to be born. Not that these movements solved their self-evoked problems but the ideas and ideals that inspired them certainly brought about a wholesome reorientation of the mental outlook of the century.

One of the causes of the all-round change in the life of man was the Industrial Revolution. It brought in wealth, and wealth gave leisure, and leisure, where properly utilized, prompted cultural creation. Industrialization gave a tremendous push to commerce, and commerce sought expansion through colonization, and colonization backed by Christian missions helped in spreading European ideas. Thus came into being colonies and spheres of influence with various concomitant problems some of which are still defying solution.

Science, which has made so much for industrial progress, is man's outstanding achievement but it has at the same time released forces far too powerful for his control. While rendering more complex the individual and collective life of man, it has been at once his weal and his worry. And when he declared that science was 'the only means of certain knowledge, and that anything unknowable to science must remain unknowable forever', he stood self-blinded, his mind self-condemned, condemned to its own limitations, shutting out from itself the higher values of the infinite, ever open to it above its own domain. Another self-created problem.

Yet science and scientific thought have considerably helped in developing two powers of man—reason and individualism. These have liberated him from much of the mediaeval obscurantism that sat heavy on his mind and soul. But by themselves they cannot lead him to the highest good, though, while serving as the necessary basis of his quest, they may point to it as some mysterious ultimate. Meanwhile, man's exclusive reliance on and adherence to them creates yet another self-defeating problem.

The eighteenth century was ringing with the cry for freedom and its first outburst was the movement in the New World that culminated in the birth of a new nation whose rapid growth in the next century enabled it to play an important role in the international life of humanity. The Revolution in France was a struggle for the attainment of great ideals none of which has been fully realized as yet in the life of any nation, or, for the matter of that, even in social life anywhere, although they were the flaming ideals of the inspired thinkers who conceived and proclaimed them as the ideals of the whole human race.

Nevertheless, what the French Revolution did was by itself

an achievement necessary at that stage of the collective evolution of mankind. The overthrow of established government in America and France, and the final consolidation of the democratic structure of the British Parliament proved to be the most powerful factors in the growth of national consciousness in the Continent. The result: liberation of Italy, unification of Germany, and the beginning of a world-wide movement which eventually brought freedom to almost all subject peoples of the world by the mid-twentieth century. Among the revolutionary ideals of the eighteenth- and nineteenth-century Europe that inspired this movement were the wonderful visions of a glorious future of mankind in the development of which each progressive nation had its own contribution to make and this it could only do in its freedom. The great Italian idealist and revolutionary Giuseppi Mazzini's vision of his country's freedom was a magnificent one; while it aimed at giving Europe a new message and a new civilization, it evoked a ready response in the hearts of all peoples struggling for freedom.

But as nations developed in their consciousness as distinct collective entities, they developed also extreme forms of national egos of which, in recent history, mankind has seen two brutal exhibitions—a third problem, perhaps the most baffling of all. A notable political step taken towards a solution was the introduction of a system of international control of affairs or congressional government which, after a series of revolutions and wars, was tried in Europe during the greater part of the first half of the nineteenth century. However inchoate, it showed a healthy and hopeful trend of things towards the future unification of the race.

In the world of thought the rise of romantic idealism in Germany was an important event. It was another cosmic force which like freedom worked in the mind of other countries —France, England, America—pointing to a brighter future for the human race. Sri Aurobindo says and Gerald Heard reiterates that Vedāntic ideas from India were an important factor in the rise and growth of this movement in Germany. And their influence in the three other countries is well known. Kant showed in his concept of 'Universal History' how the freedom of the individual to develop to his highest possibilities could be reconciled with the developing society. Hegel's thesis in his *Philosophy of History* was that man was a progressive and perfectible being. And Nietzsche was dreaming of 'a new race of Supermen'. It is well known how the ideas of the French thinkers were among the inspiring forces of the French Revolution. A few years later Condorcet declared that man is capable of 'infinite improvement'. Human ills can be mitigated by progress, said Comte in France; by the spread of knowledge, said Buckle in England. Darwin's theory of evolution and those of others on the same subject showed, however vaguely, the continuity of man's growth. Spencer identified progress with evolution. The English romantic poets discovered something of heaven in things of the earth. Some of them, called by Sri Aurobindo 'the poets of the Dawn', saw visions of a new world of freedom and harmony, and sang of its glory. The spiritual impulse is even more marked in the poetry of Whitman, Carpenter, Yeats, A. E. and Tagore, the forerunners, according to Sri Aurobindo, of the coming new age of the Spirit. In America the transcendentalists of Concord echoed the Vedāntic idea that 'within man is the soul of the Whole. . . . Man is a stream flowing into the ocean of infinity'.

The nineteenth century is also marked by the growth of socialistic ideas. The 'birth cry of modern socialism' broke out from its two famous exponents whose influence on human mind is wide but not deep in that the more important of their prophecies with which they popularized their doctrines are belied by later developments. Socialism has, however, awakened the masses to a consciousness of their rights as human beings and as equal citizens of the State. And Nature is perhaps using the movement as an indirect medium of their preparation for a larger awakening in the coming age of the Spirit.

Another remarkable idea that governed a number of progressive minds is the so-called anarchistic thought—that much misunderstood but inevitable phase in the development of the human spirit. Its inner meaning lies in the evolutionary nisus or impulse of man's soul to break through all artificial, mind-made bounds to a wider consciousness which is for man to develop as the condition for a higher life. It started in England, was echoed in France, but found its larger expression in Russia, maybe because of the mystic element in her social make-up, as pointed out by Nikolai Davilisky. It was a great ideal which Nature held up before Europe to see how she would respond. The ideal is still there awaiting its hour of realization when it would be a dynamic force contributing to the growth of the spiritual revolution through which man will rise to a higher consciousness. But the revolution itself may largely be a subjective one with subjective results. The collectivist anarchists, or as they are called 'social idealists', have nihilism for their extreme school of anarchism.

The ideologies of nihilism, anarchism or revolution aiming at re-making society into a perfect form imbued the minds of most of the world-famous Russian writers of the nineteenth century who vindicated the sovereignty of individual freedom, and portrayed the struggle of man's soul against the ills that afflicted him. The world-wide influence of their works was certainly a new force in the nineteenth-century upsurge.

While the poetry and thought of the nineteenth century were in the main romantic and idealistic, its art and literature showed a marked tendency towards realism. The impressionist was realist, although somewhat etherealized, determined to paint only the visible. He was vitally interested in the scientific interpretation of nature. Realism, as a distinct literary movement, began in France. It had its exponents in England, Germany and Russia, who laid bare the hidden springs of human action in all their bare reality. Some of them suggested that human nature might change through the creation of a better order of society.

The principal ideas that motived the movements developing in Europe did not take long to spread to countries beyond, particularly to those with which European nations had already come into contact through their political and commercial expansion. European civilization began thus to extend its influence all over the world, rapid means of communication accelerating the process. But with these ideas also arose and grew insistent their inevitable problems. If Western culture today is a dominant element of world culture, its problems too are equally pressing world problems. This is the main justification for the reference made here to the extraordinary cultural phenomenon of the nineteenth-century Europe with which resurgent India is intimately bound up. In fact, the cultural upsurge of the nineteenth-century India forms part of the world upsurge in the same century.

Both in the world of culture and commerce Europe and Asia knew each other from very early times. China's silk-route carried not only her silk but her ideas to Western Asia and Mediterranean countries. India's historical connection with Greece and Rome from pre-Christian times continued for centuries. The contact between Europe and Asia in modern times was more or less a revival of old relationships, though in the beginning it was of a different nature and not so happy so far as Asia was concerned. Yet it is an event that seemed to have been decreed by Nature for the future progress of the human race. Asia and Europe must unite so that humanity might advance towards a new cycle of life in the One World governed by a new synthesis of Asia's spirituality and Europe's materialism.

Whereas the impact of Europe on India took its definitive turn about the middle of the eighteenth century, it started in Japan about the middle of the next. But Japan being a free country, European culture could not very much penetrate her life. A Japanese writer once said, 'We borrowed their machine, not their Shakespeare'. Nevertheless, the influence was there and was growing, though it never attained the form of a cultural conquest. Japan, as indeed any Asian country, never lost her soul and its characteristic inclinations distinguish her life and culture even today. Yet Japan is the first Asian nation to acquire technological modernity and become a modern nation.

Soon after America's entry into their country for purposes of trade, the Japanese realized that they might profit by their contact with America. And when their leaders overthrew the military rule of the Shogunate and restored the emperor, and then used the imperial authority to overthrow feudalism and introduce Occidental industry, the New Japan was born, whose rapid rise in the present century is a phenomenon of great significance. With much of what was really beneficial to her, Japan imbibed some of Europe's evils too, the worst of which was imperialism and something of her 'mechanism'. But conditions have changed and seem to be changing fast towards a betterment of her relations with others. As one of the great peoples of Asia, Japan has her contributions to make in the creation of a New Asia, and along with it, the New World of tomorrow.

In the beginning China looked upon the Western impact as 'the White Peril'. Through her contact with the nations of Europe that entered China for commercial and missionary purposes, Western ideas began to enter the Chinese mind, and the movement that started in the nineteenth century resulted in the establishment of the Chinese Republic early in the present century under the leadership of one who was a Christian. Whatever China may be today, she has a great destiny to fulfil for which she has lived on through the ages. Her ancient idea of the whole human race as one family in the cosmic Mother of Tāoism has certainly a great bearing on the future unity of mankind.

In India the nineteenth-century upsurge started first in Bengal, 'chosen by the Śakti of India as her first workshop',[1] where she threw up new forces and new personalities that became makers of a new epoch, bringers of a new dawn in every sphere of national life. Plastic in her mind, open in her heart, intuitive in her soul, 'Bengal has eminently the gifts which are most needed for the new race that has to arrive. . . . She has a mighty will-power which comes from the long worship of the Śakti and practice of the Tantra that has been part of our culture for many centuries.'[2] Naturally therefore Bengal soon grew up into a centre of wider awakening in the whole country. The progressive movements that had their birth in Bengal began to expand to all India and prepare her for the great work she is destined to do for the spiritual regeneration of the human race.

Historically speaking, the nineteenth-century upsurge in Bengal could be traced back to the eighteenth century, in 1757. Here the overwhelming superiority of organized resistance

---

[1] Aurobindo, *The Renaissance in India*, p. 60.
[2] Aurobindo, *The Brain of India*, pp. 33, 35.

was undermined by the great betrayal. Then followed the Sannyāsī rebellion of a dedicated band of freedom-fighters. Next the Midnāpur uprising—that unique popular revolt—and the outbreak of 1857: the first bullet at the foreigner went off from Bārrāckpur in Bengal. Isolated instances, no doubt. But they showed the will to freedom that had never deserted the race.

Bengal was the first in India to receive Western culture. In the beginning its reactions seemed to disrupt her own order of life and culture. But she did not take long to work these out and become herself again. What she achieved then is her splendid history of recent times. 'It is Bengal', says Sri Aurobindo, 'which first recovered its soul, respiritualized itself; forced the whole world to hear of its great spiritual personalities, gave it the first modern Indian poet and Indian scientist of world-wide fame and achievement, restored the moribund art of India to life and power, first made her count again in the culture of the world, first, as a reward in the outer life, arrived at a vital political consciousness and a living political movement not imitative and derivative in its spirit and central ideal.'[1]

All these and many more Bengal was able to achieve because she had in the nineteenth century a galaxy of luminaries who illumined her sky from horizon to horizon. About a hundred in number, they were men of outstanding genius in art and literature, religion and mysticism, science and philosophy, law and politics, who along with their compeers in other parts of the country enriched the world of culture in various ways and made wonderful contributions to the growth of resurgent India. It was indeed a springtide of cultural activity that has left a rich legacy of their inspired labours. The leading figures in these movements were not only pioneers but makers of a New India with her part to play in the making of a New World.

The world-wide upsurge in the nineteenth century threw into prominence the scientific and materialistic character of Western civilization, of which reason was the very soul and centre. And it is by the cultivation of reason that the mind of

[1] Aurobindo, *The Ideal of Human Unity*, p. 260.

modern man has been very near fulfilling its utmost possibilities through which, and afterwards exceeding which, man would grow in readiness for a higher power than reason, the next destined step of human evolution. Here ends the basic work of the West and begins the yet greater work of the East.

But before she sets about it the East must have a knowledge of the essential truths of Western civilization, a direct experience of its ways of life. Hence the impact on her of the West—the impact which gave to the somnolent peoples of Asia a rude awakening, an awakening to their own ancient heritage in whose immortal ideals they found the source of their strength, the strength that had sustained them through the long millenniums of their history. The experience of the shock of events and the return to the moorings of their soul started them on a new life inspired with a new sense of hope and confidence. But to their ancient ideals the Asian peoples, especially the Indians, began to turn with their reasoning mind sufficiently quickened by their contact with the West.

All these point to a new movement that was to grow and ultimately lead towards the creation of the spiritual civilization of the future. Notwithstanding the fact that modern Western culture is the mother of many progressive ideas which are more or less intimations of a greater future for humanity, it has raised also serious problems that are now confronting both East and West and causing world-wide tension.

These problems are fundamentally problems of harmony, of peace, freedom and unity culminating in harmony. Intrinsically, this harmony is the harmony of the Whole that exists in the home of the infinite Truth where One is All and All is One and which is far beyond the world of mind. Man has therefore to rise to a consciousness above the mental and discover there the truth of this harmony. The soul of Asia enshrines this vision, and as India is the hoary guardian of this Asian idea and its profound spiritual secrets, her reawakening in recent times is part of the world movement which is India's portion to foster, first, by herself revisioning the ancient Truth, and then declaring it to others, and herself living it so that the most glorious synthesis of the greatest achievements of the mystic East and of the pragmatic West may find their highest fulfilment in the coming age of the Spirit which will see the birth of a New World of truth and light. This is the underlying reason of the resurgence of India that started in the nineteenth century and that has since been, under the veil, gaining in strength from moment to moment.

28

SIDNEY KARTUS

World Unity

THE IDEAL OF HUMAN UNITY

SRI AUROBINDO, the prophet of modern India, laid down his political pen after his early leadership of the struggle of India for independence from the British Empire. He took it up again only when the first world war made urgent and necessary all the vision that mankind could summon in order to prevent such catastrophes in the future and to make human unity possible.

To this end and for this purpose, he wrote his book entitled *The Ideal of Human Unity*, published serially in the *Arya* from 1915 to 1918, and in book form in 1919. In 1950, after the conclusion of the second world war, and in the last year of his life, another edition of the book was published with revisions made before the second conflict and a postscript chapter written after it.

The writings of Aurobindo for Indian independence at the beginning of the twentieth century had been so powerful and distinctive that, even when published anonymously, the British knew that only Aurobindo could be the author. They imprisoned him thrice to silence his pen and voice. His book written for human unity in the world has all the power and uniqueness in this wider field that his polemics of an earlier period had for the liberation of his own people on the sub-continent of India.

The Western world knows far more of Marx's call to the working men of the world to unite than it does of Aurobindo's message to humanity to unite. Yet it is a message such as that of Aurobindo with which humanity must become familiar and which it must heed in order to attain human unity. In this book of enormous scholarship and prophetic vision, Aurobindo traces the rise, mutations, and decline of the civilizations of man from the facts of history and sociology. He begins by saying that 'our whole thought and action with regard to our collective life is shallow . . . it does not base itself on a firm . . . and complete knowledge. . . . The moral is not the vanity of human life . . . and of the ideals it pursues, but the necessity of a wiser, larger, more patient search after its true law and aim. . . . Today the ideal of human unity is more or less vaguely making its way to the forefront of our consciousness . . . is evidently a part of Nature's eventual scheme and must come about.'[1]

Having thus begun with the thesis that human unity will be attained, Aurobindo next takes up the question of what will be the nature of the society in which such unity will exist, and of the relationship in it between the individual and the social group. He arrives at a compatibility in which there is no clash between the two but a harmony and proportion of each in its respective sphere and in conjunction with the other.

'The perfect society', he writes, 'will be that which most entirely favours the perfection of the individual; the perfection of the individual will be incomplete if it does not help him towards the perfect state of the social aggregate to which he belongs and eventually to that of the largest possible human aggregate, the whole of a united humanity.'[2]

Aurobindo then considers the question of what form this largest possible human aggregate will assume, what means of organization it is to embody, along what lines its political machinery is destined to operate. In social aggregates there are always two types. One is state supremacy over the individual; in the other the state yields as much as possible to the 'freedom, dignity, and successful manhood' of the individual. The former would lead to a dominant world state, the latter to a world union. Under one or the other of these two types of global government the human race is fated to live as it draws physically closer together and becomes constantly more economically interdependent.

Aurobindo, *The Ideal of Human Unity*, pp. 2, 7.   [2] *Ibid.*, p. 8.

At present, the first type, state supremacy, is plunging ahead under the banner of a socialist world state. Yet, declares Aurobindo, the idea of a world state is inadequate. It would not unite humanity, nor hold together its hegemony, socialist or otherwise, even if temporarily achieved. Founded on compulsion and ruled from the centre, such states or empires have decayed and fallen throughout history. Reaction against the compulsive nature of a socialist world state might well bring on a greater conflict than any which the world has heretofore experienced, one from which mankind might not emerge. If civilization did survive, it would resume its progression towards human unity on a sounder basis.

A world state is therefore to be avoided. But the idea of a world union of free nations is adequate and sound. It would be a true world democracy against which there would be no reaction. It would unite humanity, and preserve the unity that it brought about. It would not be a source of final conflict but a chapter of final peace. In the words of Aurobindo: '. . . freedom is as necessary to life as law and regime; diversity is as necessary as unity to our true completeness. Existence is only one in its essence and totality, in its play it is necessarily multiform. Absolute uniformity would mean the cessation of life . . . diversity is essential for power and fruitfulness of life, unity is necessary for its order, arrangement and stability. Unity we must create, but not necessarily uniformity.'[1] 'Human society progresses really and vitally in proportion as law becomes the child of freedom; it will reach its perfection when, man having learned to know and to become spiritually one with his fellow-man, the spontaneous law of his society exists only as the outward mould of his self-governed inner liberty.'[2]

The ideal solution, says Aurobindo, is a free grouping of mankind. This made its first appearance with the League of Nations. The league failed, but it was succeeded by the United Nations Organization in which the idea survived and persisted and gained strength. Such a powerful nation as the United States elected to stay out of the league, while today all nations desire to be members of the United Nations Organization and

[1] Aurobindo, *The Ideal of Human Unity*, p. 181.   [2] *Ibid.*, p. 185.

knock at its door to be recognized and admitted, a notable progression in attitude between the demise of the one organization and the birth of the other.

The same urge for unity which joined warring tribes in the larger aggregates of great nations is moving to join the nations of the earth in world union. The same process which worked to bring the ideal of the nation to the forefront of human consciousness will bring forward the ideal of world union. That union when fully formed and realized will enjoy all of the devotion once reserved to the nation, the latter not yielding in the process anything that will not be to its benefit to yield. Such will be the steps of evolution toward a peaceful society and a united world. In it the individual, the smaller unit of government, the nation, and the world union will live and be free in a diverse unity.

The prototype of such a union is being evolved in the United States. Having instituted a central federal government to unite a number of sovereign states, with power to maintain its authority, preserve order, provide for the general welfare, and to control inter-state commerce and international relations, the founding fathers hedged it about with constitutional guarantees of individual and local liberty and a judiciary empowered to enforce those guarantees against the legislative and executive branches. Thus nature's law of diversity within unity was preserved inviolate in the organic law of the newly independent nation; thus it must be preserved in the world which will achieve its independence in the future.

ECONOMISM

In modern social development, writes Aurobindo, 'the economic conception of life overrides all others'.[1] Church, aristocracy, military, letters, and culture have surrendered their former pre-eminence to economism. Time has seen the levelling out of many inequalities among men. The gap has been virtually closed between monarchy and nobility, and between nobility and the middle class. Today the struggle is between the middle classes and the working classes who stand at the

[1] Aurobindo, *The Ideal of Human Unity*, p. 263.

bottom of the social ladder and on whom the curse of poverty, and lack of learning and opportunity, rests most heavily. It is a struggle which dwarfs all of its precursors in scope and intensity; it is world-wide and may become interstellar. This, says Aurobindo, is because economic equality is necessary to existence itself, and therefore is that equality which Nature allows to be violated with the least impunity.

It is questions of 'the proper organization and administration of the economic life of society' which are 'preparing the difficulties of the future' . . . the propertied, and professional classes and the bourgeoisie who governed in the name of the people',[1] but in recent years labour unions 'have attained an equal power with the other classes'[2] and an equal voice in the decision of these economic questions.

'Capital and Labour . . . are now engaged in a . . . conflict for sole possession in which the completion of the downward force of social gravitation, the ultimate triumph of Labour . . . seems to be the visible writing of Fate.'[3] This 'will be a change from one side of economism to the other, but not . . . from economism to the domination of some other and higher motive of human life'.[4] Yet such a change is inevitable; a higher motive is evolving as a religion of humanity.

THE RELIGION OF HUMANITY

Aurobindo says that this religion of the future stems from what he terms the 'intellectual religion of humanity' mind-born in eighteenth-century Europe, mainly in France. From it, the ideal of individual liberty, happiness, and equality, has been impressed indelibly on the human race. But this motive or religion must become something beyond what it has been if that ideal is to be perfected and if the ideal of human unity is also to be perfected and indelibly impressed on human consciousness. This to which the past of mankind owes much and to which the future will owe everything, Aurobindo sums up in the following stirring passages which form the climax of his book:

[1] Aurobindo, *The Ideal of Human Unity*, p. 152.
[2] *Ibid.*, p. 243, footnote.   [3] *Ibid.*, pp. 262–3.   [4] *Ibid.*, p. 266.

War, capital punishment, the taking of human life, cruelty of all kinds whether committed by the individual, the State, or society, not only physical cruelty, but moral cruelty, the degradation of any human being or any class of human beings under whatever specious plea or in whatever interest, the oppression and exploitation of man by man, of class by class, of nation by nation, and all those habits of life and institutions of society of a similar kind which religion and ethics formerly tolerated or even favoured in practice, whatever they might do in their ideal or creed, are crimes against the religion of humanity, abominable to its ethical mind, forbidden by its primary tenets, to be fought against always, in no degree to be tolerated. Man must be sacred to man regardless of all distinctions of race, creed, colour, nationality, status, political or social advancement. The body of man is to be respected, made immune from violence and outrage, fortified by science against disease and preventable death. The life of man is to be held sacred, preserved, strengthened, ennobled, uplifted. The heart of man is to be held sacred also, given scope, protected from violation, from suppression, from mechanization, freed from belittling influences. The mind of man is to be released from all bonds, allowed freedom and range and opportunity, given all its means of self-training and self-development and organized in the play of its power for the service of humanity. And all this too is not to be held as an abstract or pious sentiment, but given full and practical recognition in the persons of men and nations and mankind. This, speaking largely, is the idea and the spirit of the intellectual religion of humanity.[1]

The intellectual religion of humanity already to a certain extent exists, partly as a conscious trend in the minds of a few, partly as a potent shadow in the consciousness of the race. It is the shadow of a spirit that is yet unborn, but is preparing for its birth. . . . Democracy, socialism, pacifism are to a great extent its by-products, or at least owe much of their vigour to its inner presence.[2]

But still in order to accomplish all its future, this idea and religion of humanity has to make itself more explicit, insistent, and categorically imperative. For otherwise it can only work with clarity in the minds of a few and with the mass it will be only a modifying influence but will not be the rule of human life.[3]

. . . the enemy of all real religion . . . is human egoism, the egoism of class and nation. These it could for a time soften . . . : curb their more arrogant, open and brutal expressions, oblige to adopt better

[1] Aurobindo, *The Ideal of Human Unity*, pp. 362–3.
[2] *Ibid.*, pp. 361–2.   [3] *Ibid.*, p. 365.

institutions, but not to give place to the love of mankind, not to recognize a real unity between man and man. For that essentially must be the aim of the religion of humanity, as it must be the earthly aim of all human religion, love, mutual recognition of human brotherhood, a living sense of human oneness and practice of human oneness in thought, feeling and life . . . which was expressed first some thousands of years ago in the ancient Vedic hymn and must always remain the highest injunction of the Spirit within us to human life on earth. Till that is brought about, the religion of humanity remains unaccomplished. With that done, the one necessary psychological change will have been effected without which no formal and mechanical, no political and administrative unity can be real and secure. If it is done, that outward unification may not even be indispensable, or if indispensable it will come about naturally, not as now it seems likely to be, by catastrophic means, but by the demand of the human mind, and will be held secure by an essential need of our perfected and developed human nature . . . achieved, as an outward expression of the larger inward life. . . .[1]

Yet is brotherhood the real key to the triple gospel of the idea of humanity. The union of liberty and equality can only be achieved by the power of human brotherhood and it cannot be founded on anything else. But brotherhood exists only in the soul and by the soul; it can exist by nothing else . . . freedom, equality, unity are the eternal attributes of the Spirit. . . . It is the practical recognition of this truth, it is the awakening of the soul in man, and the attempt to get him to live from his soul and not from his ego which is the inner meaning of religion, and it is that to which the religion of humanity also must arrive before it can fulfil itself in the life of the race.[2]

Since the eighteenth century this religion of humanity has been ethical and rational. All else has been pushed aside as in the realm of the speculative or mystical. Rationalism, either professed or unprofessed, rules the world today. It is no accident that Paine referred to it as that 'rational world' of which he was the 'friend of its happiness'. But two world wars have now proven man's inability to cope with his problems by pacts, agreements, political devices, and organizational methods of a rational order alone. Rationalism is nevertheless determined, and with justification, not to surrender its hard-won forts or to give up what it has so recently wrung from the stalwarts on

---

[1] Aurobindo, *The Ideal of Human Unity*, pp. 365–6, 368.
[2] *Ibid.*, pp. 368–9.

the mystic side, and one thing that rationalism will not permit man to do is to suffer again what he has suffered in the past at the hands of dogmatic and inquisitorial religion and autocratic government.

But the rationalist is not faced with a choice between the past errors of religion and government and the impasse which his rationalistic world has reached in such a short period of time, a world now capable of more incredible confusion and more terrible suffering and damage than any with which it could be previously charged under mysticism.

The rational world can turn instead to that more imperative religion of humanity which will not violate the tenets of rationality or the theories of science. The political scientist, like the physical scientist, will then find himself face to face with a realm not divided from his own but greater and all-encompassing from which 'the truth of the Spirit may step in and lead humanity to the path of its highest possible happiness and perfection'.[1] Such is the philosophy of Aurobindo from which arises his conception of human unity and brotherhood. His philosophy affirms the reality of universal being, variously expressed and diversely creative, an enlightened awareness of the spiritual unity of our existence through which enduring world unity can be achieved.

[1] Aurobindo, *The Ideal of Human Unity*, p. 379.

29

TARAKNATH DAS

The Political Philosophy of Sri Aurobindo

Aurobindo was the greatest intellectual of our age and a major force for the life of the spirit. India will not forget his services to politics and philosophy and the world will remember with gratitude his invaluable work in the realm of philosophy and religion.[1]

THE above passage, a tribute from Dr Sarvepalli Radhakrishnan, India's Vice-President and world renowned philosopher, gives an estimate of Sri Aurobindo as a man who in his early life gave his services to the cause of the freedom of India, not for India's aggrandizement but for humanity's welfare and progress. Today the world knows Sri Aurobindo as the Saint of Pondicherry, who worked for spreading a philosophy of life, based on the teachings of the Ṛg Veda, the earlier Upaniṣads, the Vedānta and the Bhagavad Gītā and supported by the modern scientific knowledge of man's potentialities for greatness. But Sri Aurobindo also made distinct contributions in the field of political philosophy, which would vastly influence our course of social evolution.

I

Man's religious, social and political ideals or philosophies are interwoven into a whole; and these cannot be compartmentalized. Thus a man's political philosophy is a segment of his total world-view which he cherishes or which is in the process of transition. His philosophy of life is the product of the cumulative heritage of the group in which he is born and it is

[1] D. Mackenzie Brown, *The White Umbrella* (Berkeley: University of California Press, 1958), p. 124.

modified by inner evolution of the individual as influenced by outside forces—local and world-wide. This was also the case with Sri Aurobindo.

Aurobindo was the product of Indian renaissance during which the most enlightened of her people were consciously engaged in reassertion of the best of Indian thought and at the same time interested in assimilation of the best of the West. This renaissance of India began in Bengal roughly from the time of Rājā Rām Mohon Roy (1772–1833), the founder of the Brāhmo Samāj movement (reformed Hinduism), a pioneer in the field of comparative religion and an advocate of political and social reforms in the India of his time. Sri Aurobindo was born in a most cultured family of Konnagar in Western Bengal. His grandfather was a leader of the Brāhmo Samāj movement and was a pupil of David Hare of Calcutta, noted for his educational activities. His father, Krishnadhan Ghose, after receiving medical education at Calcutta, was sent to Aberdeen University for higher studies where he took an M.D. degree. After his return from England, he entered the Indian Medical Service and served as Civil Surgeon in various parts of India. He was a cosmopolitan and his home became a common meeting place for Europeans and Bengalees.

Aurobindo was born in 1872, some fifteen years after the outbreak of the so-called Sepoy Mutiny (1857) which was an effort to overthrow British domination in India. In 1885 the All India Congress movement came into existence, but during the quarter of a century between the Queen's Proclamation (1858) and the inauguration of the Congress movement, the spirit of the intelligentsia of India was permeated with activities for cultural, social, economic and political regeneration of the people.

Aurobindo's father believed that India must adopt western methods of civilization. He felt that his children should be given the best of western education. Thus Aurobindo got his early education in the Loretto Convent, Darjeeling. In 1879, Aurobindo and his brothers were sent to England for further education which was entrusted in the care of Mr and Mrs Drewett, then residing in Manchester. Mr Drewett was an accomplished Latin scholar and he inculcated the study of

Latin and Greek in him. In 1885 Aurobindo was sent to St Paul's school in London. After five years' study in the school and making remarkable progress in classical studies, Aurobindo obtained a senior classical scholarship, and proceeded to King's College, Cambridge. 'Soon after entering Cambridge he appeared for the Indian Civil Service Examination and was given record marks in Greek and Latin. . . . Aurobindo passed the first part of the Classical Tripos Examination in the First Class at the end of his second year at Cambridge, and during these years also managed to spend part of his time studying modern languages and in writing Greek and Latin verse, *for which in one of the years he won all the prizes given at King's College.*'[1]

II

Aurobindo was at Cambridge to enter the Indian Civil Service, but things happened that changed the whole career of the man. During his stay in England as a student at King's College he absorbed the political theories and ideals of freedom and at the same time felt very keenly about the condition of the people of India, an enslaved people under foreign domination. After fourteen years in England, at the age of twenty-one, in 1893 Aurobindo left for India. But it is said that while a student in London, he had joined a secret society entitled 'The Lotus and Dagger', dedicated to the cause of Indian freedom. At the age of twenty-one Aurobindo was actively engaged in carrying out his political creed of freedom for man by championing the cause of freedom of the people of India.

In 1893 he took an appointment in the Civil Service of the State of Baroda where he worked for nearly thirteen years. During the latter part of his stay there, he was Vice-Principal of Baroda College, which is now Baroda University.

Fourteen years spent in England (from the age of seven to twenty-one) for education, laid the foundation of his future career as a man of vision and world perspective. But thirteen years spent at Baroda were spent not merely for the service of

[1] G. M. Langley, *Sri Aurobindo* (London: Royal India and Pakistan Society, 1949), p. 14.

the State (Baroda was the most progressive of all Indian States, specially in the field of education), but for self-education in the field of acquiring clear comprehension of India's legacy in the spiritual field and for the formulation of a revolutionary programme for Indian freedom as a necessary factor to the freedom of Asia and the spiritual regeneration of the world.

III

It may be interesting to note that the year 1893 is the most important one in the history of modern India. It was in 1893 that Swami Vivekananda came to the Parliament of Religion held at Chicago and represented Hinduism. Vivekananda's speech at the Parliament of Religion created a sensation all over the world, specially in India. The message was simple but revolutionary. The young Hindu *sannyāsin* proclaimed the old truth of the ancient sages that there are many ways to reach the destination of man's supreme interest in achieving God-consciousness, and that no religion has the monopoly of salvation. Every individual has the potentiality of divine existence and the thing that is necessary is to develop this 'God-in-man' through one's *sādhanā*. The human soul is immortal and thus it never dies and the true nature of man is the source of all good and beyond all fear. This was the message of freedom and fearlessness in search after truth as was being taught by Vivekananda, the disciple of Sri Ramakrishna. Aurobindo recognized the significance of Vivekananda's activities—in a sense, conquering the thought world. This gave him double inspiration to drink deep at the fountain of knowledge of the ancient sages of India. As a student of Greek philosophy he was quite conscious of the fact that through knowledge man may become free. But in studying the Upaniṣads, the Bhagavad Gītā and other works of the ancient Hindus, he was deeply impressed with the teachings of karma yoga. At this stage of his life he was thinking in terms of activities leading to the freedom of India.

Sri Aurobindo, during his Cambridge days, was deeply interested in Indian politics and later he became the leader of an Indian revolutionary movement. If the teachings of

Ramakrishna and Vivekananda gave him the firm spiritual foundation for political activities, it was Bāl Gangādhar Tilak, one of the Congress leaders, but later on termed as the 'extremist' leader of the Congress party, who roused the spirit of political activities, not merely for some small concessions to be given to the Indian people towards self-government, but for freedom of the land from a foreign yoke. In Hindu philosophy a man's liberation is not based on grace of somebody, but is to be attained by action. To be spiritually free there must be 'the will to be free'. Tilak represented the school of Indian political thought which advocated that if India were to be free then there must be a resolute will to be free, supported by actions which might lead to suffering. A political leader must be a *karma yogi* and not an opportunist. It is not the place for me to discuss Tilak in action, but I want to emphasize that Aurobindo was influenced by Bāl Gangādhar Tilak so much that he wrote an essay on 'Appreciation of Tilak' as an Indian national leader.

Another man, who influenced Sri Aurobindo's political and social ideals as well as internationalism, was Rabindranath Tagore, the first Asian to win the coveted recognition of a winner of the Nobel Prize in literature. Tagore was not only a poet, dramatist, educator, and musician, but he was a philosopher and a revolutionist. To be a revolutionist, one is not required to be a 'bomb-thrower' or a so-called 'terrorist'. A true revolutionist is a torch-bearer of truth and fearlessness. Rabindranath Tagore was such a man, possibly one of the greatest personalities of modern times.

IV

During the end of the nineteenth century and early years of the twentieth century, many things were happening in the field of world politics which had their effects upon the mind of Asian, specially Indian, leaders. The Boer War left an impression that a small nation willing to fight for freedom can carry on the struggle against such a powerful force as the British Empire. Japan defeated China and later Japan's victory over Russia shattered many of the myths regarding the inferiority of Asian peoples in the arena of international affairs and politics. While these changes were going on in the world, including Turkish and Persian revolutions, a new political force was developing in India. The All India National Congress, which came into existence in 1885 and was working for political reforms of British administration in India, primarily through the good will of the British rulers, by the end of the nineteenth century and early twentieth century was not gaining the end and there was a new demand for action such as might lead to the complete independence of India.

It was during the administration of Lord Curzon, as the Governor-General of India, that the British authorities decided to partition Bengal, the most politically advanced and the largest of the provinces in India. The British authorities thought that their programme would be carried out without much resistance; but the new spirit of India asserted itself and there was the struggle for Indian freedom. By this time Sri Aurobindo was one of the leaders of an underground revolutionary movement, a link between Mahārāṣṭra led by Bāl Gangādhar Tilak and the revolutionists of Bengal.

Here it may be asserted that the real movement for Indian freedom from British rule was under the direction of the underground revolutionists who were influenced by revolutions in various parts of the world, specially by the writings of Mazzini for the establishment of united Italy—a republic. It may surprise many western scholars of the Indian freedom movement to know Mazzini's writings, such as *Duties of Man* and other works, which were translated into Bengali; and the working principles of the Italian Carbonari Society were well known among them. The initiates of the Bengal revolutionary movement had to study the life of Garibaldi, the Bhagavad Gītā and some special writings of Swami Vivekananda. Above all the story of the Sannyāsī revolt in Bengal which happened during the early days of the nineteenth century and as it was depicted in the drama, *Ānanda Math*, was a source of inspiration to Indian nationalists and the song 'Bande Mātaram' (Hail Mother) was sung as the national anthem. 'Bande Mātaram' became the watchword or words of greeting among the youth of Bengal. At this time Aurobindo's visits to Bengal from Baroda became frequent and he played the most important role in formulating the programme and activities of Indian revolutionists who were trying to capture the Congress organization.

Aurobindo played an important part in formulating that *Swarāj* (self-rule or independence) will be the goal and this must be attained by national efforts of constructive activities of development of national industries and, at the same time, special emphasis was to be put in furthering national education, in which Indian national culture must be given proper recognition, and Indian history must be interpreted in the proper perspective of Indian national aspirations. It was through the efforts of Indian revolutionists under the leadership of Aurobindo that the programme of *Swarāj*, *Swadeshi* and *National Education* became accepted by the nation. To be sure many other prominent leaders played their role and supported the movement. It was in 1905 and 1906 that the real foundation for Indian freedom was laid.

v

Aurobindo was not a visionary and he felt the immediate need of an organ of the so-called extremists of Indian nationalists to preach the ideal. Thus a daily paper entitled *Bande Mātaram* was established with Aurobindo as its editor. The files of the *Bande Mātaram* contain many articles by Aurobindo which must be carefully studied by those who wish to understand the spirit of Indian nationalism. The Indian revolutionists, with Aurobindo as their leader, were the first who were convinced that for the success of their cause for freedom, the nation as a whole must be awakened; thus they went to villages to work among the peasants. At this time the National Council for Education in Bengal was organized at Calcutta and the first national college was established and Aurobindo was its first principal, while men like Rabindranath Tagore, Ananda Coomarswamy and others were associated with this great educational movement. This national college became Bengal National Technical College and is now the Jadavpur University, one of the foremost technical colleges in India. It may be noted that the youth of Bengal and the students at colleges and universities responded to the call which Aurobindo and his associates spread through newspapers, public meetings and secret meetings. Tens of thousands of students joined the nationalist movement. At the same time Rabindranath Tagore through his songs roused the patriotic emotions of the people verging to religious ecstasy. It was Rabindranath Tagore who prepared his concrete proposal of 'creation of a State within State' in his book, *Swadeshi Samāj*.

VI

From the above-mentioned facts, it must be clear that Aurobindo was not a visionary but a karma yogi engaged in *dharma yuddha* (fight for righteous existence or supremacy of right over might). It also makes clear that some fifteen years or longer before the inauguration of the non-co-operation movement (after the special session of the All India National Congress at Calcutta by Mahatma Gandhi), Bengal revolutionists under the leadership of Aurobindo were engaged in practising non-co-operation and organizing a 'State within the State'.

Lest there be any misunderstanding about Aurobindo's relations with terrorist activities in Bengal, it may be safely asserted that he was never personally implicated in any terrorist act; but Aurobindo was not a pacifist like Mahatma Gandhi and must have known that a section of the revolutionists were willing to die for freedom and thus giving fight to the tools of repression. In August 1907, Aurobindo was arrested on the charge of preaching sedition and inciting terroristic activities. He was kept in Alipur jail for nearly a year during the period of the trial. Ultimately he was acquitted through the efforts of his lawyer, the late Chittarajan Das. Chittarajan Das held that Aurobindo would readily and gladly admit 'having propagated the message and elucidated the meaning of national independence', and that for this 'he would be willing to suffer to the uttermost'.[1] Chittarajan's final appeal to the judges was significant:

[1] K. R. Srinivasa Iyengar, *Sri Aurobindo* (Pondicherry: Sri Aurobindo Ashram Press, 1950), p. 162.

'My appeal to you is this, that long after this controversy will be hushed in silence, long after this turmoil and agitation will have ceased, long after he is dead and gone, he will be looked upon as the poet of patriotism, as the prophet of nationalism, and the lover of humanity. His words will be echoed and re-echoed, not only in India, but across distant seas and lands.'[1]

While Aurobindo was the editor of the *Bande Mātaram*, he was reputed to be the author of a pamphlet entitled, 'Bhawāni Mandir', the theme of which is that they must build a temple to Bhawāni, the Mother, as the source of their strength; and that attached to the temple there must be a new order of karma-yogis prepared to renounce all in the service of the Mother. The work of the order must be based upon knowledge as upon a rock. What knowledge, it will be asked? The answer is given categorically—the knowledge enshrined in the mighty formula of the ancient gospel of Vedānta. And to what end? The answer is given without hesitation—to the end that India may fulfil the high destiny reserved for her. 'It is she who must send forth from herself the future religion of the entire world, the eternal religion which is to harmonize all religions, science and philosophies and make mankind one soul.'[2]

It is quite clear from the future development of Sri Aurobindo's life that while he was in Alipur jail, which he later termed Alipur Ashram, he had time to contemplate on the above ideal and what he should do for his own development and about his ultimate mission. Aurobindo wrote about his jail experience in this way: 'God seemed to whisper, "I have had another thing for you to do, and it is for that I have brought you here, to teach you here what you could not learn for yourself, and to train you for my work".'[3]

In February 1910, Aurobindo retired from Calcutta and withdrew from political movements and went to Chandannagore and a few months later settled down at Pondicherry and attracted many disciples. He passed away from this mortal world on December 5, 1950, leaving a distinct place for himself in Indian politics, and the world of philosophy and religion.

[1] G. M. Langley, *Sri Aurobindo*, p. 16.
[2] *Ibid.*, Lord Zetland's preface, p. vii.   [3] *Ibid.*, pp. 16–17.

VII

Aurobindo's political philosophy was not merely that of revolutionary changes to be brought about in the world. He felt that in order to build a new structure we may have to tear down old buildings unsuited to new conditions, so we may usher into existence a new and better social order. How should the new social order be run? It should be directed by the wisest and the best of the society and not by a privileged class. What should be the spirit behind the activities of the rulers? They should practise *'rājdharma'* or ethical and spiritual laws governing the activities of the ruler in the field of administration of a state of human relations. According to Hindu philosophy this concept of duty or self-imposed obligation of a ruler is to carry on the government of a State, to uphold the welfare of the people and to protect them from oppression, external or internal. The ruler should possess the power of intelligence and knowledge, economic support as well as support of the people so that he will be able to fulfil his obligations, but never to use power for self-aggrandizement and despotically. Aurobindo not only believed in the fundamental principles, but he practised them in his political career. The greatest tribute that was ever paid to Aurobindo was the poem written by Rabindranath Tagore extending his salutation to him, indicating that he (Tagore) and all India were willing to follow his leadership, because he was not only a political leader but a riṣi (a seer of truth).[1]

Aurobindo's political philosophy was not limited to nationalism but he was thinking of a world State in which nations will play their own part and in which their existence would be integrated harmoniously on the basis of the cultural assets of various peoples. Thus he was opposed to partitions, or artificial division of states by imperialist powers. Although he was retired from politics he expressed strong dissent against the partition of India in 1947. As he was an apostle of the infinite possibilities of individual development, so was he one of the foremost supporters of freedom of the subject peoples, and thus

[1] Rabindranath Tagore, *Salutation to Sri Aurobindo* (Pondicherry: Sri Aurobindo Ashram, 1949).

freedom of Asian and African peoples. He was opposed to racial and cultural imperialisms of all kinds and was an advocate of the brotherhood of man.

Although the world speaks of Gandhi as the liberator of India, the fact remains that all of the ideas of Gandhi, except absolute pacificism, were preached by others—specially Vivekananda, Tagore and Aurobindo; and the latter, as a revolutionary leader, preached and practised the ideal of freedom in India and ushered a revolutionary era leading to her political freedom. Aurobindo was not, however, content with the political freedom of India. As soon as he realized that the attainment of political independence was only a question of time, and that it was sure to come as a result of the rising tide of Indian nationalism combined with the pressure of favourable international forces, he devoted himself heart and soul to the task of dynamizing the opulent spiritual heritage of India so that she might make the most constructive use of her newly gained freedom toward the fulfilment of her spiritual mission in the world.

30

A. B. PURANI

Sri Aurobindo: A Brief Life-Sketch

I

OF all the Indians who have recently contributed to the moulding of man's higher values in the modern world, apart from
politicians, none is less known to Englishmen than Sri
Aurobindo. Yet, of all the Indians who have been writers or
leaders, none but Sri Aurobindo had the benefit of being brought
up entirely in the best English tradition and none dived deeper
into the profundities of Indian spirituality.

Born on August 15, 1872, he was brought to England as
a child. He became in his life the great philosopher-yogi
ranking in spiritual attainment with giants like Ramakrishna
Paramahansa and Raman Maharshi who had an entirely
Indian background. Yet, this great leader of men wrote only
in English and has given an epic, *Sāvitrī*, to the English language.

His father, Dr K. D. Ghose, had his medical training in
Edinburgh and became so enamoured with the English way of life
that he decided to bring up his children in the English tradition.
He employed an English governess, Miss Pagett, for his child
in Calcutta so that he might grow up in complete ignorance of
the Indian language, social forms, tradition and religion.

In 1879 he brought his three sons to England and left the
youngest, Aurobindo, aged seven, with the Rev. William
Drewett, a Congregational Minister in Manchester, where he
remained from 1879 to 1884.

Aurobindo did not attend any school in Manchester, but he
was taught Latin, the elements of history, geography, arith-
metic, English, etc., at home by the Drewetts—husband and wife.
At an early age he read English poetry and wrote verses for

the *Fox Family Magazine*! In 1881 Mr Drewett resigned his Church and emigrated to Australia leaving young Aurobindo in charge of one Mr Acroyd, whose name appears with Sri Aurobindo's in the Register of St Paul's School as 'Arabinda Acroyd Ghose'!!

From Manchester he was taken to London and admitted to St Paul's School in October 1884. The famous Dr Walker was then High Master and took a personal interest in him, coaching him in Greek. He proved a very promising student and won an Open Scholarship in Classics to King's College, Cambridge.

While at St Paul's, life was hard for the young scholar because remittances from his father had become irregular for some years. He also had difficulty in finding lodgings and it was an Englishman who helped him to stay in the office of the city Liberal Club and continue his studies.

This benefactor was James Cotton who was born at Coonoor in India and who took a personal interest in these young Indian boys and provided the eldest with some work in the office of the club, thus enabling him to live on the premises. This James Cotton was brother of Sir Henry Cotton who was among the pioneers of the Indian National Congress. In the office of the club, there were no heating arrangements and young Aurobindo suffered much in winter. He had not even an overcoat: sometimes he went short of food.

But no privations interfered with his thirst for knowledge, nor was he driven to seek a life of material success and comfort. Towards the end of his school career, Sri Aurobindo gave more attention to general extra-curricular reading—literature, fiction, poetry, etc. He also studied French, German, Italian and Spanish and spent much time writing poetry.

II

At Cambridge from 1890-2 he was mainly occupied with the study of the classics, with writing poetry, and with the question of Indian freedom. In 1892 he took a First Class in the Classical Tripos Part I, and obtained prizes in Greek and Latin poetry. He was selected for the Indian Civil Service, again securing record marks in Classics. However, he did not take his degree—

as it meant spending two years longer at the university, and not wishing to go through the routine of the I.C.S., he absented himself from the riding test and consequently was not selected for active service.

One of the reasons for his attitude towards the I.C.S. may have been his participation in the newly formed 'Majlis', an association of Indian students at Cambridge, in which, on several occasions, he advocated in very strong terms the cause of Indian independence. In fact, this was an indication of one of the major trends of his future career.

Writing poetry was another preoccupation. He had taught himself sufficient German and Italian to read Goethe and Dante in the original. His first collection of poems, 'Songs to Myrtilla', was published at Baroda in 1895. It was Laurence Binyon, then a student, who read them at Cambridge and pressed him to print them.

When he had finished his studies at King's the question of employment became acute. It was again Mr James Cotton who introduced him to the late Gaekwar of Baroda, then in London. As a result of the introduction, Sri Aurobindo joined the service of the Baroda State as the professor of English and French.

III

Sri Aurobindo was in Baroda from 1893 to 1905. Almost immediately on his return to India his interest in Indian politics showed itself in a series of articles in which he attacked in very strong terms the moderate policy of the Congress. He emphasized the inalienable right of Indians to freedom, and in place of the moderate policy of prayer, petition and protest, he advocated the virile policy of self-reliance, sacrifice and organization. He asked Congress to bring in the masses to support the movement of freedom. During every vacation in the college he visited Bengal, studied the political atmosphere and started revolutionary groups of young men in several districts.

The years in Baroda were not only full of formative but creative activity. He studied Indian culture and several Indian languages with the same avidity and zeal with which he had studied Greek and Latin and European culture in England. He wrote poems, some of which were later published as *Ahana and Other Poems*.

As a professor he was the idol of the students. When he came back from Surat to Baroda from the historic session of Congress, the students unyoked the horses of his carriage and pulled it to his house.

In 1906 he resigned his post in the Baroda State which was a lucrative and promising one, and in answer to the call of 'Mother India' went to Calcutta as the Principal of the newly started national college, on a mere subsistence basis.

IV

Actually, twelve years from 1898 to 1910 was the period of Sri Aurobindo's political activity, including the vacations from 1893; but for the first six years he worked from behind the scenes. Only after 1904 he began to come out openly and in 1906 he became a recognized leader when the agitation against Lord Curzon's partition of Bengal created a political storm in India. The poet and the professor became a flaming patriot and national leader.

Apart from his participation in Congress, he edited a national daily and weekly journal, *Bande Mātaram*, from 1906 to 1908, which gave to the Nationalist movement its philosophy and raised politics to the plane of spirituality. He naturally came up against the administration of Lord Minto and was charged with sedition but acquitted by the court. A second time he was implicated in the historic Alipore bomb case but at the end of a long drawn out trial he was again acquitted. As sometimes happens in life, there was strangely a dramatic irony in the situation, since Mr Charles Beachcroft, who was second to Sri Aurobindo in Classics in the I.C.S. at Cambridge, was the Sessions Judge and Sri Aurobindo was the accused.

It was then that Tagore wrote that famous poem: 'O Aurobindo! accept the salutation of Rabindra', and called him: 'The Voice incarnate of the Soul of India.'

His political work, though short in duration, made a lasting contribution to the political ideology of India at a most critical time of her history. His wide study of European history, his keen and comprehensive mind, his unrivalled mastery of English and above all his utter sincerity and readiness to sacrifice are now matters of Indian political history. It was he who, along with Tilak and Bepin Chandra Pal, first advocated the policy of passive resistance, Swadeshi and boycott, together with the constructive programme of national education and arbitration courts. He wrote a series of seven articles on passive resistance in 1907, declaring forty years ago: 'India awakes not for herself but for humanity.'

Though he approved of revolutionary activity as a right of the suppressed nation, his mind turned away from it from 1914; for, he knew that India would be free without violence. He told this to me in December 1918, when Indian freedom was not visible even on the distant political horizon: 'You can take it from me it is as certain as the rising of the sun tomorrow.'

Sri Aurobindo fully represented not only the nationalist mind of India but based his political philosophy on the true spirit of Indian culture which always stresses and relies more upon moral and spiritual forces than upon outer aids and material means. It was by stressing those inner spiritual forces of man and activating them that India has brought some of the elements of her culture to the forefront of international life today.

v

During the year of detention under trial, Sri Aurobindo found time to resume the practice of inner discipline—called yoga—for which he was longing but which his political preoccupation had prevented him from pursuing. Yoga is an inner and conscious effort at spiritual growth. It can be a very natural and normal process.

This inner discipline, consisting of definite psychological practices, gave him a very concrete spiritual experience, an illumination, in which in his cell in jail and even in the court of trial, he experienced the omnipresent Reality as the basic truth of the individual and the cosmos. He gave public utterance to this experience in 1909, on his release, in the famous speech delivered at Uttarpārā, a suburb of Calcutta. It is interesting to mention that the Government of India have now kept this cell as an historical monument.

The spiritual illumination was another turning point in Sri Aurobindo's life. The experience gripped him and he cut himself off from politics and retired first to the French town of Chandernagore and ultimately settled at Pondicherry in the South where he remained from 1910 till his death in 1950.

But this did not mean, as most people supposed, that he had retired into some height of spiritual experience devoid of any further interest in the world or in life. It could not mean that, for the very principle of his yoga is not only to realize the Divine and attain to a complete spiritual consciousness, but also to take all life and all world activity into the scope of this spiritual consciousness and action and to base life on the Spirit and give it a spiritual meaning. In his retirement Sri Aurobindo kept a close watch on all that was happening in the world and in India and actively intervened whenever necessary, but solely with a spiritual force and silent spiritual action, for it is part of the experience of those who have advanced in yoga that besides the ordinary forces and activities of the mind and life and body in matter, there are other forces and powers that can and do act from behind and from above; there is also a spiritual dynamic power which can be possessed by those who are advanced in the spiritual consciousness, though all do not care to possess, or possessing, to use it, and this power is greater than any other and more effective. It was this force which Sri Aurobindo used at first only in a limited field of personal work, but afterwards in a constant action upon the world forces.

Twice he went out of his way and found it necessary to make public pronouncements on important world issues, which shows distinctly that renunciation of life is not a part of his yoga. First, during the second world war when Paris fell, he declared himself openly on the side of the Allies and made financial contribution in answer to appeal for funds; the second time, he pleaded for the acceptance of Sir Stafford Cripps's offer by the Indian National Congress.

He wanted to discover whether this experience of the

omnipresent Reality could be made—by training—the normal part of man's consciousness. And if it could be so made, he wanted to work out the psychological result, the transformation, that would follow in the life of the individual and of the group. To him this illumination was at once the revelation of man's destiny on earth and its attainment the one key to the solution of man's problems.

From 1914 to 1920, he conducted a philosophical monthly called *The Arya* in which he published the results of his experience, experiments, meditation and thought. He arrived at what he called 'a grand synthesis of human knowledge'. All his great works, *The Life Divine, The Synthesis of Yoga, Ideal of Human Unity, Human Cycle, Future Poetry,* and original interpretations of Indian lore—the Veda, Upaniṣad and Gītā—were published serially in this monthly. It was with reference to his metaphysical masterpiece, *The Life Divine,* that the late Sir Francis Younghusband acclaimed him as 'the greatest contributor to contemporary philosophy after Bergson'.

This contribution to English literature, though insufficiently known to the intelligentsia in England, deserves study and consideration; for, he brings to his synthesis a unique detachment towards both East and West. He brings to Indian culture the rich gifts of his European training, his emphasis on the acceptance of life in any scheme of spiritual regeneration of man and the importance of collective life, the need for outer perfection and organization coupled with spiritual realization and ascent to higher levels of consciousness. To the West, he brings the true spiritual basis of reconstruction of individual and collective life, by insisting and proving that man's problem is mainly inner and psychological and can therefore be solved only by bringing about an inner change in man's nature, by rising to a higher level of consciousness beyond intellect.

In his *Life Divine* he shows that behind the appearances of the universe there is the reality of a Being and Consciousness, a Self of all things, one and eternal. All beings are united in that One Self but divided by a certain separativeness of consciousness. It is possible to remove this veil of separative consciousness by a certain psychological discipline and become aware of the true Self, the Divinity within us and all.

This One Being and Consciousness is involved here in matter. Evolution is the method by which it liberates itself; consciousness appears in what seems to be inconscient and once having appeared is self-impelled to grow higher and higher and enlarge towards a greater and greater perfection. Evolution begins with matter, goes up to life and has reached mind. This evolution is not a linear progression, it is emergent, each phase revealing altogether new powers not found in the last one, e.g. life has characteristics different from matter, mind has powers that mere life has not. Man is the representative of this mental consciousness. But evolution has not come to its end; man is not, and is not intended to be, its final product. Man is a transitional being, he has to exceed his present mental consciousness and reach the higher level of truth-consciousness, which, though supraconscient to him at present, is potential to him, and attainable. In his reading of man's future, Sri Aurobindo is the seer of the new age.

The basis of all experience is consciousness; consciousness therefore is the fundamental fact of existence. This consciousness, as seen in man, is capable of ascent and enlargement—it is not confined to one (horizontal) plane but is multi-dimensional. If in our modern outlook we accept and work out the unlimited possibilities of matter and energy, there is no reason to limit the potentiality of life and mind and human spirit.

He shows that the ultimate Reality from which creation flows is not a void, or zero or a contentless remote Absolute or an anthropomorphic God—unconnected with the cosmos. Rather, it is the omnipresent Reality immanent in the cosmos —a dynamic divine Reality—if one may say—a Mother-Consciousness as much as a Father Consciousness—that holds this creation to its bosom. It is the sustaining power of the Divine that keeps the universe going so that one day man may realize on earth his divine destiny.

From 1926 Sri Aurobindo, in response to some people's demands, started the Ashram at Pondicherry with a view to realizing the goal of divine life on earth. It has now an International University attached to it to which people come from all over the world, including Europeans and Americans.

He wrote two volumes of *Collected Poems* and an epic,

'*Sāvitrī*' extending to 2,700 lines. Throughout his long life, he retained his unflagging seeking for knowledge, his thirst for freedom and will to perfection, and never hesitated to sacrifice material prospects to attain progress. He preached and lived the freedom of man, the unity of mankind, and the divinity of man.

He represents the type of transformed humanity of the future—and in that sense is the founder and precursor of the divine race of men.

NOTES ON THE CONTRIBUTORS
TO THIS VOLUME

ARABINDA BASU. Spalding Lecturer in Indian Philosophy and Religion, University of Durham, Durham, England. Spalding Visiting Lecturer, Hebrew University of Jerusalem, Israel. Member, Committee of Experts on Translation of Representative Works, International Council for the Study of Philosophy and Humanities. B.A. and M.A., University of Calcutta.

SATISCHANDRA CHATTERJEE. Head of the Department of Philosophy, University of Calcutta. Visiting Professor at the University of Hawaii, 1952. Author of: *The Nyāya Theory of Knowledge; Fundamentals of Hinduism; Problems of Philosophy; An Introduction to Indian Philosophy* (co-author with D. M. Datta). M.A., P.R.S., and Ph.D., University of Calcutta.

HARIDAS CHAUDHURI. Professor of Indian Philosophy and Chairman of the Department of South Asia, American Academy of Asian Studies, San Francisco. President, Cultural Integration Fellowship, California. Lecturer in Indian Culture, Rudolph Schaeffer School of Design, San Francisco. Formerly Professor and Head of the Department of Philosophy, Krishnagar Government College, West Bengal. Fellow of Yoga-Vedanta Forest Academy, Rishikesh, India. Delegate to: The Silver Jubilee Session of the Indian Philosophical Congress, Calcutta, 1950; The Sixth National Conference of the U.S. National Commission for UNESCO, San Francisco, 1957. Author of: *Sri Aurobindo: The Prophet of Life Divine; The Philosophy of Integralism; The Rhythm of Truth; Prayers of Affirmation; Indian Culture* (co-editor with Dr Matilal Das); and some books in Bengali. M.A. and D.Phil., University of Calcutta.

TARAKNATH DAS. One of the co-workers of Sri Aurobindo during the first Indian Independence Movement. Lecturer in different American colleges and universities including The Catholic University of America, City College of New York, Queen's College, New York University, Columbia University, University of Hawaii, University of Southern California, University of Maryland, and Pace College, New York City. Co-founder and the present Director of Taraknath Das Foundation, New York. Author of: *Is Japan a Menace to Asia; India in World Politics; Indian Struggle for Freedom; Foreign Policy in the Far East;* and

others. A.B. and M.A., University of Washington. Ph.D., George-
town University; Ph.D.(Hon.), University of Munich, Germany.

SIDNEY KARTUS. Member of the Arizona State Legislature
(1944–56). Observer for Arizona State Legislative Council of
Colorado River Litigation before U.S. Supreme Court. Re-elected
member of Arizona House of Representatives for 1959–60. Author
of reports and articles on reclamation, historical and other subjects
including the pamphlet *Aurobindo: Prophet of Modern India.*

S. K. MAITRA. Honorary Professor of Philosophy and formerly
Head of the Department of Philosophy, Banares Hindu University. Director of The Indian Institute of Philosophy, Amalner,
1917–18. President, Indian Philosophical Congress, 1948. Author
of: *The Neo-Romantic Movement in Contemporary Philosophy;
The Philosophical Currents of the Present Day; Social Organization
in North-East India in Buddha's Time; An Introduction to the
Philosophy of Sri Aurobindo; Studies in Sri Aurobindo's Philosophy; The Meeting of the East and West in Sri Aurobindo's
Philosophy; The Spirit of Indian Philosophy; Whither Philosophy;*
and numerous articles published in different journals. M.A. and
Ph.D., University of Calcutta.

T. M. P. MAHADEVAN. Professor and Head of the Department of
Philosophy, University of Madras. Visiting Lecturer in Cornell
University, 1948–9. President, Indian Philosophical Congress,
1955. Delegate to Goethe Bicentennial Convocation at Aspen,
Colorado, and to East-West Philosophers' Conference at the
University of Hawaii, 1949. Publications include: *The Philosophy
of Advaita; The Upaniṣads: An Anthology; The Fundamentals
of Logic; Whither Civilization and Other Broadcast Talks; Gauḍa-
pāda: A Study in Early Advaita; Time and the Timeless; The Idea
of God in Śaiva-Siddhānta; Outlines of Hinduism.* M.A. and Ph.D.,
Madras University.

RICHARD P. MARSH. Lecturer in English and Assistant Professor
of Radio-TV, San Francisco State College. Formerly Lecturer at
College of San Mateo, California. Writer, producer and staff
announcer at different radio stations of Northern California.
Member of the Guild for Psychological Studies, San Francisco
and Middleton. Winner of the Aurobindo Essay Contest in
Northern California, 1958. A.B., S.F. State College; M.A.,
University of California; Ph.D., College of the Pacific, through
The American Academy of Asian Studies.

JAY R. MCCULLOUGH. Assistant Professor of Philosophy, San Jose

Notes on the Contributors to this Volume

State College, California. A travelling scholar of oriental culture in the Far East in 1956. Member, Board of Governors, American Academy of Asian Studies. Publications include: 'Indian Theism and the Importance of Moral Acts,' in *The Review of Religion*, November 1956; 'Human Understanding in a Technical Age', in *The Ananai*, Shimizu, Japan, January 1958; and others. B.S. and M.A., University of Arizona; Ph.D., College of the Pacific, Stockton, through The American Academy of Asian Studies.

SISIR KUMAR MITRA. Professor of History of Civilization and Joint Director of Education, Sri Aurobindo International University Centre, Pondicherry. Formerly Lecturer in Cultural History at Rabindranath Tagore's Viswabharati (World University), Shantiniketan. Author of: *Cultural Fellowship of Bengal; India's Cultural Empire and Her Future; The Vision of India; The Dawn Eternal; The Secret of India's Evolution; The Liberator—Sri Aurobindo; India and the World; Sri Aurobindo and the New World*.

JITENDRANATH MOHANTY. Lecturer in Philosophy, Calcutta University. Lecturer at Sri Aurobindo Pāthamandir, Calcutta. Publications include: *Nicolai Hartmann and A. N. Whitehead; A Study in Recent Platonism*. B.A. and M.A., Calcutta; Dr. Phil., Göttingen, Germany.

CHARLES A. MOORE. Chairman, Department of Philosophy, University of Hawaii. Former Member of the Department of Philosophy, Yale University. Sometime Acting Director, Oriental Institute, University of Hawaii. Chairman, East–West Philosophers' Conferences, 1939, 1949. Editor and co-author, *Philosophy—East and West*. Co-editor, Jungiro Takakusu's *The Essentials of Buddhist Philosophy*. Co-editor, *A Source Book in Indian Philosophy*. Programme Director of the Philosophy and Religion Section, the sixth conference of the U.S. National Commission for UNESCO, San Francisco, 1957. Director, East–West Philosophers' Conference, Honolulu, 1959. A.B. and Ph.D., Yale. Sabbatical study as Guggenheim Fellow in India and at Oxford, 1947–8.

HAJIME NAKAMURA. Professor of Indian and Buddhist Philosophy, University of Tokyo. Visiting Professor, Stanford University, 1951–2. Delegate to: Congress on Cultural Freedom in Asia, Rangoon, 1955; The Buddhist Symposium held by the Government of India, New Delhi, 1956. Member of The Bhandarkar Oriental Research Institute, Poona; The American Oriental

Society; The International Academy of the Jains. Editor of: *The Bulletin of the Okurayama Oriental Research Institute; Monumenta Nipponica; Science of Thought.* Author of: *A History of Early Vedanta Philosophy*, four vols. (in Japanese) (awarded the Imperial prize by the Academy of Japan); *Ways of Thinking of Eastern Peoples*, two vols. (in Japanese) (translated by the Japanese Commission for UNESCO into English); and sixteen other books in Japanese. D. Lit., University of Tokyo.

N. A. NIKAM. Professor of Philosophy, Mysore University. General Secretary, Indian Philosophical Congress. Associate Fellow, Silliman College, Yale. Member of: Executive Committee of the International Institute of Philosophy, Paris; Executive Committee of the International Federation of Philosophical Societies, Brussels; UNESCO International Committee on Inquiry into the Teaching of Philosophy; East–West Philosophers' Conference, Canberra, 1957; UNESCO East–West Colloquium, Brussels, 1958; Institute on Ethics, New York. Writer of the Annual Proceedings of the Indian Philosophical Congress. Author of: *An Introduction to Kant's Critique of Pure Reason;* the article entitled 'Realism' in *History of Philosophy, Eastern and Western; The Writs of Asoka* (under publication by the Chicago University Press). M.A., St John's College, Cambridge.

RAYMOND F. PIPER. Professor of Philosophy, Syracuse University, 1917–54. Visiting Lecturer, University of California, summer 1926. Delegate to: International Congresses of Philosophy, 1920, 1926, 1937; International Congress of Aesthetics, Paris, 1937. Member of: Phi Beta Kappa; American Philosophical Association; American Society of Aesthetics; University Methodist Church. Publications include: *The Fields and Methods of Knowledge* (co-author with Dr Paul W. Ward); *Preface to Philosophy: Book of Readings* (co-author with Chancellor Wm P. Tolley and Dr Ross E. Hoople); *The Hungry Eye:* An Introduction to Cosmic Art; four articles in *Encyclopedia of the Arts.* A.B., Wisconsin; S.T.B. and Ph.D., Boston.

A. B. PURANI. Member of Sri Aurobindo Ashram, Pondicherry. Translator of Sri Aurobindo's main works in Guzrati. Visiting Lecturer in South Africa under the sponsorship of the Tagore Gandhi Trust Association, 1954. Visiting Lecturer in the United Kingdom, 1955. Author of: *Sri Aurobindo: His Life and Teachings; On Art; Sri Aurobindo's Sāvitrī: An Approach and a Study; Sri Aurobindo in England.* B.A., St Xavier's College, Bombay.

Notes on the Contributors to this Volume

RUTH REYNA. Research scholar in Indian Philosophy in the University of Florida. Member of: Phi Beta Kappa; Pi Epsilon Theta, and the like. Author of *Contemporary Interpretations of the Concept of Maya in Hinduism* (in the press). A.B., University of Southern California; M.A., Florida State University.

RISHABHCHAND. Member of Sri Aurobindo Ashram, Pondicherry. Author of: *The Integral Yoga of Sri Aurobindo*, two vols.; *The Divine Collaborators; In the Mother's Light*, two parts. B.A., University of Calcutta.

ANILBARAN ROY. Extension Lecturer, Sri Aurobindo International University Centre, Pondicherry. Formerly Professor of Philosophy, West Bengal. Sometime member of the Bengal Legislative Council. Author of: *The Gītā; The Message of the Gītā as Interpreted by Sri Aurobindo* (editor); *Mother India; The World Crisis; Songs from the Soul; India's Mission in the World; Sri Aurobindo and the New Age;* and several books in Bengali.

INDRA SEN. Professor of Psychology, Sri Aurobindo International University Centre, Pondicherry. Former Professor of Psychology, Delhi College. Author of: *Integral Education* (compiled from the writings of Sri Aurobindo and the Mother); and *Science and Culture* (compiled). M.A. and Ph.D.

K. D. SETHNA. Member of Sri Aurobindo Ashram, Pondicherry. Editor of *Mother India*. Author of: *Essays on Wells, Shaw, Chesterton and Hardy; The Secret Splendour; The Adventure of the Apocalypse; The Poetic Genius of Sri Aurobindo; Evolving India; The Indian Spirit and the World's Future; The Passing of Sri Aurobindo*. B.A., Bombay University; Ellis Prize winner.

SRI SWAMI SIVANANDA. Founder and Director of The Life Divine Society, Rishikesh. Founder and Chancellor of Yoga-Vedanta Forest University, Rishikesh. A practising physician in the Federated Malaya States, 1913–23. A wandering monk, 1924–36. Author of about 200 books including: *Principal Upaniṣads; World Religions; Rāja Yoga; Hatha Yoga; Kundalinī Yoga; Yoga Vedānta Dictionary; All About Hinduism; Brahma Sūtras; Mind, Its Mysteries and Control; The Moral and Spiritual Regeneration of the World; Spiritual Experiences; Srīmad Bhagavad Gītā;* etc.

NINIAN SMART. Lecturer in the History and Philosophy of Religion, University of London. Former Lecturer in the University of Wales. Visiting Lecturer in Philosophy at Yale University,

1955–6. Author of a book on Buddhism and Vedānta which is shortly to appear. B.A. and M.A., London.

PITIRIM A. SOROKIN. Professor of Sociology and Director of the Harvard Research Centre in Creative Altruism. Author of: *Contemporary Sociological Theories; Social and Cultural Dynamics; Social Mobility; Crisis of Our Age; Reconstruction of Humanity; The Ways and Power of Love; Social Philosophies of an Age of Crisis;* and many other works translated into many languages. Editor of: *Explorations in Altruistic Love and Behavior: A Symposium; Forms and Techniques of Altruistic and Spiritual Growth: A Symposium.* M.A. and Ph.D.

FREDERIC SPIEGELBERG. Professor of Asiatic and Slavic Studies, Stanford University, since 1941. Former Lecturer at Columbia University, University of Rochester, University of California, Berkeley, etc. Sometime Director of Studies, American Academy of Asian Studies, San Francisco. Visiting Lecturer, Institute for Analytical Psychology, Zurich, Switzerland, autumn 1956. Publications include: *The Bible of the World* (co-editor); *Alchemy as a Way of Salvation; The Religion of No-Religion; Spiritual Practices of India; The Living Religions of the World.* Research in India under a Rockefeller grant, 1949. S.T.M., Hamburg; Ph.D., Tübingen. Fellow of Yoga-Vedanta Forest Academy Rishikesh.

RAMA SHANKAR SRIVASTAVA. Professor of Philosophy, Ranchi College, Behar. Member of the Board of Philosophical Studies, Behar University. Former Head of the Department of Philosophy, Gaya College. Author of *Sri Aurobindo and the Theories of Evolution* (in the press). M.A., Banares Hindu University; D. Litt., Patna University.

H. P. SULLIVAN. Research scholar at the School of Oriental Studies, University of Durham, England. B.D., University of Chicago.

JUDITH M. TYBERG. Founder and Director, East–West Cultural Centre, Los Angeles, 1953. Visiting Lecturer at different cultural centres in England, Wales, Germany, Scandinavia, etc., 1935–6. Research work in Banares Hindu University and Sri Aurobindo Ashram, Pondicherry, 1947–50. Professor of Sanskrit, American Academy of Asian Studies, San Francisco, 1951. Author of: *First Lessons in Sanskrit Grammar and Reading; The Sanskrit Key to India's Wisdom.* M.A., M.Th. and Ph.D., The Theosophical University, Point Loma; M.A. in Indian Religion and Philosophy, Banares Hindu University.

K. C. VARADACHARI. Reader in Philosophy, Sri Venkatesvara University, Andhra. Former Lecturer at Madras Christian College and Union Christian College. Author of: *Metaphysics of Sri Rāmānuja's Śribhāsya; Theory of Knowledge in Śri Rāmānuja's Philosophy; Living Teaching of the Vedānta; Idea of God; Aspects of Bhakti; Introduction to Logic;* and other works on Mysticism, Yoga and Psychology. M.A. and Ph.D., Madras University.

ERNEST WOOD. President and Dean, American Academy of Asian Studies, San Francisco, 1957–58. Formerly Founder and President, Wood National College, Madanapalle, 1913; Founder and Principal, D.G. Sind National College, Hyderabad, 1917; Organizing Secretary, National University of India, 1917. Publications include: *The Glorious Presence; Practical Yoga; Great Yoga Systems of India; Yoga Dictionary; Mind and Memory Training; Occult Training of the Hindus; The Bhagavadgītā Explained;* and many others.

BIBLIOGRAPHY

A Complete List of all the books published in English
by
SRI AUROBINDO

(Unless otherwise indicated, these works are published in India by the Sri Aurobindo Ashram of Pondicherry. Many are also published in Great Britain by Luzac & Co., and in the United States of America by E. P. Dutton & Co. Inc.)

Ancient Scriptures: Commentaries and Translations

On the Veda. Sri Aurobindo International University Centre, 1956.
Hymns to the Mystic Fire. 2nd ed., 1952.
Isha Upanishad. 5th ed., 1951.
Kena Upanishad. 1952.
Eight Upanishads. 1953.
Essays on the Gita. 1949. New York: Sir Aurobindo Library, 1950.

Philosophy

The Life Divine. Sri Aurobindo International University Centre, 1955.
A Glossary of Sanskrit Terms in 'The Life Divine'.
The Mind of Light. 1953.
Ideals and Progress. 4th ed., 1951.
The Superman. 4th ed., 1950.
Evolution. 5th ed., 1950.
Thoughts and Glimpses. 5th ed., 1950.
Heraclitus. 2nd ed., 1947.
The Supramental Manifestation upon Earth. 1952.
The Problem of Rebirth. 1952.
Thoughts and Aphorisms. 1958.

Yoga

The Synthesis of Yoga (complete) or *On Yoga.* I. Sri Aurobindo International University Centre, 1955.
The Mother. 8th ed., 1956.
The Yoga and its Objects. 6th ed., 1952.
Lights on Yoga. 6th ed., 1956.
Bases of Yoga. 7th ed., 1955.
Elements of Yoga. 1953.

On Yoga II, Tomes One and Two, Sri Aurobindo International University Centre, 1958.
The Riddle of this World. 4th ed., 1951.
More Lights on Yoga. 1953.
Letters of Sri Aurobindo. 1st series, 2nd ed. Bombay: Sri Aurobindo Circle, 1950.
Letters of Sri Aurobindo. 2nd series, 2nd ed., 1954.
Letters of Sri Aurobindo. 4th series. Bombay: Sri Aurobindo Circle, 1951.
Letters of Sri Aurobindo on the Mother. 1952.
The Hour of God. 1959.

Nationalism

Foundations of Indian Culture. New York: Sri Aurobindo Library, 1953.
Bankim Tilak Dayananda. 3rd ed., 1955.
Bankim Chandra Chatterjee: An Essay. 1954.
The Renaissance in India. 4th ed. Calcutta: Arya Publishing House, 1952.
The Ideal of the Karmayogin. 7th ed., 1950.
A System of National Education. 3rd ed., 1948.
The National Value of Art. 1953.
The Significance of Indian Art. 1953.
The Spirit and Form of Indian Polity. Calcutta: Arya Publishing House, 1947.
The Brain of India. 4th ed. Calcutta: Arya Publishing House, 1948.
Uttarpara Speech. 5th ed., 1950.
The Speeches of Sri Aurobindo. 3rd ed., 1952.
The Doctrine of Passive Resistance. 2nd ed., 1952.

World Affairs

The Human Cycle. 1949. American ed., 1953.
The Ideal of Human Unity. 2nd enlarged ed., 1950. American ed., 1953.
War and Self-Determination. 3rd ed., 1957.
Messages of Sri Aurobindo and the Mother. 1949 and 1952.
After the War (World War). 1949.

Literature, including Poems and Plays

Vyasa and Valmiki. 1956.
Kalidas. 1950 and 1954.
Views and Reviews. 2nd ed., 1946.

Letters of Sri Aurobindo. 3rd series. Bombay: Sri Aurobindo Circle, 1949.

Letters of Sri Aurobindo on Savitri. 1951.

Life-Literature-Yoga: New Letters with Questions. 1952.

The Future Poetry. 1953.

Conversations of the Dead. 1953.

The Phantom Hour (a short story). 1951.

Collected Poems and Plays. 2 vols., 1942.

The Herod and the Nymph (Vikramorvasie). 3rd ed., 1952.

The Century of Life. 3rd ed., 1948.

Love and Death: A Poem. 4th ed., 1948.

Baji Prabhou: A Tale of Mahratta Chivalry in Verse. 3rd ed., 1949.

Poems, Past and Present. 2nd ed., 1952.

Chitrangada (a fragment). 1949.

Songs of Vidyapati. 1956.

Poems from Bengali. Sri Aurobindo International University Centre, 1956.

Savitri: A Legend and a Symbol. Sri Aurobindo International University Centre, 1954.

Ilion: An Epic in Quantitative Hexameters.

The Birth of the War God. 1952.

Last Poems (with facsimile plates). 1952.

More Poems. 1957.

Perseus the Deliverer: A Drama. 1955.

Vasavadatti: A Dramatic Romance. 1957.

Miscellaneous

Sri Aurobindo on Himself and the Mother. Sri Aurobindo International University Centre, 1953.

Sayings of Sri Aurobindo and the Mother. 1952.

Food and Life: A Selection from the Writings of Sri Aurobindo and the Mother.

Science and Culture (selected extracts). 1951.

The Message and Mission of Indian Culture (selected extracts). 1951.

GEORGE ALLEN & UNWIN LTD

London: 40 Museum Street, W.C.1

Auckland: 24 Wyndham Street
Bombay: 15 Graham Road, Ballard Estate, Bombay 1
Buenos Aires: Escritorio 454–459, Florida 165
Calcutta: 17 Chittaranjan Avenue, Calcutta 13
Cape Town: 109 Long Street
Hong Kong: F1/12 Mirador Mansions, Kowloon
Karachi: Metherson's Estate, Wood Street, Karachi 2
Mexico: Villalongin 32–10, Piso, Mexico 5, D.F.
New Delhi: 13–14 Ajmeri Gate Extension, New Delhi 1
São Paulo: Avenida 9 de Julho 1138-Ap. 51
Singapore: 36c Princep Street, Singapore 7
Sydney, N.S.W.: Bradbury House, 55 York Street
Toronto: 91 Wellington Street West

SRI AUROBINDO AND THE
SOUL QUEST OF MAN

NATHANIEL PEARSON

Sri Aurobindo, the great Indian philosopher who died in 1950, opens out new realms of spiritual truth in his great work *The Life Divine*. He saw and wrote from a universal vision which traversed many paths of knowledge, and this makes it difficult for the reader to follow the main theme without becoming lost in an intricate maze of by-paths. Nathaniel Pearson, who has been a member of the Sri Aurobindo Ashram for the last six years, has made an intensive study of *The Divine Life*. His book deals with the first twelve chapters, which are of fundamental importance, and provides a clear and illuminating exposition of the basic metaphysical principles of Sri Aurobindo. He was in close personal contact with the great spiritual teacher and was able to have his views corrected according to the actual meaning they were intended to convey.

The three steps to spiritual knowledge with which he deals are the fundamental stages studied in the twelve chapters. The first step is to establish the Divine Unity of all things; the second is to reveal the soul of man as forming the basis of a higher development; and the third is the knowledge of the Divine Nature.

Nathaniel Pearson shows how the new spirituality propounded by Sri Aurobindo bridges the gap between the ancient and the modern knowledge, particularly in the scientific field. In his refreshing approach to the subject of modern man in search of a soul he has subjected some of the current scientific theories to critical examination.

'Mr Pearson writes well and seems to have thoroughly absorbed Aurobindo's views; and he manipulates the formidable mass of "other-worldly" terminology with dexterity and precision.' *Philosophy*

Demy 8vo. 10s. 6d. *net*

THE BRAHMA SŪTRA

RADHAKRISHNAN

The illustrious scholar-statesman Dr. Radhakrishnan, to whom we already owe many standard works on religion and philosophy, here gives us another classic. The spiritual tradition of India is based on the three-fold canon *prasthānatraya*, the *Upanisads*, the *Bhagavadgītā* and the *Brahma Sūtra*.

This study of the *Brahma Sūtra* is a notable contribution to the development of solidarity in thought to which our world is committed. It is no exaggeration to say that this book in its theme and in its serene prose will prove invaluable to all those who are interested in the problems of man's spiritual quest and fulfilment. A book of the highest erudition and authority.

Demy 8vo. 42s. *net*

GEORGE ALLEN & UNWIN LTD